No Ordinary Words

The Real Life Wisdom Of Women

Written by 33 women, edited by Kelly Herrick

This book is dedicated to all the women who have gone before us, and all those yet to come.

There is something deeply strengthening and nourishing about creative weaving. Couple that with honesty and love and you have a recipe for beauty made visible and a resource to return to again and again. This book, crafted from the heart of women and TreeSisters globally is a celebration of womans lived wisdom, passed on like life gifts for the taking. Enjoy.

Clare Dubois,
Founder, TreeSisters

I was very touched by the courage and wisdom of the souls who shared their stories and verse within. In today's world, it's easy to feel that the burdens we hold are ones we carry alone. However, after a careful read of the soul-baring accounts within, you will find solidarity in realizing others experience seasons of deep pain, confusion, or trauma too— but have also found paths of hope to overcome their steepest life challenges. These authors have given me hope and made me feel less alone in the struggle of life, and I trust that they will impart the same inspiration to you.

Kirby Trapolino,
Founder & Director, She Has Hope

Contents

Introduction

This is an imperfect book.

The imperfections are what make it real. We are real women sharing our lives with you on the page, hoping to show you that we are connected, that we can rise, that we have an abundance of wisdom that will help change the world.

There will be chapters that speak to you and some that don't...yet. Yes, we could have had a greater representation of women, yes, we could have covered more topics, but we didn't want to be paralysed by perfection when we had truths to tell. Any woman speaking up in love and wisdom is a voice to be treasured.

No Ordinary Words started whilst watching my dear friend and author Danielle Macleod speak about her story online. I was suddenly hooked with an intense curiosity; I knew all the women watching along with me had wisdom to share and I wanted to know their stories too. The title of Danielle's book *Remarkably Easy*, was like a wakeup call. It might be a challenge for many of us to write a book alone, but it could be remarkably easy if we did it together. I asked who wanted to write the book with me and overnight our literary sisterhood was born.

The honesty with which we have written this book hasn't always been easy. Many of us have been through a sort of writer's therapy with our chapters, finding a healing from writing our words. Yet we have held you in our thoughts at every stage dear reader, and, as you read, we hope you feel a conversation flow between us.

Our aim is to create a book that is of service to others, and it is with this intention that all proceeds are going to two women's charities; TreeSisters and She Has Hope. Both these charities commit to incredible change in the world, and we thank you for buying this book to support them.

All our lives are extraordinary, sometimes we just have to take the time to share them.

Kelly Herrick
Editor

Womb

Bethany Carder

"What we truly are does not lack anything, does not seek or need anything, because it is already being everything." ~Monica Gagliano, Thus Spoke the Plant

When I was born I was cleaned up and placed in a bassinet. I did not feel the touch of my mother or my father. In my earliest moments, I was held in the arms of life. I have always felt a sense of something beyond what I could see. I have this feeling that I am surrounded by ethereal beings. I talk to them. I laugh with them. I find strength in their presence. But, I dare not speak of such things for fear of sounding completely unhinged. I keep this truth of my life wrapped up tight, so as not to reveal my connection to realms unseen. This has often kept me from acknowledging the wholeness of who I am and what guides me in this reality of being an earthling embodied as a woman.

The day before my birth my mother spent the afternoon floating with her belly to the sky held within the waters of the Saline River in Benton, Arkansas. It was the fourth of July, and the southern summer heat was exceptionally brutal that year. She was with a couple of friends and they were keeping cool in the river in the midst of the intense heat wave. Once the waters had soothed her she returned home to nap before the evening firework festivities planned at her church. The church building was only a few steps away as she lived on the same lot. At dusk she made her way over to the field behind the fellowship hall where the festivities were taking place. She was entranced by all the colorful displays of light as brilliant flashes of purple and red lit up the night sky. At one point during the display the loud boom of an exploding roman candle resulted in a fierce leap within her belly that made her whole stomach bounce. She was startled as she realized I had changed positions and that I could hear everything that was going on around her. Apparently that was all it took to get me curious enough to arrive a week earlier than expected.

My dad awoke before dawn the next morning to attend his morning prayer circle. He made his way across the lot to the church. My mom stayed in bed resting a bit longer and then got up to begin her day. As she did so it became clear that she was going into what she believed to be early labor. She was told by her midwife that during early labor she would have time to get up and walk around to help ease the intensity of the birthing process. After walking around the house a while she began to feel that something was wrong, so she called the church. No answer. She then decided to get dressed and walked out her back door the few steps to the back door of the church building. As she opened the church door one of the men in the prayer group saw her and instantly alerted my father that something was wrong. She closed the door and went back to the house with my dad close behind her. Once home he immediately called their midwife and doula.

The doula, my parents' close friend Jo, lived just two blocks away, so she made it over quickly. Upon her arrival she began preparations for my birth by boiling water and dressing the bed with sterile sheets and a plastic cover. While she was prepping the bed she advised my mother to go to the bathroom to labor more comfortably. My mother went into the bathroom with my father, and she sat on the toilet. My dad knelt in front of her so she could hold his gaze and find comfort through the immense pain that she was feeling. Jo was listening to her from the adjacent room and felt that my mother sounded as if she was in transition, not early labor. Transition is the last stage of the first phase of labor. In a normal birth it follows early and active labor. At this point, there is a swift progression as the cervix dilates from seven to ten centimeters, and the baby's descent begins. Since my mother had just started to feel the pains of labor Jo thought she couldn't be this far along and began to grow nervous. While in the bathroom my mom told my dad, "if this is early labor I am not going to make it. You are going to need to pray for me." As he began to pray, Jo heard the sounds of my mother bearing down and she rushed into the bathroom as my mother dropped me from her womb into the basin of the toilet. I just fell out. She did not push, once. Mom looked at Jo and said, "I think I had my baby. I feel something." My mother had just experienced a precipitous delivery. The contents of her uterus had emptied in a split second as the cervix went from one to ten centimeters rapidly. I was still in a foetal position in the toilet, and I was covered in blood.

Jo and my dad were both trying to remain calm, even though they were clearly alarmed. The placenta was delivered shortly after my birth. I am told that I did not make a sound when I was dropped from my mother's womb. It all happened so fast. Jo picked me up from the toilet, cut the cord and cleaned me up. At this point she had to decide if she would stay with me or help my father with my dying mother. Jo was growing increasingly alarmed as my mother began to lose consciousness. She laid me on my side in a nearby bassinet. She placed me in this way so that if I spit up

I wouldn't choke to death. She said a prayer for me and returned to my mother. Jo told my mom she had a baby girl. Mom said she could not see anything. Her eyes were wide open, but she was blind. She was in shock and was bleeding heavily from a concealed haemorrhage behind the placenta. Jo and my father called 911 and alerted the midwife to come as quickly as possible. Then they picked mom up and brought her to the bed as they anxiously awaited the arrival of the ambulance. After the ambulance arrived, they were off, and I was left with Jo until the midwife arrived.

I think about those first moments of my life and my newborn self. How was she making sense of an entirely new experience? What did she feel? Was she scared? I imagine myself laying there, eyes closed. I had become bound, heavy; made of flesh and blood. I had transitioned from the womb to the outside world in an instant. Did I feel an awakening to the inner depths of desire to be touched and held? Did I find comfort in the stillness as the shadows of the morning sun danced across my newborn body? Could I feel the power of my breath reverberating through me, moving my bones and the flesh of my body? Did I feel soft? Did I feel solitude? Did I feel surrender?

Once in the hospital the doctors gave my mother a blood transfusion. She had six pints of blood. The doctors decided to perform a dilation and curettage (D&C), a surgery to remove abnormal tissues in the uterus and continued to try and stop the bleeding. After they did the D&C she was moved into the Intensive Care Unit (ICU). While she was in the ICU Dad and Jo could only visit her room for five minutes on the hour. Dad went to look for the doctor to find out how she was doing. The doctors informed him that they could not stop the haemorrhage. They told him and Jo that they needed to say their goodbyes. Jo thought, "What are you talking about, are you talking about Liz Carder? There is nothing you can do?" And Dad said, "There's something I can do." He went to the chapel and began to pray asking for her life to be held here on earth. As he prayed he felt released. He had a deep sense that she would pull through. The five minutes they were allotted to visit Mom in the ICU did not encourage him. She was barely conscious. He laid his hands on her and felt a strong presence there with them. He knew she was going to make it. At this point, he had to leave the room. When he and Jo returned for the next hourly visit, my mother was fully conscious and fully aware. The bleeding had stopped, and her sight had returned. She had been singing the words of my father's prayer over and over in her mind. She said it was as if a song had washed over her. She felt deeply that she was held in life, and this was not her time to go. She was released from the ICU into a regular room, and we were reunited in the hospital chapel three days later.

My mother fully recovered and went on to give birth to three more healthy children. Some of my earliest memories are of dancing, singing, and creating plays for my siblings and dressing them up in costumes so we could perform for our parents. I was homeschooled until the age of fifteen. For years I wondered what it was like to be in public school or in the "secular" world, but now that I am older I am beginning to appreciate how my relationship to my home life has given me the self-discipline and sense of self-exploration that I find so fundamental to my present experience. I have endured many struggles, as anyone living has, and I am returning to the cultivation of these creative practices from my youth to find a sense of grounding in my true essence.

When I was in my early twenties, struggles with my reproductive health led me to study my body in a more in-depth way. I enrolled in a massage therapy program in Las Vegas, Nevada and began studying energetic healing and muscle manipulation therapies. From here I moved to New York City to play music with friends and eventually met my life partner, who also happens to be my band mate. We bounced around the country for a year or so living in our car and playing shows to keep us fed and fuelled. This led to a short stint of farming in Georgia, a stopover in Arkansas and an eventual move to Portland, Oregon. While farming, I had become obsessed with plants and eventually returned to school to study the science of life through the lens of ecology. In my younger life I was educated through religion and spiritual practice, but I hadn't yet had the experience of studying science in an academic setting. My studies filled a place in my heart that longed to understand the connectedness interwoven through all organisms. However, the competitive and fast paced system in which these studies were taking place was slowly deteriorating my health and mental well-being. The course of my life changed dramatically just days after I graduated.

I was diagnosed with cervical cancer June 14th, 2019. I still don't really know how to talk about it. I write and write and write as an endeavour to integrate the experience, but all I am doing is describing the scenery around me. I find myself recounting what time of the day it was, or what room I was in, or who was in the other room when I got the news. In reality, I am trying to describe an indescribable feeling. I knew something was wrong when the doctor did not leave the results of my colposcopy on my voicemail. They just said to give them a call back as soon as I could. I could feel the tension in my throat coupled with a tightening in my chest. My mind felt frozen. One thought began playing over and over. "I have cancer." That's when I quickly began to realize the fragility of the everyday. What have I been doing with my time?! Am I being who I want to be?

After confirming my diagnosis with my primary care physician, I was referred to an oncologist. As the doctor explained all of the possible treatment options and the subsequent risks, I could feel my head growing faint. While breathing deeply, I tried to imagine myself post-treatment healthy and recovering with all my remaining organ systems intact. This did little to calm my nerves. After the visit I had to decide what option to pursue. During this time many people reached out to me to give their advice.

Up to this point I had no desire to have children. I wanted to pursue a career in science and fill whatever remaining time I had with music, but this diagnosis brought up so much around what it meant to be a woman. I dove deep into online rabbit holes watching women talk about how without our wombs we lose our sacred connection to Mother Earth. Some people would send me messages about how if I were to just meditate or juice cleanse, I could beat this. Such messages carried the implication that if I were diligent enough I could overcome this diagnosis with no need for surgery or any invasive treatments. I was overwhelmed with possibilities. Who am I without a womb? What value do I have to this world or to my culture? If I chose surgery am I somehow choosing to not trust in my own body? But what if I don't have surgery? Will I die of something that was completely operable? These days would end with me crying in the bathtub unclear on who or what to believe and who to trust with my body. In the midst of all of this I saw an online post from a woman preparing for chemotherapy by nourishing her body with healthy food and gentle movement practices. This inspired me to seek some grounding in myself which led to my decision.

I chose open abdominal surgery, the most invasive procedure, because the recovery rates were so high when compared to the other procedural options. The surgeon suggested this as the course of action because nearly all women who had this procedure recovered with no recurrence of cancer within the first five years. This meant a lengthier recovery period. This put my plans to work in the field of habitat restoration, which requires a high degree of physical labor, on hold until I could recover my strength.

The surgery was a success. In one month I had graduated, gotten cancer, beaten cancer and was now in the process of recovering. I keep trying to find the best words to describe the pain of losing my womb, having a shortened vagina, and having to relearn how my body works. I was told that I may never be able to have an orgasm again. And then, when I could have sex, how might that feel? Sometimes I think that since my cancer came and went rapidly that I don't deserve to be upset about it. I did not need chemotherapy or radiation as many close to me have endured. I had cancer, and then I didn't. I should be over it, right? I didn't know how to talk about what was happening inside of me. I had many friends and loved ones willing to help, but I didn't really understand how to ask for help. Death was calling, and then death was gone. I felt transformed and was unsure how to make my way back or forwards or anywhere for that matter. How would I live my life now?

My immobility during recovery led me to deeper stillness. When the television shows became boring and I had watched every film I could think of, I began to sit in silence. I began to listen to the sounds around me. I began to hear the voices of those that had been there all along. I heard the voices of the birds, the squirrels, and the neighbors. I heard the voices of the wind dancing in the trees. They showed me what it meant to be alive. The more I sat in stillness, the louder my habituation called to me, but I kept showing up for myself in new ways. I took small steps each day to allow the healing to unfold. The transformation of my world was swift, but the transformation of my days was a practice in self-discipline and immense self-compassion. When the "shoulds" would come knocking on my door, I would have to fight to remain in the space of self-awareness that I was striving to cultivate. It was and remains one of the most difficult challenges of my life. I struggle to show up for myself with love and empathy and self-forgiveness for the times that I have cowered in the face of the oppressor. I contend with the lies of what and who I am. I fight to remember that I do not need to contort myself into some ideal that was not even my choice. I am me: vibrant, messy, strong and capable. I long to learn the song of this planet and to share in the collective harmonic frequencies of the cosmos. I find solace in the stars and the galaxies when the human world feels so broken that it seems beyond repair. But, I know that it takes each of us to change the course of our collective lives.

I lost my womb to cancer. I was at the threshold of mortality, just as my mother had been in the earliest moments of my life. I was asked to choose how I would spend this precious existence in this body that remained, for this time, on earth. I strive to befriend my fears and to stop hiding the truth of who I am. I have to make this choice daily, with each breath, with each thought. I am learning to trust that I am held in life and in the arms of all who seek change in this world through acts of self-responsibility and true self-love. I will no longer cower to the lie that I am not enough, I am too strong, I am too weak, I am too vulnerable, or I am too much. I will no longer hide my connection to the ethereal world, to this planet and all earthlings. I will trust in the unknown as an act of devotion to the mystery of life. I will do so by practicing trusting myself and following the divine thread that is guiding me towards the truth of who I am here to be. I know that this is not the end of my story.

The Reluctant Author

Jean Ferguson

"Would you like to be part of a book of wisdom of women?" asked Kelly.

I could imagine nothing more outside my comfort zone. I love structure and processes. My tool of choice is an Excel spreadsheet not a pen or a paintbrush. Even my chosen craft, cross-stitch, has straight lines. It was scary.

"Yes", replied Jean.

Taking part felt like it would be a great way to do something different and stretch myself. Plus, I'd be working with fabulous women. I jumped at the chance to be on the production team – project management is very much my thing. I set up doodle polls and zoom calls. I encouraged others. And I waited for inspiration to strike. For my story to come along and announce itself. After all, everyone is supposed to have one book in them…aren't they?

I talked to my lovely book buddy, and for a little while got excited about writing a letter to my 30-year-old self. I wanted to share all the things I wish I had worked out earlier in my life: not working for a company that did not align with my values; staying there too long to look after my team, which of course gave them completely the wrong message (it took me seven years to work that one out); not acknowledging that I am a remarkable woman until a "Remarkable Women" workshop epiphany when I was 59 years, 3 months and 22 days old. I thought about you, my lovely readers. Why would you want a lecture from me? Crossed that idea off.

Could I write about mother-daughter relationships and the guilt I still feel about taking myself to live across the water in Scotland? My move made it so much harder for my Mum to see me and her grandchildren. I put myself and my children first. Northern Ireland was not the best place to bring up children in the '80s and '90s. The ingrained importance of family that my mum had so carefully nourished also worked against her. Thinking ahead, I did not want my children to leave me and go to Scotland. Of course they would, because I'd be encouraging them to go to University away from home. It was a big risk that they would not come back and I did not want that. Guilt – yes. A lesson for others? Maybe. I regret the pain I caused, never the decision. Do what is right for you.

I thought about writing about my beautiful daughter – I am so very proud of you. You're like me in so many ways...ways that hurt as I see you suffer many of the pains I did. But oh so much better than me too. You're a better mother, so calm and loving to your two babies. You're so patient and less likely to explode in frustration at the end of the day. And you're so good for the environment, with your cloth nappies and wipes and your second-hand family clothes, because it's the right thing to do.

I need calm, quiet and uncluttered surroundings to feel peace and joy. I also need to be always learning new things. Two small children brought some of the latter, and I so loved learning with you...but they also brought little calmness and too much clutter. For my own sanity, and because I needed the challenge, I returned to work full-time when you were five, your brother three. This showed you that women could have a career, but it also meant I was less available to you. Was that the right thing to do? Somehow it has worked out OK and the absolute joy I have now sharing time with you and your babies soothes my soul. Where is the lesson in this story? Do not panic when your beautiful wee girl turns into a horrible teenager – a teenager who sat with her back to me at the dinner table because I chewed too loudly and whose bedroom floor was a foot deep in clothes, books, homework and debris including assorted apple cores. Like the very hungry caterpillar, you were building a cocoon around yourself and at the end you came back as a very beautiful butterfly.

None of the ideas I had seemed good enough for you dear readers. I took my problem to Kelly. After a few helpful thoughts she tossed off the comment "why not write about why you find it a challenge to write?" Oh my goodness, the power of a great mentor. Words are now flowing as I write on this train rolling through the beautiful glens of the west of Scotland.

Why have I never had a mentor? That was another idea I had dismissed. I am a natural problem-solver. It is how I define myself. I never ask for help. I am always the one to be supportive, to offer advice, to solve problems. Maybe even sometimes when the recipient just wanted a listening ear. My lesson here is that asking for help is good, gives joy to the giver and succour to the receiver. I commit to doing more of it. More recently I have become really aware of how many times I start a sentence with "What you need to do is…". I have also committed to give people more space to solve their own problems whilst still being there for them.

Let's come back to why I found it so hard to write anything. I am a recovering perfectionist and have been for quite a few years. I grew up with my Dad's favourite saying ringing in my ears and heart: "If a job's worth doing, it is worth doing well." Alongside "measure twice, cut once" which makes me cautious and sensible. I am a voracious reader, consuming a hundred novels a year. I know what good writing looks like. If I could not write anything wonderful, inspirational, memorable, then I did not want to write anything at all. The last few years of my full-time career I taught continuous improvement skills and one of the mantras I shared was "do not let perfection be the enemy of good". Try, learn, improve. I am still working to replace that early message from my Dad with the new one. I have come a long way from the 39-year-old who threw a tantrum (yes, a proper meltdown) when the builder installing double doors between my living and dining rooms sank a metal keeper for the bolt into my fabulous new wooden floor. Luckily the builder was not there at the time. So, here I am, bravely sharing my less than perfect writing. It's a patchwork of random musings – perhaps hoping that just one might connect with each of you.

My lesson here is to chill, let go and think about what really matters. Four years after that tantrum I had breast cancer and that changed my perspective. I made a big effort to work less, and carry less stress in my life. Over the intervening years I have strayed often, even in the last year giving more to a volunteer role than I set out to at the start. Just because I *can* do something that needs to be done does not mean I *have* to, despite that sensible upbringing. Try, learn, improve. And my daughter and her babies are constant reminders about what is important.

Having just reached 60 years old, I have entered the last phase of my life. I am not religious and have no expectations of there being any "after". My intention is that every moment left brings me peace and joy. Why not? It seems a very sensible way to live. For such a sensible girl, why did it take me so long to learn? I ask myself regularly "will it bring me joy?" It is a great tool for decision-making and tossing away so many wrong things. It has also made me really think about all the small things that do bring me joy – today it is the glorious red of the autumn leaves in my garden. Asking this question has also helped me ward off perfectionism which rarely brings me peace or joy.

For my last lesson, I invite you to ask yourself: "does it bring me joy?" Often. Recognising that something, whatever it is, does not could be the first step to both tiny changes and big brave changes too.

Facing My Fears and Following My Calling

Barbara Brown

I would like to tell of my journey toward the realization of my life's calling, the manifestation of the project that now fills my life with such purpose and satisfaction. This is my *SYLVAN REFLECTIONS* project of *Wanderings, Paintings & Ponderings From the Forest*; sharing my love of the forest through visual art, writing and film. It's a journey of facing fears and embracing joy; it's about becoming the artist I always knew I was meant to be.

I'll begin my story about fifteen years ago. I was in my early fifties, and no longer fulfilled creatively by my work; but always resisting, or somehow never pursuing, the deep-seated urges I always felt toward making art.

There was at that time a year of many deaths close to me, beginning with the death of my mother. And then the next year I was myself diagnosed with lung cancer. And in these losses, and in the facing of my own mortality, I awakened to a new level of awareness of what this life is all about. It is about embracing it as the wondrous gift it is, as fully as I am able. It's about finding deep joy and sinking into those depths.

I made the decision to sell my home-based business—I had been producing annual tourist and street maps of my region for twenty years—and to re-invent myself as the artist I needed to find out if I could be. I felt like I was jumping off a cliff...and I was going to need to learn how to fly.

I remember feeling like somehow my whole being— even my past selves and ancestors, my future selves as well—all were crying out to me saying: "It's TIME!" I had no idea what it was I was going to do with these creative urges; all I knew was that I had to give myself the time and space to see what wanted to percolate up from deep within me.

I attended a Hay House 'I Can Do It' conference, without even knowing really why I was there, and barely speaking to another soul, but being immensely inspired by the likes of Louise Hay, Marianne Williamson...and Wayne Dyer with his "Don't die with your music still inside you" message.

So I decided to free up my life to begin painting. I hadn't done a painting in twenty years; I had huge resistance to the actual act of painting; I didn't even know what I wanted to paint; but I knew I had to. I knew I had demons I would need to face. But I felt I had promises to keep that I had made to myself way back in the mists of time.

I registered as a participating artist in our local ArtWalk, knowing that if I had a deadline, involving a commitment to other people, I would meet it. I started listening to webinars by inspirational speakers. I created rituals to help me to break through my resistance, using music and aromatherapy...and the wearing of what I call my 'power necklace', that I made for the purpose from Raven bones and amber and a feather from the forest.

I've never told the story of this necklace before, at least not publicly. It's the story of a young fledgling

Raven I came upon one day in the forest; he was on the ground, dying, with a broken wing.

It was early Spring, small patches of Winter's snow were still in the most shadowed nooks and crannies of the forest. I was on my daily walk a little ways up the mountainside, passing through an open forest glade where Cedars grow tall and the forest floor is mostly clear of underbrush. To be honest I have always felt a hush of enchantment in this glade.

On this day I was deep in thought, as I was in the throes of selling my little business, without knowing what I would do next to keep body and soul together—jumping off that cliff, knowing I was going to have to learn how to fly. I wasn't watching where I was stepping and all of a sudden the most raucous alarmed squawking startled me, shattering the peace of the place. I looked down to see a young Raven, downed, crippled, defenceless and terrified of me. I had almost stepped on him! It broke my heart to see him so hurt, and to see that I was causing him such distress. I left quickly and as calmly as I was able, leaving him to die in peace.

I wanted so badly to comfort him, to heal him and see him fly free…but he was so frightened of me I knew I couldn't without causing him too much more anxiety. And it is my belief that death is not a bad thing; it was his time to go; Nature takes its course.

I felt it to be a sign. Raven is a totem of mine—the name of my business has always been 'Raven Creations'. This shiny black young life, cut short and landed into my own life in such a dramatic way; I felt it must be a gift, a strong message, medicine, meant for me. He would never fly. Could his life and his flight somehow have been a sacrifice? I vowed to do my

best to learn to take flight in my own life, in honour of
him.

Weeks later I returned to the glade, found what
remained of him, bones and feathers; and created a
rustic shrine and protection, surrounding him with
fallen Birch branches. That Summer and Autumn I
returned often, tending the site and communing with
him. Over the Winter a deep blanket of pristine snow
covered him. As the following Spring approached my
business sold, I had committed to ArtWalk, and I had
to get painting! Raven emerged as the snow melted,
and on the Equinox I gathered up his backbone—
eighteen vertebrae bones. I took them home and
cleaned them with hydrogen peroxide and sunlight. I
collected eighteen small stones of jet from an old
necklace of my Mother's (jet, black & shiny as Raven,
is formed of fossilized trees; it protects against
anxiety, and is used magically to open portals to
other dimensions). I found two beads of amber
(millennia-old tree resin) and a black feather carved
from bone; and I strung them all on a leather cord. I
did this all as ritual, with the intention to honour and
make sacred; to create a talisman that would aid me
in finding the wherewithal to achieve my ambitions.

It is a remarkable looking necklace—the stark white
bones interspersed with the shining black-as-black-
can-be jet beads, and set off with the touch of amber.
I feel the power of it. I wear it every single time I go to
paint.

This young life, cut short just as he was about to fly,
helping me to fly free with my creative life. Somehow
reborn in my paintings.

Donning my new 'power necklace' I began
experimenting with watercolours & pastels, colour

schemes, figure drawings and symbolism and landscapes.

Then at one point I simply asked. I asked myself—my higher self, I asked Raven, I asked the universe...I asked what it was I was meant to do. And then I did my very best to step back, to get out of my own way, to let go, trust and surrender...to let the answer come. I gave myself the time and space needed to allow the answer to arise. At one point I asked myself the question: "Well, what is it that you love the most?" and that was when the answer came: "I love spending time in the forest."

I had been walking in the forest as a daily practice for nigh on two decades, ever since I had seen a psychologist, seeking relief from the chronic low-grade depression I had suffered from for most of my life; and one of the first and best things she said to me was: "Well, do you want to be depressed or do you want to go for a walk every day?" I began walking every day in the forest where I live—in the fairly remote and wild forest of the Slocan Valley, nestled in the mountainous southeast corner of British Columbia, Canada. This walk immediately became the best-loved part of my day. It became 'who I am', the activity I most identify myself with. As my connection with the forest deepened, all aspects of my life—the physical, mental, emotional and spiritual—all experienced deeper levels of well-being.

A realization came to me while I was in the woods, being awestruck every day at the beauty of nature, feeling so blessed to live where I live and have this amazing gift right outside the front door of my cabin. I realized that while I was spending time there, walking, or sitting in mindful stillness, I was always imagining sharing it with others. In my mind I had an audience to whom I was showing the beautiful images and telling my stories, of animal encounters and the finding of treasures and the feelings of reverence and connection I was experiencing. I wanted to share all of this. It was a feeling of being filled up to overflowing, so that it had to flow out of me and be shared.

For my last painting completed for ArtWalk that year I thought I'd try my hand at oil painting (it had been thirty years since I'd done an oil!). There was one particular Grand Fir tree on the edge of the forest that struck me every day with the gorgeousness of its great and graceful boughs sweeping out from the shadows at its deep dark core, and I decided to see if I could capture this presence in oil. And I did it! It worked! I called the painting 'Grand Depths' and I knew I could happily spend the rest of my life painting the forest.

I began to write as well, following these same urges to share. I wanted to offer the experience of the beauty and the wonder of the forest to people who weren't so lucky as I was to live within it. The book began to take shape, and then the website...all with the idea of bringing the forest to people. I had in mind especially elders, or people house-bound or bed-ridden, or even just city folk; people who can't easily get out into the forest themselves and might like to join me, vicariously, for a walk in the woods. Three years later I published the book.

It begins: "Come, let's go for a walk together, in the forest...if you are unable to spend time in the forest today let me take you there; come along with me. I'll be your eyes and your ears, your nose and your skin. Come drink from the creek with me, get a little wakeup slap on the cheek from a tree branch in passing...."

It is my hope to inspire and to soothe, by bringing to people the beauty and the wonder of nature; to inspire others to deepen their own connection to the natural world, and thereby with themselves, for we are ourselves Nature.

But of course the publishing of a book is really the very beginning of the journey, as then comes the work of finding the people it can touch, and sharing it more widely out into the world. More fears to face! I am an introvert, and public speaking was an old old terror of mine that I knew I was going to need to face down. So I joined my local Toastmasters group, shaking in my boots...and learnt I could do it after all and even enjoy it! All along with this project I am learning that these fears so often hide the joys; that where the fear is felt is where the real juice lies in life; that what I am afraid of is, more often than not, exactly the direction I should be moving in. I've learnt to feel the fear and do it anyway.

And as the years go by the project keeps deepening and broadening and feeding my soul. I found a local filmmaker and produced a film, full of gorgeous forest footage, as a companion to the book. I am now working on Volume II, with a second series of forest paintings and writings; and a second film to go along with it. With this second instalment I am delving further into the human experience of beauty. The film begins: "Let's contemplate Nature's Beauty...let's revel in the Beauty of Nature and ponder the Nature of Beauty...as we come to it in the forest."

It's my mission to inspire people to bring the beauty of nature into their everyday lives. Let us fall back in love with Earth and all her wonders. And let us then treat her with the awe and reverence she deserves.

I still have hurdles to cross, fears to face and challenges to rise to. I still feel I don't have the confidence to pull all this off. I still feel I'm a fraud, just pretending I have the talents and skills needed to do this work. I still feel that I am nowhere near 'enough' to be presenting myself to the world in this way. On the one hand I am taking all the steps I'm capable of to bring all this to as wide an audience as possible; and on the other hand I tremble in fear at baring my soul to the world. There's a voice within me that is still saying "Who the hell do you think you are, and why would anyone be interested in what you have to say?"

But aside from all this chatter there is a deep joy in sharing, to the best of my ability, the love that I feel for the forest and for all of life in its wondrous beauty. And, aside from all the chatter, I do believe we all have gifts we are meant to offer; and I believe I am finding what mine are...and that is deeply gratifying.

I am learning that if I acknowledge the fears I can then usually set them off to the side, calm them, and carry on with what needs to be done–carry on with what my soul truly longs to do. I am learning that the feeling of fear, more often than not, can actually be excitement in disguise.

I am learning that by leaning into ritual I can raise the strength I need. And by turning towards Nature's offerings, opening myself up to what she is bringing to me, feeling her love for me, watching for signs and synchronicities; she will drown out my negative self-talk, giving me the courage to shine my light–after all it is her who has given me this light to shine. By paying attention, and tuning myself to resonate in harmony with Nature, the way will come clear and beckon me on.

It is a surrender, really, to the calling of my soul.

Play

Rachel Herzig

My first morning at the Abbey, I walked out the front door to see a tall monk strolling up and down the gravel driveway with a coffee cup sitting on top of his head. His gold and red Buddhist robes gleamed in the sunshine only slightly less than his bald head did. Other monks and nuns passed by, paying him no mind. I was delighted. I had no idea why the cup was on his head, but the fact that it was, and no one batted an eye, boded well.

I come from a lineage ripe with playfulness, at least on my father's side. A case in point: We lived in the Southern California foothills, without air conditioning, and in the summer the temperature could climb to well over 100 degrees. On such days, my professor father would grade papers, or prep for classes, reclining in bed with his shirt off. One afternoon when I was six, my younger sister and I were hanging out on the bed with my dad when my sister decided to delicately pour part of her cup of water into my dad's belly button. My dad did not miss a beat. He set his papers aside, put a hand on each side of his generous belly, and squeezed its sides together so that the water squirted out as if from the blowhole of a whale. "Ah-oogah!" my dad yelled. "Ah-oogah!" we screamed back, giggling maniacally. "Do it again, do it again!"

My mother's approach to life was different. In one of my earliest memories, colors rush by me: pink of dawn, blue of sky, green of grass, dapple of sunlight through maple tree leaves. At four years old, I had

Rachel Herzig

not yet separated this and that, subject and object, self and world. Spinning was the joy of this, blurred into kaleidoscopic color. I spun, as the earth spun, regarding one another. Air on body, body on air, light on body, body on light. I did not know these words or these distinctions. There was only the felt sense that this was right, this was alive, this was good. Then came my mother. Yelling, disdainful. Dancing outside without clothing was not allowed, was bad, indecent. The neighbors would see. The neighbors would mind. It was not, somehow, safe. Neither the dancing, the abandoned glee, the nakedness, nor the joy—neither parsed from one another nor in a delicious heap like new puppies. All must go.

A few years later, I told my mother I wanted dance lessons. She said no. She lumped in dancing with Barbie dolls and cheerleading, all things girls were relegated to and I would not be. Even then I appreciated that this made sense regarding Barbies and cheerleading, but I knew she was wrong about dance. Nonetheless, I now felt dirty, immoral, for wanting it. I was urged to do gymnastics instead—it was sufficiently rigorous and sufficiently unbeautiful as to be acceptable. But I hated the regimented, uncreative movements required for the balance beam and vault; I wanted to whirl. I wanted joy. As an adult, I would learn that Sufi dancers whirl to stay in conscious relation with the fundamental nature of existence: atoms whirl, blood flows, breath circulates, storms gather, planets revolve, galaxies turn. My mother, however, was raised in a fixed world. Her own mother's family barely made it through the Great Depression. Life was about grim responsibility; joy was selfish, irresponsible, morally suspect.

Dancing went underground in me, even as a desire. I also began to believe that my mother was right:

Glorious joy in one's own body out in public is a harrowing, fraught, violence-haunted thing. Playing kickball at recess aged eleven, enjoying the power of my legs, a boy grabbed me where I did not want to be grabbed. I told him to stop. He didn't. I knocked him down into the dirt. I got in trouble, he did not. I had to stand on the fence while the rest of the playground filed past me. The boy smirked going by. Boys grabbed me in junior high, even assaulted other girls, and no action was taken. My high school soccer coach, his pregnant fiancé in the next room, told me I had great legs while putting his hand on my thigh. As I walked out of a convenience store, a young man came up behind me and lifted my skirt above my head. His gang of friends laughed menacingly as I ran for my car. Incidents like this multiplied from age eleven on—boys and full grown men calling obscene things at me, grabbing me, threatening me when I resisted.

At fifteen, I fell in love for the first time. By the time I was sixteen, my first love had forced me out of his car, leaving me alone on the side of the road, in my soccer uniform, with no purse, no money, no phone; had beaten me up for speaking to a male friend; had knocked me down in my own driveway and tried to strangle me to death. When I broke up with him, he tried to run my friends and I off the road, tampered with my dad's car, came to my bedroom window at night and told me if I didn't do what he wanted he'd kill my family. My father got a restraining order and when the stalker violated it, the sheriff's deputy who came to the house pulled me aside and told me, "sweetheart, you should be happy someone loves you so much."

I managed to get through the rest of high school and went away to college. But at nineteen I had to take a medical leave because I was so undone by PTSD. When I arrived home, my mother screamed at me that I was selfish, lazy and manipulative to make such an issue out of things. I was forbidden to grieve for myself or what had been done to me. By that point, I was so trained to believe I didn't matter that I didn't think to say anything to my father, who would have been horrified, and would have helped me. Only later would I remember overhearing my parents fighting when my father hired a lawyer to go after the stalker for violating the restraining order. My father was worried that, without legal action, the stalker would kill me. My mother was worried that taking legal action would "ruin that poor boy's life". It would take me until my forties to realize that my mother's ongoing refusal to care about my wellbeing wasn't an understandable difference in perspective stemming from her upbringing; it was abuse.

By the time I got to the Abbey at thirty-one, if you had asked friends to describe me, playful is not the word that would come to mind. Serious, sombre, intense, perhaps. But fun loving? Not so much. In truth, I was anxious, depressed, and terribly traumatized. I had not gotten the psychological help I needed as a teen and struggled all through my twenties with escalating PTSD. I had gotten myself counselling but this was before PTSD was well understood, and before it was known that somatic techniques are necessary to heal it. Talk therapy only seemed to make things worse. I clung onto something resembling function only by taking myself to a park, sitting at the base of a tree, and staring into a rushing creek for four hours every morning. It took me that long to calm myself down from the nameless, amorphous dread I always woke up with so that I could go to work.

Over several years, sitting at the base of my tree, I evolved a meditation practice. Meditating gave me a kind of peace and comfort while I was engaged with it, but this evaporated once I headed back into the world. I hoped that if I found a meditation teacher, I could learn to stabilize what I experienced and bring it into the rest of my life. I read about the Abbey, and after much consideration, decided to quit my job and move there. I imagined the Abbey would be a serious, quiet place, full of serious, quiet people, where things would be somewhat rigid and so uniform as to be bland in tone and manner. I was apprehensive about this, but so desperate to gain control of my mind and mood, to reclaim my own voice from the yammering terror in my head, I was willing to put up with just about anything. My apprehensions were entirely misplaced.

Life at the Abbey was utterly disciplined. We were awakened at 5:30 a.m. each weekday by a monastic walking through the sleeping areas clacking two wooden sticks together. Then from 6 to 7 a.m. we had morning chants and meditation, followed by chores and breakfast until 8. Then we meditated until 11, and practiced tai chi until 12:30. Then lunch, followed by work from 1:30 to 5:30 p.m. I worked in the office, interfacing with the public; other residents did things like gardening, maintenance work, cooking, and fundraising. Then we had evening chants and meditation until 6:30 p.m., followed by a light dinner, then classes or free time. We practiced silence from 8 p.m. each night to noon the following day. Saturdays were our days off from Abbey routine and from silence. On Sundays we meditated and stayed in silence all day long. These disciplines weren't arduous for me. Instead, it was like slipping into a warm bath, buoyed on all sides by a routine and structures that suited my temperament well.

Residents at the Abbey observed both the Buddhist precepts and monastic rule. This meant that, with a few exceptions, the distractions and entertainments of Western culture were deliberately absent. There was no drinking, no drugs, no music, no television, no radio, no fashion, no general access to computers or phones, no sex. There was, blessedly, sugar, caffeine, and thanks to the tall, cup-bearing monk, a regular supply of chocolate, sent monthly by friends. We did get a newspaper, but we were so remote that it took two weeks to get to us, and by that time there was no use getting riled by whatever was in it. There was a library excellently stocked with Buddhist and world wisdom, and with one wall of children's books, which we all relished reading. There was a cat, who sometimes deigned to be cuddled, a huge orange, fluffy creature. He was rumoured to be the reincarnation of the Abbey's founder because he liked to lurk, seemingly asleep, until you lapsed into mindfulness, whereupon he would leap up and jab a claw into your leg or arm.

Play snuck into my life at the Abbey before I realized what was happening, and the more I played, the less anxious I felt. One Saturday morning, we woke up to snow so high we could jump right out of our second story bedroom windows, so we did! Other winter Saturdays we could be found in the kitchen banging on pots and pans, only slightly more melodiously than three-year-olds. In the spring, we played freeze tag, created treasure hunts, and played pranks. In the summer, we found secret paths to hidden coves, played hide and seek, and walked hours to town to get ice cream. In the fall, we wore wildly-patterned, mismatched socks, the only option for sartorial individuality in the communal sea of red and gold. We made cakes with crazily colorful frosting and built fairy houses in the woods. We collected rocks and feathers, flowers and twigs. We finger painted and drew with crayons. We played baseball badly and soccer with many turned ankles. We made bonfires and told stories.

We did not feel silly or that we were too old for these things. We stop playing as we grow up not because we have lost the desire, or the need for it, but because our playful nature becomes muffled and layered over by what we have been taught—by family, by culture, by life experience. Meditation and mindfulness clear away artifice and any pretence to knowing how things 'should' be. When I no longer felt I had to tamp down my reality like my mother demanded, no longer had to pretend to be a high functioning thirty-something, and allowed that it was okay to be an anxious mess, or to not be a mess, or to be anything at all, there was space for play. Being oneself, it turns out, is a necessary ground of play.

Everything played at the Abbey. I think because everything felt safe to be itself there. Three red foxes played chase on the lawn with the orange cat. Two teenage moose chased each other around the far yard. Momma moose stuck her head in the open kitchen window and hoovered up any food left on the counter. Squirrels ran up and down porch railings and up and down arms. Wild horses nuzzled up for snacks. Even whales came right up to the edge of the sea below our cliffs, the air so still at times you could hear their blowholes spout, sounding remarkably like an amplified version of my dad's water-expelling belly button. Even I, believing the stalker would not find me in another country, in the wilderness, could go for a walk alone in the woods, see some lovely, springy green moss, take off my clothes and roll around on its softness, fearing nothing.

I left the Abbey in the end because I wanted to have a family, something monastics were not allowed. I took a job as an assistant college chaplain and moved to a small city in New England. I was not yet conscious of the fact that play was so important for me, but I did love most the parts of chaplaincy that were artistic and playful, designing rituals and services that were full of music, song, dance, art, poetry and deep quiet. For several years I was happy and at peace. Then, when I was in my mid-thirties, my beloved father suddenly died. Then my true high school sweetheart, a young man I met after the stalker, and to whom in my heart of hearts I had always believed I would return, also died suddenly. Then the stalker found me again.

My world crashed in, and I handled it as my mother had raised me to: by denying my pain and making as though nothing significant had happened. My mother valued productivity, responsibility, duty, so when my boss resigned and I was promoted only months after my father died, and staff and volunteers to my office were simultaneously cut from four persons to two, I took up the slack, working 80-100 hour weeks. I became too exhausted to cook, but I went to work; too exhausted to see friends, but I went to work; too exhausted to shower, but I went to work. I then, unsurprisingly given the tsunami of trauma in which I had been awash for so long, became ill. Very, very ill. I had to leave work and for the last fifteen years I have been in and out of bed, sometimes with limited function, sometimes with none at all.

Five years into this new life of disability, while dancing for all of five minutes at a healing retreat, I heard a very loud, very clear internal voice: "dance will heal you". I knew by then to listen to such voices, but I was still so ill, struggling daily just to survive, that I could not implement what I knew. I was too ill to access any of the ways I knew to dance--going to a dance class, drum circle, club, or party. Given the nature of my illness, I couldn't even have friends over to dance at my house. I tried to dance on my own, but could not make it a habit. I looked on the internet, but at that time, there were no dance offerings online. More years passed, during which I became even more drastically ill. But the knowing voice would not desist, and so every now and then I would again look online, hoping to find some way to dance at home but with others. Then, three years ago, I came across a notice for an online dance offering, sponsored by an organization called Interplay (www.interplay.org)

At first the name "Interplay" gave me pause. I was so removed from my playful self, so lost again to trauma, and had so internalized my mother's messaging, that play itself seemed dangerous, irresponsible. I attended anyway, and my life changed. In the Interplay community, play is regarded as a birthright, and dance joins voice, story, and stillness as a key playful practice. Interplay gatherings are improvisational, spontaneous, and one is witnessed in one's play with love. In sum, Interplay feels like dancing does to a little girl whirling outside in her front yard on a new spring morning, if she has the space and support to just be as she is, wide open with joy and wonder. Slowly, slowly, I began to feel as I had at the Abbey so many years before: Safe. Happy. Free.

I now teach Interplay to others because I have come to believe that play is at the root of creation and of joy. As such, it is both a means of personal healing and a radical challenge to cruelty, injustice, and oppression. Want to bring a new world into being? Play.

Choosing Now, Choosing Me

Naomi Puri

I take a deep breath, close my eyes, and wait. It doesn't take long for her to appear, the 8-year-old who looks like she wants to say something but can't quite find the words, or maybe she's too scared to speak them. She's calm and composed, quiet and unassuming, but look a little closer and there's an emptiness there. It hurts so much, a pain she's not experienced before, an overwhelming mix of sadness, fear, guilt and loneliness. She just wants the pain to stop. The only way she knows how is to try her best to ignore it, to keep quiet, to stay low and to be very very careful in case something bad should happen again.

It's not until the last couple of years that I've tried to reconnect with that little girl again. She needs to let those feelings of fear, anxiety, guilt and shame go - to let the grief out. And so here we are, here I am, knowing that it's time - time to choose now, to choose me. It sounds simple enough but I'm not entirely sure who me is anymore - she's hidden so well for so long it's difficult to connect with her, difficult to really see her. And it requires a lot of energy to choose now, to stop myself slipping back to the past, or worrying about the future. I am still working on this.

My story is one of grief as a child and how I've carried it for over 30 years, and how that grief became an overwhelming fear, holding me back and keeping me safe. It's about how I've (mis) interpreted my Dad's own language of love and the stories it created. I reflect on how my family home came to represent much of that grief and fear and how the simple act of selling that home has led me to start changing the narrative. It's a story, just beginning, of a girl who is finally letting go.

Reflections of a younger me

I was 7 when my mum died from cancer - my sister was 3. I can remember being told about her death and struggling to understand the finality of that sentence: your mum is dead, mum is dead, my mum is dead? I just wanted to hug her one last time, to tell her I loved her and that I was sorry for any unkind words I'd spoken. I think I was told about it in a café but that seems an odd place to be told so maybe not. I have a memory of looking out at the trees and up at the sky thinking "she's gone up there?" or was that a dream? Perhaps it's too painful to remember the order of events and feelings or perhaps it's just faded over time, memories merging to the point where I'm never quite sure what was real or not. One minute she was here, the next she was gone. And the pain grew over the years rather than become easier as everyone seems to assume it does. Not as a child. As a child you think your parents are invincible, there to look after you, to protect you, to love you. Until they're not. And that was scary at that age. I was unable to voice my real feelings and scared of what those feelings were. So, instead, I bottled them up whilst the void inside me got larger and larger over time.

And then, 10 years ago, my father passed away after suffering from dementia and ultimately dying from pneumonia. I know you're meant to say "living with" when you speak about dementia, but I can assure you that neither he nor we were living with it. So I've clung to this place where I'm sitting now, our childhood home, in an attempt to keep them both alive. It's a place to reconnect with them, as a sense of duty to my father in particular and as some weird way of boxing off my grief. It resides here, it's contained here, I can keep it separated from the rest of my life and keep me safe.

Looking back, I don't think I've really truly appreciated the impact it had on me as a 7- or 8-year-old, suddenly thrust into a more responsible and overwhelming way of being and living. I've always known and been proud of the fact that it shaped me but I am just realising it also misshaped me. The real me got lost along the way somehow. I'm only now going back to try and find her, to hold her hand and guide her into the present.

It was the '80s when Dad became a widower. His verbal and written English was poor. He never spoke to us about mum dying, at least I can't remember him ever doing so. Looking back, I can see he was overwhelmed with grief and just trying to hold it together. We never knew if mum had been buried or cremated (and we dare not ask), so for a ridiculously long time we didn't have a place to go to be with her. I could feel her presence sometimes in the flat and it gave me comfort. If I was upset I'd talk to her and was sure she was there, listening, comforting me from afar. We kept our grief to ourselves, internalising it, convinced that time would heal … but instead it created an emptiness. A missing part.

My teachers, friends and their families were brilliant and school was my sanctuary. I came to love (and need) the structure and uniformity of it: something stable, something that felt safe with logical order. I can see how this plays out in my life today. It's not a bad thing but it's important for me to recognise when I'm maybe craving too much structure, too much familiarity. It might be a sign that I'm retreating or fearing something.

As a child, and indeed as an adult, I just wanted to make my Dad proud, something for him to be happy about, something to make all his hard work worthwhile. But I felt that too often I fell short of his hopes and expectations. He had come from nothing, growing up in a remote village in Northern India, where the family worked hard to live off what land they had, where education was basic or non-existent and where family and home were central to life. My Dad saw the opportunities we were afforded in the UK and his expectations were high. Why would we not want to study all day, get straight A's and become a doctor, lawyer or accountant (the rather specific expectations of my future). But I know that he was doing the very best he could and he wanted more for us because he loved us. It's just that as a kid, and definitely as a teenager, it was often hard to see that. It felt like I wasn't being seen and I told myself that I had to change to become this successful person he hoped for, otherwise his struggles were all in vain. I felt stupid and unworthy when his expectations were unmet. I felt guilt for the time and money wasted on me. I felt *guilt for simply being.*

Dad could not afford to buy himself anything but the essentials. For him these consisted of a roof over our heads, food on the table, bills paid and enough clothes to clothe us and no more. Oh and a private education for me, the eldest, who was expected to go far, do great things and earn good money. Guilt and shame again. My Dad earned minimum wage, sometimes less when it was cash in hand. We counted my school fees in cash, £10 notes hidden under carpets. Yes, really! I can remember frantically trying to find them when Dad forgot which bit of carpet some of the stash was under. We were always late with the fees, although the school was lenient with us despite the numerous red letters we got. I felt guilt about this too and disappointment with myself for not being an A-grade student. I was gathering yet more evidence of not being good enough to be here, not being worthy, not fitting in. I felt guilty for wanting anything different to what my Dad was clearly struggling to offer us so I guess I shut down those wants. I lost my voice and that has continued into adulthood. One thing Dad was particularly adamant about was keeping the flat once he died. He wanted to have somewhere that was ours in case we had any problems and he told us very directly to keep it, not to sell it. You didn't argue with my Dad, you just did as you were told. Until you don't.

Letting go

But here I am, having just accepted an offer on the flat we once called home and I'm feeling like a protective layer is coming away. It's unnerving me but exhilarating all at the same time. The time feels right, and in choosing now, I want to say farewell to the past with love. These walls protected us through the hardest of times growing up but also hold some very fond memories.

In letting go of the flat, I'm really letting go of all those negative feelings and finally being at peace with the past. I'm finally grieving. I'm realising that young Naomi will always be part of me and letting go of the past doesn't mean I'm letting go of the love. I'm not letting my Dad down. I'm not going to forget. Quite the opposite. I'm choosing to invest that love into the life I lead now, being present for me and my family, making my own choices.

As the flat sale grew closer, I felt strongly that I just needed to leave. No more lingering, no more jobs, it was done. I was done. Time now for the new owners to create their first home, something which has given us great comfort over the last few weeks. On my last day in the flat I kissed the walls, thanking them for keeping me safe all those years ago, for what our Dad is now gifting us. I switched off the lights in the hall, glanced back one last time before shutting the door firmly, pausing, breathing it in and then the tears flowed and flowed unapologetically. Released.

I feel lighter now, having experienced severe bouts of tiredness and I've taken time to stop and rest. Some people may think it's nothing to be sad about but for me the flat was somewhere I went to reconnect with my parents, a grave if you like in the absence of a real grave for either. I have now let out a whole heap of shame and guilt for what I had done, for the daughter I had not been. But in whose eyes? Who said this to me other than myself? Nobody and yet I chose to believe these thoughts and many more. I made the best decisions I could at each stage with love in my heart. I know that much. I no longer feel a rising need to explain our decision of putting Dad into a care home when others comment how they could never do that. We did the best we could and for a long time, I felt I'd fallen short.

Selling the flat was more than something transactional. It was a symbolic moment of self forgiveness, of letting go of old stories and creating a new way of being. I now choose to respect and honour the past and not be weighed down by it and to make a path of my own creation.

Finding your strengths

My grief gifted many life lessons. My experiences in my childhood have built a level of resilience that I think most adults would find hard to muster, a level of empathy for others born from experiencing grief so deep you could get lost in it and an understanding of what it means to come from nothing and create something for yourself and your family. Through my childhood, and through helping to care for Dad when he had dementia, I've built a great deal of patience and generally can stay calm in a crisis. I guess that's no surprise when I reflect on what responsibility and situations I had to manage as a child. I was regularly on the phone on behalf of my Dad, or was dragged along to meetings, or his place of work, or looked after my sister when he couldn't afford childcare. It's these strengths and skills from a young Naomi that I'm starting to see more clearly now and want to embrace, rather than constantly battling with myself to be something else, to be a different version.

When I close my eyes now, and look again, I don't see a shy, anxious, scared little girl. I see a young girl with love in her heart for her father, mother and sister. This young girl is now a woman, a mother, discovering herself all over again, helping her daughter to navigate her own feelings of self worth - a reminder that we were all once 8-year-olds, stumbling to make sense of our feelings, trying to find our way out of the shadows and, if we're lucky, guided by love.

The Fires of Initiation

Maya Spector

What is happening in my body
is happening in and to the earth.
Fires rage, burning their way
to cleansing and renewal.
This is not easy for the people.
Lungs struggle to breathe.
Houses burn to ash.
Forests and animals are
struck down.
To the earth, we are the interlopers,
greedily pushing our way
into places we have
no business occupying.

And me?
My body has
interlopers, too.
I am being initiated
by fire.
I am becoming
a fire priestess.
I follow the burning
in and through channels
and watch things die.
I learn to stir a cauldron
bubbling over flames, cooking
down all that needs
transforming, everything ready
to melt into new form.

And so I say –
Fire, your power is
undeniable; your genius
rolls out over many fields.
Here is an offering.
My basket is empty now,
my water gourd running low.
May renewal come.

Reflections on *The Fires Of Initiation*

At first, I didn't worry about it too much. I'd had
digestive and gut issues for a number of years, but
now the pain kept getting worse. The Covid-19
pandemic was beginning to shut everything down. My
primary care doctor made some recommendations
that didn't help, and then had me message my
gastroenterologist. Even after I had to risk going to
Urgent Care, where they could only recommend
imaging, my GI doc didn't want me to come into any
medical facility due to the virus. It was probably just a
blockage. It would pass.

It didn't. Finally, after a month of pain and waiting, he
had me get a CT scan. I hadn't been home from the
imaging center for more than 45 minutes when he
called. I knew it had to be bad news, but I never
imagined this. Cancer. I would need a biopsy and an
appointment with an oncologist as soon as possible.

The shock of receiving a life-threatening diagnosis is
shattering at any time, for anyone. Having it happen
in the time of the Covid lock-down added layers of
complication and stress, including having to go into
medical appointments and procedures alone. I
remember sitting in the darkened, eerily empty
waiting room before the biopsy, the only patient there.

And also later walking into the surgeon's office, bent over in pain, having to call my husband on speaker phone so that he could hear what was happening. The diagnosis wasn't good. Stage 4 sarcoma. I had no idea what a sarcoma was. I remember naively asking, "Is that better than carcinoma?" No. It isn't. The docs made it clear that there is no cure. What they said was that they would try to extend my life.

The surgeon insisted that we needed to try to shrink the main tumor before he could safely operate, so I began four rounds (three months) of chemo. My next scan revealed that the chemo was working. Only after the fact did my oncologist tell me that only one in five patients has success with this chemo, and even then success meant 15% shrinkage at most. By the time I went into surgery, the tumor had shrunk 20%.

Unlike many other cancer patients, I never thought of cancer as the enemy. Words like "fighting cancer" or being a "warrior" never resonated with me. Don't get me wrong – cancer was not welcome. Getting the infusions, I would imagine holding up the infusion bags to the four directions, blessing it to be the medicine needed. After a lot of reflection, I began to understand that my illness was not so different from what the earth was suffering.

I live in northern California where the frequency and severity of summer wildfires has become a fact of life. Even when we live hundreds of miles away from a fire, we have learned to monitor the air quality. The damaging particles may be too small to see, but your lungs feel them. I felt as though the chemo blasting through my veins was similar to the fires running rampant across the earth's body. I never felt that getting cancer was my fault, but rather a result of what humans have done to the planet. Aren't the fires the same?

I have been fortunate to have supportive family and community, and a long history of spiritual practice. I am also tremendously grateful for having had a mentor in this journey, someone who had stage 4 pancreatic cancer five years ago, who was given two months to live, and who is still here. One of the most important things she told me early on was, "Don't make the medical establishment your home." I know my life was saved by western medicine. I have been around and been treated by some very caring medical folks. But there is much that is difficult (and even, in my opinion, wrong) about the institution. So often doctors are technicians rather than healers. I'm grateful for what they are able to do, but I know that all of us are more than statistics; that there is, of course, more to us than merely being patients.

It may sound like a platitude, but life-threatening illnesses can truly change your life. There is a choice about seeing it as an initiation, a chance to deepen into greater awareness. One thing that arose for me in these past 18 months is the understanding that I want and intend to live a more prayerful life. Prayer was not a part of my life before. I used to think of it as merely asking for what I want, or trying to make deals with the universe, God, or however one conceives of the Great Mystery. Now, prayer for me is coming into relationship with that which is greater than myself. I am grateful for my life.

My surgery and treatment were successful, for now. There are no guarantees. With this kind of cancer, recurrences happen often. But I chose to see it as an initiation into a more meaningful life, for however long that may be. I choose to consider the possibility of renewal, for myself, and for the earth.

Balance as A Dynamic Process

Martina Naversnik

Life is a bit like a seesaw and to find balance can be a real challenge sometimes. In our everyday lives as 'grown ups' there is a seemingly endless carousel of seesaws that can make us dizzy with all the ups and downs they can bring.

How do we find the right kind of balance between:

- Work & play
- Our own needs & other's needs
- Heart & head
- Gut instinct & analysis and overthinking
- Doing & being
- Things we can control & things we cannot

These are just a few examples, the list is endless and of course, different for everyone.

Personally, I had developed patterns of behaviour that were throwing my life into such a level of imbalance that it tipped me into illness. I worked far more than I played, in fact, work was all consuming. My decision making was very much based on analysis and if I am honest, overthinking. Doing was not only my preferred state, it had become a defence mechanism against feeling. There are, of course, other factors that played a role, factors that I could not have controlled, like my neighbour flooding my apartment to the extent that the building insurance paid for me to live elsewhere for several months, my father dying of pancreatic cancer or having a job that required travelling to developing countries on a regular basis.

Eventually my body decided that enough was enough and stopped me – quite literally. I developed a condition called ME. It is a complex, often chronic condition for which the schools of medicine do not have any clear answers or treatment yet. To simplify, the main symptom is a debilitating lack of energy. In healthy people a marvellous biochemical process converts the nutrients from the food eaten and the oxygen from the breathing process into available energy for that person – this mechanism does not work to a greater or lesser extent for people with ME. Whether or not and to which extent it works, i.e. how much energy is available to the person with ME is also variable and unpredictable, so the affected person may be able to function one day but not the next. Energy is required for anything you do: thinking, speaking, having a shower, eating and digesting food, getting up and making yourself breakfast or a cup of tea. So, the less energy you have, the less of those things you can do. Your choices become very limited. As it is a spectrum disorder some people are able to work but then are not able to do much else, whereas others are bed bound and need 24 hr care. I was not bed bound but ended up pretty much house bound.

Initially, I fought hard to get my body to function the way I was used to and wanted it to. I tried to force it to comply with what I wanted, but it did not play ball – to remain in the image of the playground. In fact the more I tried to force it the less energy it made available to me. I eventually resigned after 12 months off sick and another year trying to work part time.

Once I surrendered to the situation and started to listen to my heart and my emotions, I found a way to re-balance. Through painting, I found my way out of frustration, anger and depression. I felt less useless when I could see something tangible develop that I was creating. It didn't matter how many ten-minute sessions it took to complete one painting because in the beginning that was all I could manage. I am still not 100% back to full health but I can see a way forward even if I never get back to my previous energy levels, without giving up hope that I will recover fully. After all, if some people do it, I can do it – I don't give up easily!

It is always difficult to find a new perspective when you are in the middle of a challenging situation. When I was given my diagnosis I was faced with a debilitating potentially chronic condition, that if it was chronic would change everything. Looking back at my journey so far I developed a concept about balancing my life that I think might be helpful to share. Sometimes it helps to try and clarify what is going on by trying to write things down or chart them somehow, especially if you are the visual type. You might want to try and chart the axes of the circle of your life.

Draw a circle and start with one horizontal line through the centre. Label one end with a direction you feel pulled into, e.g. work, and label the opposite end of the line with the opposite direction, in this example play. Keep adding extra lines through the circle until you feel you have the main factors that you want to achieve balance with. Try using different colours for different areas of your life. You may have to play with this for a while until you feel you have captured the 'forces' that determine the dynamics of your life. The axes may also change over time - so it's worth repeating this exercise once in a while.

This is what my circle would have looked like before my body stopped me.

You can then mark where you are on each axis. Your life is all work and no play? Put the cross close to the work label. Mark your position on the other axes to reflect how you feel about those life situations.

When I was contemplating this, the other image that came to mind was that of a roly-poly toy. You know, one of those figures that have half a sphere, with a weight inside it as their bottom half, try as you might you cannot get them to lie down, they wobble about for a while and then they are upright again.

So, depending on where you have marked yourself on the axes, you would get an idea how much you are wobbling about in your life, or how out of balance you are. The closer your markers are to the edge of the circle, the higher the amplitude of your movements and the less in balance you might feel.

As adults we also learn that we need both ups and downs in our lives, for there is no up without a down. If we were up all the time we would assume up was the new normal and it would soon lose its appeal and positive notion. So, if we accept that some level of up and down is actually required, the question becomes one of amplitude. How high and how low do we want the overall line of our lives to go? What is the right level for us? What are we comfortable with?

If we put the two images together we would end up with the circle we have drawn illustrating the issues we want to balance, sitting on top of the half sphere that makes us move along the axes all the time to balance and stay in the game. I would imagine there is a protective bubble over the top, which stretches as we approach the edge, but if we stretch it too far it is likely to break and take us out of the game for a while until the bubble can be restored.

I have come to the conclusion that balance in life is not a state, it is a constant process and we get to decide to an extent how turbulent we want that process to be. Of course, some of the things we cannot control, can really throw us off balance, but it is our awareness and reaction to such situations that determines how far off balance we get thrown and how long it takes us to get back into the range of 'dynamic' balance we have decided is comfortable for us.

What are those curve balls, those events out of our control that throw us out of balance? Perhaps losing a loved one without any warning, or being diagnosed with an illness that turns any life plans upside down, or the break up of a relationship you saw potential in – I'm sure you have your own experiences of such events that you did not see coming, but that devastated you. You will find several examples on the other pages in this book.

Being in static balance would mean we are standing still and whilst being still in meditation can be a wonderfully relaxing and recharging experience that helps us gain clarity, peace and calmness, most of us are not in this state permanently. What we do want though, is awareness of what is actually happening and a way of influencing our situation so that it works for us.

So, if you have actually gone ahead and drawn that circle and marked your position on your chosen axes of life, look at each position you have marked and whether you want to be in that position or somewhere else on that line. If the answer is I'm ok where I am, move on to the next axis. If the answer is, this position is not good at all, think about what you can do to move yourself to the position you want to be in. Some position changes might be massive and will take time to achieve, but whether they are massive or subtle they start with the first step. What step can you take now? Right now?

Maybe it is 'only' the commitment that you want to keep an eye on this and therefore will keep this weird drawing somewhere where you will see it regularly. Maybe you can do more straight away, who knows?

The size of the step is not what is important, it is the consistency of taking action. Thinking about what you want, bringing into awareness what influences the dynamics and then setting priorities for actions and taking action again and again and again … one step, after another, and another, and another, towards the life that you have decided you want to create.

Lots of short 10 minute sessions of painting add up to a finished work on a big canvas, even if after the first 10 minute session it doesn't look like anything, because you have just put a base layer on that helps the actual paint to adhere better. You could get frustrated and say this makes no difference, I might as well give up, or you can keep going and each little 10 minute session will contribute to the final piece of art. It's the same with each little step you take to address the imbalance; keep going and you will get to where you want to be.

The power is in the process, all those little steps add up. Imagine one of those massive balls in the gym. On your first day at the gym you probably would not be able to stand on the ball and keep your balance (PLEASE DO NOT TRY THAT!). Metaphorically it is the same, it takes time and practice to develop awareness of what the axes are in the first place, then how they determine the dynamics of the balancing act that is life for you to then be able to decide what strategies help you to get to the desired dynamic or amplitude. We may find that when we get to where we were aiming for, we do not like it after all and set a new goal.

Though, if the described dynamism is what we are expecting it will lead to less disappointment and perhaps the mindset of 'whatever happens, I can find my way back to my chosen dynamic balance'. With each step you take you are training your 'life balancing muscles' and the longer you do it consistently, the easier it will get.

We will also accept that there will be curve balls thrown at us on occasion and will give ourselves the time it takes to re-adjust and to finding a new equilibrium.

If you are reading this you are likely to have a 100% track record of survival, you have got this! If you have just slid to one side of your axis and feel out of balance, take a deep breath and a break, if you need to, and then get back up and decide where you want to be and make it happen. You are stronger than you think.

Ideally, I'd highly recommend not to wait until you feel extremely out of balance. I managed to re-balance but it took me quite a while and I was probably not the nicest person to be around. Start taking action earlier and do it consistently, so that you can hopefully avoid the challenges I went through.

Violent Consequences

Dr Jacqui Leaman-Grey

There has been much in the media recently about violence and women which caused me to reflect on how many acts of violence I had experienced personally. I was shocked to add them all up and to recognise how these experiences shaped my view of the world.

My mother cautioned me from a young age not to take sweets from strangers, not to talk to them, not to go with them because 'bad things can happen'. I learned to be fearful of the intentions of others, particularly men.

Aged 3 – 8 I experienced 'Inappropriate touching' by my grandfather – I learned that love comes at a price and that you can't trust men. I didn't tell anyone.

Aged 11 A Man stopped his car going in opposite direction, when I was walking 200 yards from a bus drop off to my grandmother's house, and tried to get me to get in, but I ran. I learned my mother was right, and that it wasn't safe to be out after dark on my own.

Aged 12 A Man exposed himself to me on a train – I learned not to sit in single carriages, not that they exist anymore, when travelling to school. This happened more than once.

Aged 14 In a Tunisian market – a local man in robes picked me up by putting his arm between my legs and lifting me off my feet and ducking down an alleyway in plain sight of my parents. A tour guide caught him just in time. I learned to fear travelling without chaperones.

Aged 15 – 18 I developed 'boobs' on my dancer's body. I went out and socialised a lot with my older (very protective) brother. Still, men of all age groups repeatedly touched me, groped me, tried to have sex with me at social occasions. I believed this was normal.

Aged 15 I was attacked by a motorcycle gang in a pub car park. I ran into the road and tried to get someone to stop – they stopped and then drove on despite my obvious distress. I fought, bit screamed and eventually an older girl they knew stopped them. All but one backed off, I bit his hand and he punched me in the face. He tried to attack me again a few weeks later 1:1 in the woods. I didn't tell anyone because I was ashamed it was my fault because of how I was dressed and because I was at a pub my parents didn't approve of. I was bruised and beaten but afraid of the consequences of speaking up. I learned to stay silent and 'get on with it'.

Aged 18 – 20 Men repeatedly 'hit on me' in bars, or tried to have sex with me at the end of evenings out. Several of my friends were forced to go further than they wanted. One was raped. We all stayed silent. I learned to fight them off with words. I fell in love with an older guy, who slept around and put my health at risk. I believed it was ok to treat me that way and eventually married him.

My 86 year old grandmother was attacked on a bus because she said the wrong thing and was hospitalised. I learned that women of all ages are vulnerable.

I spent most of my social time in rugby clubs – it was where I met my husband - and learned to take the 'banter' that is prevalent and to be honest I enjoyed the attention. I hate overly 'woke' behaviour and the stamping out of good natured humour, but there has to be a line. The danger of my upbringing was that I learned coping strategies that weren't always helpful. I learned to flirt to get what I wanted, to use sexuality as part of making my way because it worked. Some of the experiences I had would be regarded as abuse today but I recognise I played a part in my own experience.

Aged 20 working in Turkey on a yacht, a local man attacked me in a Market – he hit me and pushed tomatoes in my face when I wouldn't buy them, my then husband hit him and was almost arrested. I saw a man abusing some kittens, throwing them in the sea for fun, and terrorising his toddler. Again, my husband intervened, I learned to believe that I needed men to save me. I felt paralysed with fear in the face of so much violence.

Age 23+ finally in the world of work I learned how to hold my own amongst men, despite outrageous flirting, innuendos and occasional put downs or not being taken seriously. I climbed the corporate ladder despite them. I learned to use humour to diffuse difficult situations. I learned to stand up for myself as no one else would.

To summarise, I learned to believe the following:
- It isn't safe to trust
- Love and affection come at a price
- Sensible women don't go out in the dark on their own/to far flung places alone
- Sensible women don't wear provocative clothing unless with groups of other women or a male protector (and they generally don't like provocative clothing on 'their' women)

- It's OK for men to say and do things that sexualise me
- It's OK for men to touch me inappropriately as long as its friendly fun and they 'don't mean anything by it'
- Certain men will protect me – but when they leave, I feel unsafe.

I have no doubt some of my early experiences wounded and damaged my feelings of psychological safety, whilst others made me more resilient and able to navigate my way. I do believe 'what doesn't kill you makes you stronger' but why should we have to go through this? Sadly, I know that most women have had multiple experiences of the same sorts of things. I am not unique, and many women have endured much worse. Sadly, the things I learned are the messages many women have taken, and it constrains our ability to fully experience the world. I now believe it is safe to trust, that love doesn't usually come with a price tag, that I can wear what I like and will speak up when men overstep the line. I don't need men to protect me. The only one I still let constrain me is that I don't tend to walk alone outside at night and there are definitely places I choose not to go because I don't deem them safe. I am not sure what would change these perceptions for me as I also don't want to live in a police state where every move is monitored.

I have studied Existential Philosophy and researched the human sense of self, psychological safety and our relationships with others. I have also worked with social neuroscientists and the concept of 'Threat and Reward' and what happens in the brain when it perceives we are under threat. Basically, we experience an 'Amygdala hijack' where the limbic system (sometimes known as the animal brain) takes

59

over the logical thinking part of the brain, known as the Prefrontal Cortex or the PFC and we become emotional and unable to think. The stress hormone Cortisol is released which is very harmful to the human body over time, especially for women. When we suffer the same type of experience over and over our brains form biases and filters through which we see the world. These filters affect our beliefs and perceptions about others. My repeated experiences with men formed a filter which meant I had difficulty in trusting others, especially men, I became attracted to men who were emotionally unavailable to me, and an expectation that they would hurt me in some way. Something that took years to overcome.

I 'brought up boys' and I know they are respectful of women and would step in if needed to challenge the inappropriate behaviour of others. I don't believe these things are caused by all men but by a small proportion and it isn't enough to just not do it yourself. Women must take men on the empowerment journey with us. Men are victims of their personal experiences as well but without the fear of physical violence, or at least to the same degree. Their life experiences and the way they were taught about women, and the interactions they have with friends at school, their parents, the media, all affect how they view the world and their subsequent interactions with others. They may potentially do things that scare women even if it's unintentional.

I remember once crossing the road to avoid a gang of scary young men in hoodies and then realised it was my future husband's younger brother and his friends who were lovely and only 15 but they really scared me when I didn't know who they were. We know that some behaviours are more sinister. Nevertheless, I choose to believe that most men are good and want to do their best in this imperfect world. I now live with my second husband who is kind, would never hurt me, and who spends his working life helping others.

This is not just a personal problem but a systemic one. Many men are asking what they can do to help. They need to engage in the conversation and actively notice when things are not ok and to say so. To root out where inequality exists in their own worlds. Not to be patriarchal heroes and saviours but just to play their part in societal change.

Why I am hopeful

The world is a different place to when I was growing up. We only have to look at TV programmes representing the 50's/60s and 70's like 'Mad Men' or 'Life on Mars' to see how much. It would no longer be acceptable for men to treat women the way they used to inside or outside of organisations. The focus on feminine nature-based leadership in service to healing the planet, plus the 'me too' movement and Inclusion generally has led to greater awareness of people's rights and a new set of societal values. Stereotypes are no longer entrenched in terms of sexuality or what it means to be a woman. I believe that the Millennials and later generations are leading the way. We must listen to them.

What needs to be done?

- Parents and schools need to educate young men around consent and what is OK and not.
- Societies like sports clubs and male dominated environments need to look at their culture and what they need to do to ensure they are not reinforcing outdated stereotypes.

- We also need to educate young women (including all non-binary people identifying as such) in holding boundaries and what to do in difficult situations, that they have rights and that they don't 'have to put up with it', or 'over allow' behaviours they don't like. They need to work on their confidence and step up. They need to step into their power, to have a voice, and to be clear when things are not OK. (See how at www.feforte.com)
- Organisations employ many people around the world. Greater attention must be paid to stamping out inequalities and they must train their people in Unconscious Bias and Inclusion. Some sectors are already stepping up and are better than others, but we can all do better. Shockingly, the dates for when we will reach parity in organisations is currently set at 61 years in Western Europe and 165 years in North America! (World Economic Forum 2018)
- We all need to watch the stereotypes we are playing into. We need to think about the messaging we give to our children and to the world about how we deal with systemic abuse. I am learning all the time as I unconsciously see the world through the lens of a 'middle class mother of boys' which is not always OK. I heard a female presenter of my age say on breakfast television 'I just learned to get on with it but younger women just won't have it will they?' The younger guest said 'yes but they shouldn't have to be the only ones fighting back'. I think she's right.

Maiden

Heather Pearson

When I was a young girl, I never felt like I had the time to just be a child. I never felt like I had the opportunity to just be *me*. To be free.

My parents loved me, but of course, they were imperfect. My dad was kind, but he had a terrible temper. I feared him; I felt his subtle distaste for the messiness of life - of *me*. I only felt loved when I was a 'good girl'— when I was smart, sensible, and quiet. And so I was always smaller than I truly was.

My mum, I loved dearly. But when I turned six, she lost her mind to schizophrenia. She never left home, apart from brief stints in a mental hospital, and she made a great recovery—but it felt like, ever since that day, I never saw her again.

Being a mixed race girl in a small town with a small-town mind, I never felt like I belonged anywhere, and I was badly bullied. My peers could never place their finger on me, couldn't understand me—how I was so familiar yet so other, that abject feeling of confusion and disgust. I didn't meet another mixed white and Asian person until I went to University at eighteen. Even now, I still struggle to feel my roots.

I deeply hated school - though I greatly loved to learn. There were teachers who saw my potential, who tried to coax it out of me, who recognised my brilliance in English and Music, but I could never let them in, I never felt safe enough or just *me* enough to let *anyone* in, and they could only do so much.

When I left school to go to Sixth Form College, amongst a sea of new people in a slightly bigger, more accepting town, it felt safer to shine. It felt like it was my time! I discovered my style—and had great fun experimenting with my gender expression, with my long black hair, red lipstick and glittered eyes, and magenta suit and tie. I had my first boyfriend, a sweet boy whom I loved so much; yet the unresolved pain of my past meant I pushed him and his love away the whole rocky two years we spent together.

I made true, lifelong friends in the corner of my Philosophy class, and I left the ones who talked ill of me behind my back. I went off to University, and after a lonely and tumultuous first year, I finally found my tribe. It felt like, for the first time in my life, I was free to have fun! And I did, and I did so many great things for myself and others, but I was chipping my life away with addictions: drinking, and drugs.

I was naïve; I had convinced myself I was starting to pave a way out of my past pain, but I still carried it with me, dragging it around my feet like a ball and chain, in the form of my addictions. The addictions effortlessly morphed between substances and people, and with my lowered defences I was vulnerable to people who would take advantage of me: my early twenties were ravaged by abusive, addictive relationships that drained the life force from me like a leech sucks blood. One with a woman I thought I could trust, and another with a man who I knew I could *never* place my faith, but his danger, cruelty, and volatility felt strangely safe. That 4-month whirlwind of a 'relationship' with him was a cyclone that destroyed the very ground I walked on, shattered me to pieces with ricocheting debris and left me—literally—battered, bruised and abused.

That night, as I watched him being carted away in a police car, with only a yellow blanket draped around my purpling body, I didn't feel like I'd hit rock bottom. It felt like the end: the end of the darkest night, and the beginning of the brightest dawn. It felt like I had *finally* become my own light at the end of the tunnel. It felt like I had *survived*, and I knew it was now the time to take the reins of my life. I was hopeful; I knew now was the time for *me*.

That evening, as I feared for my life, I returned to my faith. I prayed, because after being so completely pillaged by this man, all that seemed to remain was my Soul - the eternal light that can never go out. My prayers that night were not desperate, they were Divine.

As a spiritual seeker, I knew, cognitively, that 'I' could never die. I knew, cognitively, that angels were always on my side. That fateful night, it was time to put it into practice. It was time to bring mind down into body and *through* Soul. It was time to Feel, and to Know, not just understand, that this was the Truth. In those moments I was alone, my Soul beamed forth and told me to have faith, that my life as I knew it was about to end; but not to worry; even if I was to be killed, my Soul would never die. And so, I didn't give up hope. I surrendered.

 And I felt them there: my angels, and *Her*, the Goddess. It truly was nothing short of a miracle, that evening, in a cottage in the middle of nowhere, with no signal and certainly no access to my phone, that the police arrived. I managed to escape his grasp for just ten minutes whilst he was distracted, and in a moment of resourcefulness, logged onto my laptop and filed a police report online. My heart sank when I saw the confirmation message: 'it may take up to a week to get back to you'. At that point, I didn't give up hope, I surrendered. My body felt weaker than it ever had, but my Soul felt as strong as a mountain. I continued to pray and felt my eternal essence, my Soul, beam out of me. Even though I was afraid, I knew 'I' could never die. That Truth saved me. In no miraculous coincidence, the police happened to catch the online report as it was submitted, sensed the danger, and arrived two hours later. I was safe; for the first time, it felt, in a lifetime.

**

And now, as I write this, barely a year has passed. I'm twenty-four now; I'm still so terribly young, but life has left me weathered by the most severe of storms. The climate of my recent and distant past could have hardened me, left me cold, cut off, fearful, resentful, and lost. And I have felt this...sometimes, at an intensity I thought would debilitate me.

But that night, my faith returned, and She never left. And so, with Her help, I am beginning to flourish again.

I had always found it hard to feel any sense of pride. I thought it was arrogant, or that I didn't deserve it. But now, I can truly say that I am so utterly, and unbelievably, proud of myself. After the event, I received the greatest help I could ever ask for: from the police; from local domestic abuse services; from my parents, for taking me in again; from my friends, for loving me unconditionally; for the new people who came into my life to empower me, guide me, and restore me to Life; and from Her, the Goddess, for sparking the remembrance of my eternal, ancient, and mystical power, re-aligning me to my sacred purpose here on this earth.

I received so much help, but without the tenacity, determination, bravery, and courage that I managed to muster from myself, I could have never stopped the cycle.

What helped me was to live my life embodied as Soul. My ego had taken too many hits to take the front seat. My Soul took over and She showed me the way. She showed me grace, and my Heart softened and spoke to me; and so, I began to listen.

And because of that, I was reborn into a Queen.

I married my delicateness with discernment.
My gentleness with grit.
My innocence with instinct.
My softness with strength.

And so, I became like the Greek Goddess Persephone: the Spring Maiden who was kidnapped into the Underworld. When it was time for her to leave for the light, she carried her darkness and light as One. She became a Queen. And that is what birthed the seasons—the cycles of life—the grace of the descent, and the grace of the ascent, always spiralling towards the light.

Then I began to realise, even though it felt like ever since I was a child I was never allowed to just *be* one—I never lost that youthfulness. I never lost that young Maiden, that glimmering, eternal beam of light. She was just hiding: in her own little world, she was playing, laughing, singing, and smiling. She never grew old. She could never die. And in enough time, with enough safety and support, she managed to come out again.

I hold her hand now, and we walk side by side. She is with me in every smile, laughter, and permeating sense of Joy that can lighten up any room and heart. She is soft, sweet, kind, and gentle. But my Queen is always around to take the reins, to keep my head held high, to be discerning of danger, to speak up for and stand up for my worth, to unapologetically prioritise my pleasure and pursue my passions, and to keep us both safe, and thriving.

Even though I am a woman now, the young Maiden is still within me. She could never grow old, for she is the purest light of the Soul, and even though She hid away, it never stopped her from shining.

She illuminates my life now. The Joy that keeps my blood pumping and gives resolve to my bones. I speak for her, I dance for her, I write for her, I live for her. I do this for my younger self, my inner Maiden, the girl who never felt like it was safe to be her. It is safe to be you, now, sweet one. This is for you.

***

as pure as snow
and as effervescent as the stars
in the sky,
the Maiden archetype
represents our innocence;
unpenetrated, yet,
by the dark of the world—
the young girl, within,
that never grows old.

brilliant and bright
she shines through her eyes;
open, curious and wide—and
her smile; soft and sweet
and shy and tender,
the Maiden sparks
remembrance
of the light of the soul,
our eternal radiance,
that never grows old.

youthful, fervent and fresh,
you'll find her amongst flowers
in flowing Sunday best,
dressed in joy and jubilance
exuberance and enthusiasm
as she dances with the rabbit,
the deer - the animals of Spring,
her season; sheer bliss without reason,
she is the muse of life,
she is the breath of new,
she is the beginning of the
cycle that always unfolds,
she is that sweet Maiden,
that never grows old.

*****

but in every Woman
there was once a girl,
an unsuspecting Persephone
seized straight into the underworld.

swept off her feet
and straight onto her knees,
forced to face her shadow
by the light of Hades.

though a painful initiation
for her sensitive heart,
her body finds surrender
and makes love to the dark.

enlightened by the night
and all her Self seen,
thus completes the rite
from Maiden to Queen.

*****

though crowned and older
and wiser now, Her joy is a
wellspring the never runs dry -
excitement for life need not
be quelled by experience,
no need to wear our resilience
like armour around the heart -
may we soften through every Spring
and fresh start,
may we reign with the fierceness
of the lionheart and the gentleness
of the lamb,
may we hold her hand through every
fire and flame,
may we return to Her
sweetness and reclaim
our Innocence, our essence,
the pure light of our Soul—
the Maiden, within,
She never grows old.

To Be Resilient Is To Be Resourceful

Sarah Pepper

My life now tells me that being resilient has led me to develop a superpower in being resourceful. Allow me to elaborate on that theory…

It started in 1982.

My mother was a daughter of a working-class mother whose father came from Yorkshire to work in the Nottinghamshire coal mines, and her father was a textile worker who studied to become a university lecturer in textile technology. My father was also the son of a coal miner.

My mother and father had been married 3 years and were much in love. My mother had recently been made redundant. In 1984 my sister arrived. My mother's mental health deteriorated and the lifestyle events that had happened to her over the past 5 years; loss of job, marriage, a motor-scooter incident, two children, and a second house move. All took their toll on her shy, meek, timid nature, like straws from the game Kerplunk being removed one by one, unable to retain the marbles in the upper container – and she was diagnosed with Schizophrenia.

In the early stages of my mother's prognosis, there was a disconnect between my father and my grandparents regarding the type of care and support she needed. Mental illness is often a taboo subject and talks of her being sectioned are mentioned. A story once shared was on a day when my father returned home from his 12-hour shift, in a non-summer month, to find my sister and me in a paddling pool in our garden alone – we were about four and two. Prior to this, I add, I fell out the bedroom window, and luckily landed in a bush. I share these stories to tell the tale of a much unattached parenting style that we experienced. We soon moved closer to both sets of grandparents for support due to these events and the pressure of the illness upon my mother and father's relationship. My earliest memories of being a responsible child were looking after my sister. Walking her to primary school approximately one mile through residential pathways, finding dinner money where we could within the house, washing our clothes and then using the (coal) fire to dry them with a 50% success rate of not burning them. My dad, a sportsman, played football, refereed football, umpired at cricket matches, worked, did whatever was necessary to provide but also to be busy and to be "needed" away from the home – to "reduce the stress" on my mother

The times when we were not at school, my sister and I would walk to grandma's approximately 1.5 miles (2.41 km) (country lane with no footpath) to be fed, for company and for immense unconditional love. My grandma (on my mother's side) was a nurturing, empathetic, loving soul with a huge deep heart, with a greeting of Woo hoo whenever she entered a room. She made the best chips (from a chip pan – they were the rage in 80/90's) followed by the mandatory choc ice (another snack fashioned by the 80's/90's). She also gave the most loving hugs and sung us, 'You are my Sunshine' as we lay with her.

My grandad (on my mother's side) was then retired. He was strong, disciplined (we occasionally clashed (both Taurus)) and he was very handy and was always in the garage. It was there I learnt to drill, clean my bike with paraffin, disassemble and reassemble all sorts, make things for our toys. He drove a navy-blue Ford Capri Laser 2.0 with subtle orange stripes, and I loved it.

Entering teen hood...well, that's a rollercoaster for us all at the best of times. When I was 14 my father informed me on the way back from a football match I had played in) that he was splitting up with my mother, which I thought, due to her need to be cared for, would never happen. Seventeen years of marriage ended in a few months. Looking back, we had Christmas' where we would be at grandma's and my dad would be at his parents...as a child, one just thought Santa mislaid my dad's presents, hence him being there to receive them.

At the age of 14 I was in a relationship with a guy ten years older than me, and due to my years of responsibility and awareness, felt no age gap. To the outside world, this was not a normal relationship; to me, I formed a security blanket, and we lasted four years and bought a house. I was the breadwinner at 16, and I was the alpha female in the relationship.

I played football for a ladies' football club and then started refereeing. These were opportunities my dad provided for me to unleash the anger and keep me out of trouble. We also tried jazz dancing and horse riding – my dad was a huge advocate for providing opportunities to try things out (be busy) and to be open-minded about unknown challenges.

When you're a daughter of a mentally ill person you become very resourceful and learn quite quickly that you're not a priority, nor can you be. Their illness is the priority, then them, and then their environment and support network. My sister and I have a great relationship; we are a team. She is the carer, and I'm the doer and fixer when looking after our mother. I love her more than she knows (and more than I let on).

It is here where I would like to explain that woe cannot be allowed to enter your demeanour. To be woeful in my childhood environment may have been seen as self-inward or adding emotional pressures to others, which is something in our home environment could not be addressed or calculated for. It was also a wasted use of an emotion. As I aged, being woeful could be a scary place to enter, as you could be trespassing into the realms of mental instability. This was a place where, as I grew, I definitely did not want to dwell, so over-compensated with positivity and smiles. This energy is resilience and with resilience comes being resourceful to find strategies to exist, appear normal, to function into today's society, to meet the demands and needs of the day. We had to become resourceful, we had to become resilient to survive.

I can remember coming home from being out with my mates around 15 years of age and my mother had had a drink as she was mourning the breakdown of her marriage. At the time I thought it was because she was mentally ill and careless with her approach, but as an adult I know it's a normal thing to reach for the "bottle". There was sick everywhere and an unconscious mother. I cleaned up, cried that I just couldn't be allowed to be a child, not even for a moment, and covered her with a blanket before sleeping on the sofa to ensure she was ok through the night. Then, off to school I went the next day, calling grandma to check in on mum for me. My sister made the move to live with my dad. I felt it cruel to leave mum, but it was hard, and soon realised my sister had made the right choice. My GCSEs were looming, and I was the main live-in carer for my mother – but who cared (or knew) outside our family. It felt like no one. The mental pressure took its toll, and I also moved in with Dad just before my GCSE's. It got too much mentally, and the freedom I had wasn't worth the mental torture of someone needing constant care and attention. Who knew a teenager would come to that conclusion herself?

I became self-preserved, resilient, a sponge for information to do things well, and I became inwardly angry and intolerant of needy (normal) people, people that were loved and looked after. I am a pleaser. I've always put other's feelings, experiences and wants first and I over-analysed people's state of mind and their reactions, constantly reacting to their actions, judging their profile. This takes effort, and it takes a mask, profiling others to understand their personalities, their triggers. I reflect, knowing I did this from a young age. It's an emotional and social intelligence strategy used to quickly temperature-check the environment and the person's demeanour, so you can react, read them, and then act accordingly. One amends tone, body language, and vocabulary based on the person's current state in a hope for a positive transaction and outcome.

Dad soon moved in with his new partner, and my sister and I were relocated to her parent's house to live. It was unconventional, but it was practical in our circumstances. They (now step Grandma and Grandad) were disciplined, there were rules – I obviously rebelled. There was organisation and a demand for respect, something we had not had before. I then started college and did a GNVQ (equivalent to 3 A-levels in the UK or an AP in the US) in IT (Information Technology).

As I reflect over that period, it was an odd set up, but I felt I survived that unorthodox era and soon obtained an IT Job in Sheffield after passing the college course. For my sister, it had a more lasting impact to be refuted from the stability of a parental home.

My relationship with the older guy ended. (We had been engaged). I realised I had outgrown him and was losing respect for him. I was mean with my tongue and realised being nasty to loved ones isn't a nice trait, so the relationship ended with me being honest and frank with him that I no longer loved him. I briefly moved in with my dad in his new marital home and didn't stay long. Months later, I moved to Sheffield to live with a new boyfriend.

This was another relationship that I controlled, steered and led the way. I thought I could, mother my partners. I wanted to. It took me a while to commit to this relationship: it was only a car accident that spurred me to value the relationship I had with him, and I proposed to him. After a counselling session, I soon learnt this is a coping mechanism of me saying I want someone to care for me and to continue the control I had over my life and others (my sister and mum). I threw myself into work – my safe space – and that relationship quickly ended in divorce. I thought I would be married for life and wouldn't be the cliché, broken child that equals broken relationships. I found love again (I'm a romantic at heart and a traditionalist) and so far we're enjoying each other's company and sharing the journey of life with our two children. We have a very equal relationship. Some days it's easy, sometimes I struggle with not "owning" it; he gets my outburst and understands my need to control and to lead.

As I now reflect on my life, and its chapters, I enter the Autumn of life (0-20 Spring, 20-40 Summer, 40-60 Autumn, 60-80 Winter) approaching four decades of age. My childhood gave me the freedom to roam, and the detachment from my parents allowed me to fuse relationships with many friends and have free rein of my nights – no scheduled play or clubs for us. It meant I entered circles that as a parent I shiver for my children to enter in. It also meant I had to use my gut and moral compass to make the right decisions, as there was no one to protect me. My stories of my day were unheard, and my relationships were for me to deal with. Money was hard, we were poor: we had school vouchers and free dinners in secondary school. Occasionally had a mother who would appear at our classroom windows to see if we were ok and if we wanted anything from the shops. Sometimes we were embarrassed, and sometimes it was nice, funny to see her. I look back, and it's not the childhood I want anyone to go through, but at the same time it gave me freedom, independence, responsibility, consequence and crafted the conscientious woman I am today. I am slowly becoming more true to myself and others, but it's taken time and life events to get to this position.

The wisdom I share is that when you find your CHAKRA – your warming central happy space, hone into it and listen. I surround myself with people that make me feel 6ft tall, cheer me on, stretch me and challenge me. I'm grateful for every new friendship that is created and formed because we all have something to share and learn from one another. I'm a huge advocate of supporting women and trying to make the angry less angry or at least understand the root of their anger with informal coaching sessions. Why did you react like that? How did that/it make you feel? How did it make the other party feel? What is the purpose? I believe as women, we should be kinder to one another and reduce our social bias towards one another. Why can't a mum go nightclubbing or work away, but the father can without judgement? And, find your CHAKRA – inner peace, surround yourself with people or find a place, an environment that helps get you that balance of peace or seek that balance by walking, to rest yourself from society's biases.

I've changed/evolved, as we all do, due to experience, love, and hate from relationships along the way. My first turning point, and my pinnacle moments, were my divorce, helping me reflect on what I think I want versus what I actually want. The second is children – this really broke my anger and made me more empathetic, less of a control freak, less pedantic. At times, I felt pathetic, insecure, vulnerable, because as a parent you have, IMO, regular failures– you turn up late, your child has clothes mishaps, they have unplanned toiletry requirements. Because of the extra responsibility in our adult lives, we have to ask for more help (I especially did with my mother), which means coming to terms with priorities and triaging the requests being made of me. Who gets my care and my time, my attention? What impact does it have on them and you if they are not first but last on your list?

As I see it, our lives are a "beautiful" journey – let's make our lives meaningful, purposeful or (I'll drop the controlling element) just enjoy the ride and the privilege of existence. Leave a legacy, and the best way to leave a legacy is the effect on how we can make others feel in a positive way.

All lives have purpose – what is yours?

Losing What I Never Held

Rhianna McGonigal

I'm beginning this chapter exactly one year to the day that my first miscarriage began. We decided we were ready to start a family just ahead of the first lockdown while we were on on holiday in Lanzarote, relishing the sunshine and excitedly planning for a whole new year of plans and adventures ahead. Starting a family was the biggest adventure of all, and we had finally decided we were ready. We didn't want to put too much pressure on it, just hope for the best and see if we were lucky enough. Sure enough, it wasn't long before we found out we were pregnant. We were both terrified and excited, and couldn't believe it had happened for us so soon.

On June 8th 2020, I was around 6 weeks pregnant, and it was on this day that I started to bleed. We'd only known for a couple of weeks. Stupidly excited the day we found out, I'd made my husband watch *What to Expect When You're Expecting*, I'd already googled prams and the reusable nappies I was sure I'd use, I downloaded an app and marvelled at the size that the foetus was already. We'd discussed names (they'd been prepared for a while), I'd called the doctors to let them know, and we'd excitedly told our parents, in a way we hoped would be memorable and fun, so we'd all look back and laugh at how funny and lovely it all was.

Reality hit on the 8th, when I was hit with the worst kind of pains. The ones that cripple you, and it doesn't matter how many painkillers you take or how many hot water bottles you push against your abdomen, the pain goes nowhere and doesn't release. I furiously googled how much blood is normal to lose in the first trimester, frantically reading blogs, medical essays, searching on Google images (always a bad move). I called the prenatal team at the hospital and explained what was happening, hoping for words of encouragement, but unfortunately in this situation there is nothing they can say or suggest to make you feel better. I called one of my closest friends, and announced the pregnancy, but with a lump in my throat and tears in my eyes as I knew deep down it was in hopeful desperation. Looking back I probably made light of the amount of blood I was losing, because I was desperate to believe that this couldn't happen to me and that I would be one of the lucky ones, everything would be ok. I just had to sit and wait.

It took several days of bleeding for me to finally accept that my first baby was gone. I'd taken many pregnancy tests in that time, feeling hope in the fact that they still said positive–later learning that it takes around two weeks for your HcG levels to drop, so I wouldn't have the confirmation that I'd lost the baby officially until then.

For the weeks that followed, every pregnancy announcement, be it by a friend or celebrity, every Instagram post detailing happy child's development and lives felt like a stab to the heart. It feels awful to say you feel like this, and the guilt you feel for your envy of others coupled with the grief of your own loss is unbearable. It feels wrong to feel so empty when seeing others' happiness. You begin to blame yourself for the heavy bag you lifted, the food you ate that you didn't realise you weren't meant to; your body for not being able to perform the miracle that others' can. And you're internalising it all with your partner, as you're not meant to talk about any pregnancy this early on, so it's a journey you take on your own. It's very isolating.

Amazingly, only a number of weeks after the miscarriage we fell pregnant again. It's interesting how our mindsets had already changed. Before we began trying for a family, it was all very relaxed. 'It'll happen when it happens, we're not in a rush, we never want to feel like there's pressure.' Suddenly once you've miscarried, everything changes. It feels like your fertility window is closing in. There is only so much time, and if this happens again, then what? What if this isn't possible for us? What if we have to suffer this again and again? Have we started too late? What are the other options?

This pregnancy gave us fresh hope. I made it past six weeks, I was getting symptoms, wretched nausea, the metallic taste in my mouth, everything you expect, and even what I hoped was a hint of a bump. We told our family, a couple of friends. It wasn't the excitable announcements like the first time around, this time it was approached with more caution. It felt like the more excitement we felt, the harder we could fall. Other pregnancies happening around us no longer felt like a burden for me, they felt like the joyous occasions they should be. The excitement bubbled week on week as we got ever closer to the 12-week mark. My symptoms began to lessen around week 9 or 10, but I was ok with that, as I'd read they can begin to diminish from this point, and I felt a confidence that this time it would all be fine and we'd make it over the first major hurdle.
We were in a hotel in the Cotswolds, relishing our newfound freedom post covid lockdown when it happened. We were off to Bath for the day, before moving on to Devon to be by the sea for a few more

nights. I went to the bathroom prior to leaving the hotel room, and that's when I noticed, one tiny droplet of blood. So tiny that it wouldn't have been noticeable if I wasn't already hyper-aware of every change in my body at that moment. Pure horror and a wave of nausea hit. Such a tiny droplet of blood but holding the most significance for our situation. That morning I was scheduled to have my first official call with the midwife, to go through how I was feeling, medical history etc and to book in my 12-week scan, something I had been so excited for moments earlier. We pulled into a layby when my phone eventually rang, and I sobbed down the phone, explaining through heaving breaths that I was spotting. The midwife was amazing, encouraging and calm, explaining that spotting can be completely normal in the first trimester, just to keep an eye on it and see how it developed. My scan was booked in for the following week.

Feeling reassured as it didn't develop any further, it continued as spotting, nothing like the first miscarriage I'd had. We finished our holiday, still hyper-aware but calming each day when the bleeding didn't worsen.

On the Saturday after returning home, feeling more relaxed and re-energised after a change of scenery and some fresh sea air, I was excited to be attending one of my closest friend's baby showers. A low-key event, she hadn't wanted anything major, so we gathered at a friend's house, ordered some pizza, played a couple of games and gave some presents. I relished in the knowledge that I was also secretly pregnant (only she knew), so the excitement for her was also selfishly a little bit of excitement for me, knowing that one day not so far in the future I'd be feeling the same level of anticipation and energy for the new adventure my husband and I were about to embark on.

It was later in the evening when I began to feel incredibly bloated. This wasn't unusual for me, so I didn't give it a second thought. I nipped to the bathroom and felt a new rush of panic when I noticed new, fresh blood. Not a huge amount, but enough to set the alarm bells going. Rushing downstairs, I sent a text to my friend across the room to let her know what had happened, and then one to my husband, panic beginning to rise. I ran back upstairs to check again, and as I ran up the stairs I felt a rush of blood. Staggering over to the toilet, it happened again, and at that point I felt completely empty, and completely numb once again.

The 24 hours that followed is a bit of a blur. I know it began with me sitting with my head in my hands on the toilet, sobbing like I've never cried before. I couldn't flush the toilet. I couldn't let it go. I wanted to sit there as long as I could so I didn't have to watch it disappear, that would make it too real, and at that point that little baby would be gone. My body was wracked with grief. It had happened again, but this time, very little blood in the lead up and no pain. It was completely out of the blue. At my friend's baby shower. I couldn't get my head round it. It was so different from last time.

As my friends began to discover what was happening, I felt the shock and shared grief in the house. I was offered fresh clothes, sanitary towels, and support, but all I wanted was to feel that my baby was still there, growing inside of me. That I could still feel hope and that the worst hadn't just happened. I was surrounded by people that I loved but felt so completely empty and at that moment, devoid of any hope. Numbness enveloped me.

My husband came to take me home, and we called 111. I was advised to go into hospital due to the amount of blood clots I'd lost. Due to the covid pandemic, my husband wasn't allowed into A&E with me, so I sat alone, my mind racing. All I wanted was to be at home with my husband and my dog and pretend it had never happened. After blood tests I was taken down the corridor to be assessed, and it was on the way to the doctor's room that I felt a rush of blood again. Another clot followed. Another ounce of hope lost. The examination confirmed that I had miscarried the baby. It's strange when you're on a hospital bed being told this news. The doctors and nurses are fantastic, completely calm, empathetic and understanding but also pragmatic and practical. The complete opposite to the way I was feeling; exhausted, overwhelmed, unable to stop crying. It's like two worlds colliding for the briefest moment in time; they're doing their jobs, one patient announcement after another; whilst your world turns upside down, never to be quite the same ever again.

Once again the impact of the covid pandemic hit, as I was given a covid test by an overly cheerful nurse, just moments after sitting back up after my examination. Still red raw from crying, I attempted the swab tests but it was all too much, it felt like insult after injury, and I couldn't do the throat swab, I was gagging too much. I was told to wait following this, and that I'd be taken onto a ward overnight–they wanted to keep me in to make sure I didn't lose any more blood, and in case I needed surgery. A restless night's sleep followed, it was already around midnight by the time I got onto the ward. Connected to a drip, I spent the night tossing and turning in the strange environment, just wanting to go home. Around 5am, a doctor entered and announced that he wanted to examine me again. That's when things got even stranger.

'Your cervix is shut, you're not miscarrying.' What?! What on earth does that mean? I had a doctor telling me hours earlier that it was all over, I'd miscarried the baby and that was that. Now I was being told that I hadn't in fact miscarried? It was all too much, I felt confused and even more numbed. My husband arrived as early as he could onto the ward to sit with me. We nervously waited for the results from yet another doctor, who would explain what was going on.

A few hours later, we were presented with the results, and were told that we had been expecting twins. Twins! Two tiny little babies, our little babies, would've been born in March 2021. The ultrasound results showed that one little foetus was still in there, it hadn't miscarried, though it had lost its sibling. We were asked to wait for two weeks, to find out if the remaining foetus could grow. Neither had grown past the six weeks mark at this point so it was impossible to tell if there was a heartbeat, so all we could do is sit, wait and hope.

Two, completely agonising, weeks passed. We didn't sleep, and it was all we could talk or think about. I talked to my stomach, in the hope that in some miraculous way that would encourage the baby to grow. I began working from home again after a week, and I remember my boss calling me and asking how I was, and I immediately burst into tears. I couldn't explain how I felt, it was like my whole world had turned upside down and my perspective on what was important had completely changed. I couldn't understand why no-one else was feeling the anxiety I felt, how their worlds weren't changing, and how everyone could get on with their lives, whilst inside I was a complete mess, urging time to move faster so we could find out what was going on.

The time came for us to go back to the hospital for the scan. It's funny what you notice when you go through something like this, the nuances of your environment, the words said to you, the body language of those around you. When we sat in the hospital corridor, knuckles white as I clutched my husband's hand, knees bouncing with adrenalin, I couldn't help but notice the happy, healthy-looking pregnant women all sitting in the corridor. The only difference being that they turned left into the 'happy department' and I turned right into the department that felt cold, grey and soulless. Just like the effect of social media after the first miscarriage, it was YET another stark reminder of the difference in our situations.

I had to go in for the scan on my own due to covid restrictions. Every part of my body was shaking, I was already in tears as deep down I already knew what the outcome was going to be. Sadly I was correct, the foetus hadn't grown, and we'd lost both twins. Three babies now. Three little lives that would never be lived. Three little futures that I had planned out in my mind, as soon as I knew they were there.

After a week or so of waiting for a natural miscarriage, I opted for a medical one. For the first time since this horrific situation began, I actually felt in control of my body. A relief flooded me once the last of the miscarriage took place. I knew it was happening, I had prepared myself for it. I'd steeled myself for the feeling of emptiness, the feeling of loss.

What I didn't expect was for a year later it to feel as raw as it did when the first miscarriage took place. I have learnt a lot from this experience, how I can't control everything, how you can't *choose* to start a family, how I need to think more about the words I use as everyone around me is facing a battle of some kind. I've written this with tears, a constant lump in my throat, but with the hope that by sharing my story, I can help someone else who may be going through something similar. The biggest thing I've learnt is how important it is to share my experience, something that doesn't come naturally to a normally private person. When you miscarry, you don't want to hear the stats. To be honest, hearing that 1 in however many pregnancies end in miscarriage is unlikely to help, nor will being told that the lady down the road had experienced the same. Stats and numbers mean nothing, and yet that's often how the information on miscarriage is presented to you as you experience it. By professionals, the internet, those around you; and so immediately you feel you need to accept that you are part of those cold hard stats, you are the 1 in 3 and that is that. But you need to feel more than that. I needed to feel understood, heard; and because I shared, that is what I received. As I was with friends as one of the miscarriages happened, I was relieved of the need to tell them, but I made sure my workmates knew, my family knew, other friends knew, and it helped us get through it all, one step at a time. That's why it's important to share stories like this so that others feel heard too.

If you can feel comfortable and brave enough to speak to those you love around you, you can feel supported in a way that's indescribable, and invaluable in a situation like this. You can also help others get through their own experiences, and bring more awareness to what is still a taboo subject. None of this has been easy, it's been the opposite in fact. Even now, if I'm in a situation where I feel the need to tell the story again, I struggle to start. I look at my husband to say the words I can't say, then with a lump in my throat I nod along as he explains what happened, holding the tears back. The pain hasn't gone away, there will always be three little lives that I couldn't save, but sharing my grief and leaning on others is helping repair my heart, piece by piece, day by day.

I finish my chapter 8 days after I started writing, it's now the 16th of June. I'm ecstatic to say I have a new little life growing inside of me, and this time it feels like I just might get to the end. I am 17 weeks pregnant today, I heard the heartbeat for the first time yesterday, and my bump grows bigger every day. The experiences I've had have made this a very anxious time, where I've refused to acknowledge what amazing adventure could be at the end of the 9 months, and instead focused on the small daily changes. We told friends and family early, as I knew we'd need the support immediately if things went wrong again. I had two early private scans due to anxiety that I'd lost my symptoms again. I've analysed every change, every minute detail of my body, and until recently I've refused to be drawn into any conversations of nursery decorations, maternity clothes or kindly gifted hand-me-downs from friends and family. But now as I sit and finish writing this in the sunshine, I can say that I'm finally feeling more positive. I know I am one of the lucky ones, not everyone gets to where I am, and I'm well aware there's still a way to go. But every milestone we cross I relax a little more. So it is possible, you can have your happy ending, and I'm keeping everything crossed that my happy ending begins in November.[1]

[1] Matilda Rose was born on the 29th November 2021 weighing 8lbs2oz, much to the delight of Rhianna and her husband Ben.

She She, The Walnut Tree

Jane Toy

I found myself in the land.
I found myself in the tree.
She leans over me
peering closely
and sees her seed.

She She peers at me.
"You are so small, so wee!
Just a wee thing, a tiny spring.
So much to learn, to be.
You can be me, the crone, the tree".

She'll mentor me
for what comes next.
Autumn, winter and all that's left.
The seasons of my life;
her life.
She, great expansiveness,
age, wise giantess.
Me, learning ever so slow
to become, to birth,
to grow seed, to sow seed.
To toil, to still
to hoe, to hone…
The giantess, the crone.

She She the walnut tree.
Me. Just becoming me.

She She is the ancient walnut tree who stands as land guardian, mother tree, on a 5 acre block of countryside just outside Whanganui, New Zealand where my husband and I found ourselves in May of 2017. We were called to the land, after years of traversing a harrowing mental health journey for me, and a fraught, stress filled life running our family business for him.

On my 40th birthday, living in suburban NZ in a mid-sized town, yet feeling blocked in, overwhelmed and overrun by life, I boldly proclaimed, "If I live to be 80 I will make sure the next 40 years aren't the same as the first 40 have been".

Be careful what you ask for. By the time I turned 50 I'd been down into the abyss of mental disintegration and had spent those ten years being unpicked and stitched back together one small thread at a time.

Things just happen without your intervention sometimes. That year of my 50th birthday we took a motorcycle trip riding down, down to a remote rainforest as far south as our southern land goes. Deep in that moist quietude a mystical encounter with the ancestors of that place occurred. They came in the form of a multitude of birds, one of the most endangered and rare species in NZ. Yet we stood surrounded as they sung us into a new awareness of ourselves and our potential, voices of pure spirit calling us to go home, sell up and move to a space in need of healing as much as we were.

And then the search for a new space, although you could hardly call it a search. I saw the listing, we visited, we walked up the driveway, instinctively reached for each other's hands and knew we'd arrived home. Deal done, the sold signs went up within a week.

She She was waiting for us in the paddock. Walnuts scattered around her feet, an offering, a welcome gift. A delicious bounty waiting just for us to gather and crack and gobble. Walnuts never tasted like this before. Small and sweet, smaller than any walnuts I'd ever experienced. Delicate and nourishing; nurturing.

The house wraps itself around the flat paddocks of the property and She She is visible from every window. Her moods and seasons on display for all to adore. A focal point, a place of rest; she calls to all. The goats, sheep and alpacas rest under her gloriously thick foliage from the summer sun. Autumn sees the magpies spend hours purposefully stabbing their dagger beaks into cracks to get to the sweet meat inside. She serves and nurtures us all.

The day she and I formally met for the first time, I stood beneath her colossal branches and gazed upwards. 'My word you're stunning", I thought. And as I sat down at the base of her trunk, in a little hollow that perfectly fit my body shape and leaned back feeling her knobbly support, I felt her say 'You're so wee!'. Not heard with my ears you understand, but felt in a much deeper place than mere words can access. I felt myself let go, to release myself to her, to accept her deep and ancient knowledge. I looked at the land, sick from years of over-pasturing from its past life as part of a large-scale dairy farm. Tired, drained, chemically altered, a dull beat of what it once was residing somewhere beyond the now. A mirror image of myself. "This is up to you now", she said.

Words, feelings, thoughts, questions, prayers; so much to learn from such a wise teacher. She is the crone, the hag, the ancient divine feminine. She She has taught me the value of the strong moment of patient waiting. That which is needed to wait while the storm rips through and threatens to topple everything around you. That which you suspect might rip you clean out of the ground. "Turn your strong side to the wind and allow your branches to dissipate the updraft while you grow your roots deeper into Mother Earth. She won't let you down but you must hold fast and trust."

So, She She listens to my many questions and I'm sure shakes her branches in wonder at how little her 'wee' friend knows of the great mysteries that she, as Tree, has complete understanding of.

I believe in the sentience of all species and in the wisdom of listening to those great ones who have seen the passing of many seasons, tragedies, celebrations, births and deaths, comings and goings. Who else but the trees can hide so much from human sight while communicating with the whole cosmos of life beneath the soil. Who else shares their very breath with us. We breathe them in and become them. Who else can offer their leaves to the sun, and then feed so many others with that richness. As a woman I have shed my last blood, yet I am but a mere sapling in comparison to She She. "There is more to being a woman than a pretty face and soft skin", she says. Then she enigmatically turns to face the sun and says, "run along now. I've got sun to catch and you've got seeds to plant".
I hug her and feel like a small thing. And that feeling is good.

Wish Bold, Wish Big, The Universe is Listening

Claire Frame

Have you ever created a mood board or a wish list? Magazines use them to share a look that's in fashion, guiding us to buy the dream.

You may know them as design boards or dream boards. You may also know this as manifesting.

In the early stages of my design career, I dabbled with mood boards, creating a look to be presented at the next creative meeting, to win the bid, to create the vision to sell the product. To be successful.

My story that follows is overall a joyous one, with both heart-warming rewards, darker moments and challenges too. I want to bring you along on my journey to offer suggestions of how to manifest and create some magic in your life, too. From creating mood boards with magazine cut outs, photos and embellishments to represent your dreams, to conversations, trust and perseverance, all will help manifest your dreams into reality.

Us

In the early days when my husband was my boyfriend, I recall seeing a framed mood board hanging on his wall. Shiny planes, fancy diving watches, patterns and textures, locations, clothing, all staring back at me. I came to realise that some elements on that board were being realised in the form of Me. I looked at the pattern on some new clothes I had bought, clothes that I bought to wear with him, and quickly saw they were exact replicas of patterns on that mood board. His manifesting was working.

Our time living is SE Asia gave me the opportunity to say YES to opportunities and explore new pathways as they presented themselves to me. During those 6 years, I returned to the UK with my husband for 2 years. We put together a 5-year plan for ourselves. We gave thought to where we wanted to be, what we'd like for ourselves, family consideration, friends, our passion for more travel yet still putting down roots in our home country. Five years of storage unit logistics: costs were high, not just financially but in mental health. We knew location would be the biggest challenge. Lists were made in notebooks, conversations had together and shared with loved ones, Pinterest Boards were created, new Instagram accounts followed. Even buying new magazines and frequenting local places and getting to know the residents. Asking questions, joining clubs…these things all helped us build up a vision of where we wanted to be.

It was a challenging time, navigating new cities, learning new languages, finding somewhere to live, discovering local resources for healthy food, and understanding new transport systems. I did always wish to travel. All these topics are par for the course and every single one reaped many magical moments creating lifelong memories. Difficulties were outweighed by the fun we had. Often these difficulties were approached with going out for a coffee, sitting in our favourite pizza parlour "Pala" and watching the world go by. We'd sit and tap into conversations about expanding comfort zones one subway stop at a time, trying a new food at the local market, learning a new word and finding ways to use it. Coming to a stop and taking one day at a time is a rule we both live by to this day.

Things on the manifestation list for us included: green space with amazing countryside views; a field for a long awaited glamping business; a barn for cars and workshop; creative space for me; a converted barn; no neighbours; being within driving distance to the airport; and, the icing on the cake: either space for a runway, or to live on one. I know, I know…I hear you laugh a little—or perhaps out loud—but I kid you not, it's something that would be utterly magical. Imagine having your own runway and being able to fly light aircraft from your own back door. I am allowed to dream and that's exactly what I'm doing.

This is the fun of wishing big. Play with it. Wish bold.

Them

My Parents had spent 15 years living in France and had already doubled their own plan of how long to stay. They already had their own plans to move back to the UK but couldn't afford to match what they currently had in France. This sparked an idea in us: how about two properties on one bit of land? With a shared barn/workshop space, the men could work on projects together, Mum could have a little cottage garden, and I could have my glamping business, my creative space.

The four of us sat down one sunny afternoon over a relaxed lunch, and with pen and paper, we listened to each other's wants and wrote them down for each other. We still have them as they hold such potent magic.

This was a way of introducing a wish list to them. To gently welcome in manifestation. I wondered how big they would wish.

Adventures Far & Near

A new two-year adventure with my husband took me back to the Land of Smiles. I enjoyed new challenges of working professionally with Thai Clients, and new ways to expand my comfort zone in a city I'd already grown to love. I kept an eye on the UK housing market from Bangkok, and my parents agreed that if something worthwhile came up, they would go back and look. Unfortunately, that didn't happen, and I came to realise that budgets needed to be increased for what the Universe was presenting to us.

In the summer of 2018, we came home to England: a contract finished and a new one was to start in the East Midlands. Adventure and the great outdoors sealed the decision to drive home and stay in my parents Motorhome for six months.

This was also a way of keeping the dream alive by manifesting our goals and diving headfirst into countryside living. We were indeed going to wish this house into existence.

I found a private site, exclusive to five units only, that would afford us more time to house-hunt. We were now presented with learning how to live *Tiny*. Compact living full-time in a unit 24ft long by 8ft wide presented us with many issues. We rose to these challenges with vigour and have wonderful stories to tell of cooking on a small stove, managing moisture levels, compact storage, towing our car, waste disposal management, blue (men) & pink (women) jobs, oh and so much more. On arrival we were greeted and welcomed into what was to become our home for the next 3 years!

The site where our pitch was waiting for us was nestled on a whole acre of green field, with stunning countryside views. While I sit and write this, I smile and totally see how we got part of our dream. All the wishing of fields into our lives had brought us here. We would drive by fields and laugh and say "that'll do" or "what about that one?" or "he's a nice one!". It was the view too, including the most magnificent sunsets and sunrises. Sometimes what we want most really is right in front of us.

Together we explored the local area, driving past stunning barn conversions with envy. We found one locally near a reservoir, a beautiful red brick farm complex, oozing money, and with a grass runway, too. At least if we moved to this area, our love of light aircraft flying could continue. Seeing property like this confirmed to us that at least our wishlist existed out there, if in a bigger size.

We both vowed to try and find something like that within budget.

Dream ticking

Six months passed, and no house. With a holiday booked, we spent 3 weeks in New York State flying light aircraft, visiting friends and making more dreams happening in abundance. We stayed in a fantastically luxurious American RV courtesy of our friends Richard & Judy (not THE Richard & Judy for those old enough to remember who they are, but an amazing couple who own Kittyhawk Flying School, who we fly with when we visit).

I was blown away by their RV and had never seen such a beast except on TV. Three nights we had in her, and they were the best 3 nights in terms of comfort and style over the whole holiday.
My husband exclaimed, "How can we get one of these in our lives?" His manifestation had begun.

After 10 months of Hymer living, it was agreed an upgrade of space was needed, and after exploring renting a house and knowing it was "dead money", we invested in our very own American RV. We call her the Wendy Bus. We made her happen. Research, photos, talking as if we owned one, taking the talk, joining the clubs, sharing the dream, visualising her with us, looking for houses to accommodate an RV…we totally manifested her into our lives. We took little steps each day to move us closer to the dream.

And with that, our Wendy Bus became our asset and our home. Boy did we wish big on her!

Time

I lost track of the amount of houses I viewed. I remained open to each one and viewed it as offering us some of what we wanted. Some, I got really excited at, but the disappointment was difficult to manage when they were either too big, too small, had a shared driveway, had neighbours, too close to town, not close enough to town, too remote, too much work, terrible decor… Sadly most of these reasons were not our own but those of Mum and some of Dad.

Daily, I would tell myself that with each property that wasn't right, and there was a message from the Universe reassuring us that Our House wasn't ready for us yet. It was out there, but when it was ready, it would reveal itself to us. This kept me positive and kept the dream alive.

With the help of others' insights, I now see that Mum was never going to leave her French house. The desire was there but the reality didn't match that. Well, Mum finally left her house for good in mid-October 2019 on an unexpected one way trip to hospital. Sadly, she passed away in Bordeaux of a massive aneurysm.

...and here is where my world stopped. Even as I write, my heart is racing, my writing flow halted. How does one pick back up and move on? The light changed. Everything changed. It was as if a huge Pause Button emerged and was stuck in the pressed position. Grief was a new challenge for me. It immediately overtook everything else. I've realised that until that direct loss happens to you, one doesn't fully understand it. I couldn't do this alone yet did want to be totally consumed by it; life does go on after all.

The clock doesn't stop ticking.

Reaching out to loved ones, professional therapy, self-care, taking a day at a time, sometimes one hour at a time, writing, immersing myself in nature—this all helped me manage this new emotion. It's a journey in itself and will always be present in my life, but it won't govern my outlook. That's remaining positive. Often, one little positive action helped my day enormously.

Quite understandably the 5-year plan had changed in an instant.

So, with a revitalising breath and a swig of coffee, I'll resume my writing… months passed in a blur, back and forth to France, not looking seriously at houses, although dabbling without direction. While I sat under the Indian Bean tree on the front lawn at Dads, I gently explained that we needed a house. Dad's life was now changing daily, and ours needed stability. Dad was in agreement that a new plan was needed.

It was set. I was to resume house-hunting immediately for something we could afford and would perhaps tick a few things off our original list.

Such massive compromises were needed with a budget of less than half of the original we were to contribute. Still with an open creative mind and the love of a project or 3, the challenge was set. The Glamping Business would take a back seat, and maybe there's still room in the future for that. Four years' worth of research, planning, and purchasing things to build is a great investment already.

Wish Big

When we first arrived in the area in 2018, I wished for a network of local friends. I walked into a very local cafe and asked the lady there what goes on socially in the area, and that I wanted to make new friends and get to know the place we were trying to plant roots in. I was welcomed immediately and told to consider her and her colleague my first new friends. And they are, to this day.

I also volunteer at a local non-profit zero waste company (and am still there to this day) and am enjoying many growing friendships. I have created a great network of friends and work associates which firmly ticked that challenge off the list.

One afternoon, I received house details, sent with excitement, "what about this one?" from the owner of where I volunteer. She doesn't want us to leave.

There was an air of familiarity about this place, but I couldn't place it. A viewing was arranged. A spark burned brighter somewhere inside.

On arrival, we immediately knew we'd been here before. This was the place that inspired us to keep going to trust something was out there for us, the one we were green with envy over, the one we joked and said, "that'll do nicely". This is the one that had the runway. The ultimate item on the list. This was the place that reminded us our Wishes existed.

We wished big for a *character barn conversion*. We wished boldly for a barn/workshop. I wished big for *creative space*. Bold wishes were sent out for amazing countryside views and rural location. My husband wished for a big for a runway. We both dreamed big for a Victorian walled garden, and space for our Wendy bus (aka our American RV) emerged too.

Our manifestation came to life in bite-size proportions before our very eyes. The universe had indeed listened. Being a tiny home, our experience of motorhome and RV living helped us overcome challenges such as managing storage, making the most of a small space, addressing our actual needs versus wants.

The Universe gifted us with a little bit of everything we wanted for ourselves. Keep believing.

I have since dared myself to re-ignite the glamping dream, to explore possibilities presenting themselves right in front of my very eyes. I'm going to get those wishes back out there. Bigger and bolder than before. I know the Universe has my back on this one. It's like a treasure hunt and being gifted some clues. I just need to piece them together.

Wish Bold

When I get into alignment with my positive thoughts, I create magic. When I believe in myself, in the Universe, sparks are ignited and simmer away until they are ready to burn bright for me to see. With reflection, I really see how my wishes come true.

There are days too when it's cloudy and visions are hard to focus on and wishing bold can be hard. On days like these, I reach out for help, and surround myself with loved ones who have my back and know my journey. I take time to nourish and nurture myself. Self-care plays a massive part in my life and enables the clouds to clear and the visions to shine bright.

I ask questions too. Am I moving in the right direction of my dreams? What is unfolding for me right now? What is one simple thing that I can do today to help move me in the right direction of my dreams? Finding answers to these questions helps me in my own responsibility with commitment and being able to take action towards my goals.

I fully believe in the power of my thoughts. I get that I AM my thoughts and work hard to keep these positive. Difficult times are acknowledged and worked through, and whilst challenging, are often broken down into bite bite-size, easy to manage portions.

I aim to own my outcomes, to have trust, and to trust that the Universe is indeed listening. A golden rule I

103

am still living by is to take one day at a time and be open to manifestation in my life.

Let's break it down to manageable chunks.

Set intentions. Ask the Universe clearly for what you want. Be positive. Take small easy steps in the right direction. Be present and take self-care. Be gentle. Trust in the magic.

What will you manifest? What will you wish big for?

"The whole point of my Inner Roadtrip, and this Joyride to Freedom, is to see what happens if I dare to follow up on my INSIDE JOB."

Lou Niestadt, Transformational Writer, Visual Philosopher & Speaker

Under The Bed

Sara Lesley Warber

Fears come in lots of forms. Much of my life is stitched down at the edges by fears from long ago. Do you feel it too? Here's one of mine…I'm in grade school, a time when learning is fun; a time of summery days in the lakes, the fields, the woods, and the dense hedge-fort under an arched roof of branches. Life is really pretty easy. But…there is a witch living under my bed. She means me no good. I purposefully surround myself with stuffed animals, my beloved tawny dog, Woofy, closest to me. His worn plush body protects me. Another favorite, the life-like and tricky chimp, guards my other side. The rest are arrayed out to both edges of the bed. I snuggle safe amongst them. I am precise in keeping my feet and hands from straying over the edge of the bed. If my arm hangs down, she will grab my hand and pull me under the bed into her lair. I complain to my mother about this harrowing witch; Mother announces, "she is not real". I want to believe her, but I know my room better than she does. There is magic in here, something dark and deep under the bed. I even catapult into the middle of the bed from the floor, quickly pulling up my feet to make sure that witch does not snag my ankle.

I'm an aged woman now, still robust. But I crash into my legacy of fear just as I try to flourish, as I try to bring one more sweet dream to life that holds meaning and motivation. I feel the cold dread hem me in. It dawns on me that I STILL carefully keep my hands and feet from straying over the edge of the bed. No splaying of limbs in glorious exhaustion for me! Do I think that witch is still under the bed? Do I

105

still fear her violent malice? Her bottomless cavern? Is there something else, more insidious than habit that drives my self-imposed constriction?

Witch or wise woman: My young self knows witches from stories, powerful cautionary tales. Grimm's wrinkled woman in the woods, like a spider, suddenly alert to the echo of children's steps reverberating through the web of forest roots, the flare of a gnawing hunger about to be satisfied. Or the terrifying arrival of the flying chimps heralding the looming, inexorable entrance of that deformed, malevolent, cackling, green Witch of the West.

Witch or wise woman: In the heady freedom of college days, I throw a wild thought into the sky one wintery night, while crossing the campus in the flatlands. What if I became a white witch? Is that possible? For someone so recently bound to teachings of redemption and sin, it is vital to imagine a pure form. What ancient part of me awakened that night under the silver ice-tipped stars, while elemental snow blew off the plains into my face?

Witch or wise woman: Someone reads my palm; just here there is a clear marked square, the sign of a healer. Something hopeful turns within me, remembers another life, remembers a promise. Hard living years tumble from the blown pages of calendars. I stumble from welfare to maid to bus driver to homeless. I land in the underground tunnel between hospital buildings, knowing I am coming home. My mind expands and I delight in the understanding. A feather found, guides me into the halls of medicine, where I gaze into bodies and trees, awed by their branching similarities. In my soul pack, then, I carry all I have learned, ready to meet and comfort whoever appears, no matter how ugly or embarrassing the wound.

Witch or wise woman: I hear the call of the plants. I lie on my back in the remnant greenwood surrounding an abandoned city lot. I learn the kaleidoscope pattern of leaves overhead. I think I must know how to survive, how to make medicine. I learn their names, the plant sisters; I draw detailed pictures, find and save the hidden knowledge. I learn the heart of the forest, the spirit that animates the trees. Inchworm teaches me a soft, but relentless persistence. My body turns with the light of the moon. I come into alignment with stones and water's restless sway. I am suspended floating between earth and sky. I dream and the dreams take shape.

Witch or wise woman: Drifting in half dreams, I lie with my hospital pager, she screams; I spring into waiting clothes. Steamy noir jazz flows over me, a creature of the night, careening down abandoned rural roads into lonely city lights, flashing aimlessly. I reach out to the mother-being-made; help her call in her own dark animal self for strength. Blood runs down the aqua drapes; I settle deeper into prayer, connected with the life emerging. Alert, bonded with all, yet alone and afraid, blessing the empty space that awaits blood-wet matted hair, the slippery body oozing into the foreign air, the longed-for cry, the brimming breasts.

Witch or wise woman: In the history of the world we are imprisoned, burned, drowned, tortured. We are shunned, misunderstood, but in the night, or the quiet day, one or many come reaching out for a simple, a concoction, an explanation, a plan, a bit of magic to heal their lives. We are feared or revered: role-defying women of earth and forest, wild women of moon and night, bright-minded women of secret knowledge, strong-hearted women steeped in ceremony, in ritual, in that which must be done to ensure the fecundity of the broken world.

Now, I practice putting my hand, my foot over the edge of the comfy bed. My tired bones sink into softness and I dangle my toes in the pregnant air, as I once dangled them in summer waters. My hand cascades down, escaping covers and boundaries. Waves pound and push the sand. I am ready to be pulled under, into the deep. I am ready to enter the dark and magical place where dreamers and tawny dogs, wise women, and all that is wild, still cavort. Will you come too, patiently unstitching the secure quilt of old fears, of memory and experience? Will you, too, add your unfettered and newly courageous voice to the laughter of others, fresh from freedom, giddy with energy, and singing sweet life into the new made earth?

Looking Within, Looking Without

Nüv

I was asked why I wanted to write this story…at first, I thought I didn't know, in reflection the truth is throughout my short lifetime I've been in prolonged darkness, deeply confined to my agonising mind, with aggressive thoughts and battles of high emotions, a space of total isolation with a painful sense of aloneness. Many times, in my experiences of self-pain I was aware of the battle and also aware that no one should suffer a mind alone like that. Even with a partner, children, a large family, good friends, I would ask how could I feel so alone?

I wrote this to reach out to anyone that feels lost or alone in their minds, because deep down I wish I'd come across some kind of relatable connection for myself back then, it would have saved me a hell of a lesson learnt!

The bigger picture is I'm not alone, how can I, you, or we be alone really? We live in a beautiful magical universe filled with millions of living breathing beings and most of them are HUMAN! We're not alone, and I saw in my experience that all I needed to do was reach out….and IN!

The feeling is growing stronger and stronger, I'm intensely unhappy.

Deep within me there is something that I can't identify, not past or future, it's in my now.

My soul is calling out to me, I can't hear what she's saying but I know she's begging me to listen.

109

I can feel her pain from the faint whispers of screams.

Something needed to shift, I had to take the reins and make some changes, and it made me ask why it had taken so long to reach this transition in my life, why did I allow myself to reach a point of explosion before I really considered to look at myself with deep reflection?

I reached my mid to late 30's and I'd never before stopped and paid attention to me, that me described above, the gentle pure wise me that resides in the very core of my being. I'd also never taken a risk to change my life, never consciously made a decision or actively sought an alternative way of being to improve my lifestyle or more importantly my inner peace. I was simply taking what life was throwing at me, not being happy about it, but sucking it up and numbing through it anyway!

Why didn't I (and so many others) know before the edge of explosion that actually I don't have to suck things up, that I absolutely can create a life where things are not in the least bit sucky?! My theory...or at least my story, had me in this space because I stayed in my own head and never used my voice.

Our eyes see a thousand pictures, our minds hold a thousand thoughts, our hearts feel a thousand emotions, and our lips yearn to speak a thousand words, and together we stay silent.

We all know that human experiences of stories, thoughts and feelings are more than a thousand, each of us could write an entire book alone (and more) based on our stories, but we don't, some of us not even sharing with those closest to us...why?

It wasn't until I got to my 40's, and after I had done several years' worth of self-reflection and growth that I learnt, not one tale is better or worse than the other, because no matter what we experience, the feelings emotions and mental positions that sit behind the differing experiences are all the same. Love is love...deep, passionate, unconditional. Pain is pain...heart wrenching & unbearable. Joy is joy...warm, light, uplifting. Shame is shame...dark with regret & self-hatred.

So, if...no matter what our external experiences are, the internal chaos is always the same, then why don't we share?

In my experience it was because my mind had me believe that I was alone. I held myself separate from everything and everyone, I thought my situation was unique and special. I went through life thinking that no one could truly know my endurances because they wouldn't understand and they couldn't help me. And fear, fear of what others may think, how they will respond, and most of all how it will impact and hurt them.

The trouble with being alone in my head, not only taking away the opportunity to be helped, I in turn didn't help myself, as a result I battled internally with my mind for years and eventually went into a full-fledged war!

I never played victim in my mind, never played the, "I feel sorry for you" card to myself, or asked, "why me?" Instead, I enlisted straight up to Fight Until You Die! And it was damn exhausting. I was having a sucky life and the war with my head was sucking the life out of me!

When I finally reached the point of seeing that there was a different way of being, I asked myself why the fuck I didn't know or wasn't taught it before? Duh…if you don't speak or share then how is anyone supposed to help you?

For me, through not sharing, speaking, connecting and coming together with others meant the mental war also had me dressing for the role, I wore armour, wrapped around me to conceal my truth, guarded, never truly letting anyone in, AND never dealing with what was going on inside, suppressing, pushing, running, hiding…. tinned up in war gear standing fierce like the hard North London girl I was. And ironically pissed off that no-one really ever saw me. That kind of coping mechanism only got me so far until I learnt the painful way.

Building up my defences and growing thick skin to protect myself came with consequences. I reached a place where I had a dark confidence, considered myself to be fearless and strong, I had arrogance within me because I believed I was portraying that character to others. But that 'no fear' and strength came from a place of damaging anger.

I wanted people to fear me, I was confrontational, defensive, challenging, God help anyone who crossed my path, no matter who was in front of me or where I was, all would feel my wrath, I wanted them to feel my wrath, I dared them even! I never considered how I was hurting others with my aggressive energy and language, overall, I was a ticking bomb set in destruction mode.

I wasn't able to deal with my shit. The result…a volcano, slowly, slowly, heating, bubbling, rising higher and higher to the surface until the inevitable force of nature and explosion occurred. If I'm honest there were many mini explosions over the course of time before the big one came, moments where I looked back and said 'shit, that was a bit much', and yet I was still oblivious to my own drivers and my behaviour, until THE moment.

This story, my story, isn't the full story, but of one single incident that occurred as a result of thinking that I was alone, of not addressing my issues and trying to carry everything by myself. It's one that shows the serious impact of mental health, and how not using my voice or tuning into my soul can harm not only me but those I hold most dearly too.

The Bathroom Scene

In the book Eat Pray Love, Liz Gilbert[1] talks of a pivotal moment on her bathroom floor...I remember reading it and thinking 'Yep! I definitely know that place!'.

I often used the bathroom as an escape, to have my moments of silent tears, peace and overall me time, all while pretending I was doing a number 2 to excuse the length of time I was in there to my family!

My particular scene, the explosion, occurred roughly 12 years ago when I found myself locked in the bathroom...with a kitchen knife.

I don't remember how I got there; I don't remember taking the knife from the kitchen drawer, walking up the stairs, going in, locking the door, or even how long I'd been in there for.

All I remember is at some point I felt like I'd just woken up, it was the middle of the day, I had this sense I had lost time, from where I remembered being in the house to finding myself sitting on the toilet… (lid closed and trousers on!). In my wakening I noticed I was sobbing uncontrollably; the tears were pouring so much that my hands were soaking wet with the tears dripping off the knife. I didn't know why I was crying...let alone why I had a knife in my hands!

Moments after I came to my senses and I'd processed the situation I was in; a sudden intense fear came over me. It dawned on me that I had lost control of myself, I could no longer trust what my mind was feeding me and seeing that the mind had a mind of itself was some scary, bat shit crazy stuff!

What came next was a swarm of anger. I was filled with an intense rage at myself, how dare I, how could I be so weak, how could I be so selfish and not think of my 3 beautiful children, what sort of person was I? What the hell was I doing? I aggressively wiped away the tears from my face, trying to pull myself together, I stood up turning to look in the mirror, knife still in hand.

Looking at my unrecognisable reflection I felt sickened and disgusted at the pathetic weakness I saw, in hindsight a wounded soul crying out for help. Hating what was in front of me I thrust my fist with the knife into the mirror. My intention…to smash away what I was seeing, to make it go away, to take away the ugliness of what I was feeling, but to my frustration the reflection remained intact. FFS! I always thought I had a good arm with a fair punch, who knows what kind of material the mirror was made of, but it didn't smash, not a crack, or even a scratch! This only fed my anger more…so, I hit back, and again, and again, and again. Unleashing my inner army I went into a punching frenzy, repeatedly over and over attacking with knife and fist harder and harder.

Still, not, a, God damn, crack!

Eventually I physically and emotionally exhausted myself in the rageful attack and fell to the floor propping myself up against the wall, knife still in hand. The uncontrollable tears started again with a heavy yet silent sound, and like this I cried for some time. Eventually the self-hatred began to burn out of energy, and in its place sadness came. The sadness had an extreme fatigue, I felt myself let go, surrender even, knowing that I just didn't have the emotional strength to carry on the battle. And in that moment, just as Liz Gilbert heard her inner self gently speak to her, I too heard a stillness in my pain, a silent gentle voice stirred from my inner core, and softly wearily yet very warmly whispered "let's get some help".

And with that I understood.

After sitting for a while, acknowledging the moment, I realised and knew that it shouldn't have to be this way, that it shouldn't be this hard, that there was no way on this earth that I was gonna let myself get to that state again, and knowing I still had the good fight left in me for me, I got myself up. This time dropping the knife to the floor, I washed my face, took a few deep breaths, walked out of the bathroom picking up the knife on the way, and back downstairs placing it in the sink unnoticed. I gave my beautiful babies a gentle, deeply apologetic, grateful and promising kiss on the head and carried on with the day.

Now

Today, I still don't know what specifically triggered me, just that it was an accumulation of years' worth of inner turmoil and external factors. I also don't know how I came back to consciousness, or what snapped me out of the dark place…I strongly suspect it was my wise one ;) I'm forever grateful I returned to the physical present moment, and as part of my growth I don't look back to think what if the worse had happened.

What I do know and have learned is this…

* In order to help myself, **I** had to take action.

* Asking for help was the scariest AND bravest thing I did for myself.

* Sharing with others is a form of healing, it's a painful space to be in when you're feeling alone, sharing can help lead you to someone who can relate to you and your pain so that you DON'T have to be alone.

* It's all a learning curve, I still get it wrong or go off track, the warrior in me pops up every now and then to put on a show, but I'm more self-aware and she never gets past the opening credits!

* I'm a unique and special being, but it's not my external experiences that make me so, they're simply my experiences and not who I am at my core.

* Paying attention to my soul is vital to my being, self-reflection is the key to understanding and owning my behaviours as part of my evolution.

Of course, this isn't all I've learnt and there is so so much more, but these are the first key things I needed in order to begin a journey of release and growth.

It's hard to ask for help, it's scary, but the mind is such a powerful thing and if you don't watch the commentary or the self-talk, it can be a dangerous thing too. It's a much harder and a scarier place to be in a tortured mind than to ask for help.

The darkness still comes, but it's a balance right? 'No light without dark', the way of the universe, a cosmic duality, and I accept it. I allow it to come, I don't try to hide from it or push it way deep down, and instead I sit with it and let it be. I learnt that the darkness, like the light, holds a mirror to me, it's where I learn about myself more, understand who I am at my core, and the troubles that I still carry. It's where I see the pain or anger that still needs healing, and it's a place where I can release all the stories that are not true.

The darkness is where I grow and take root so that when I step back into the light I am stronger, that bit lighter, and everything always seems much brighter. I come out of the dark and see life for the simple beauty it is without complication, and I have a deeper sense of gratitude for everything around me. And each time I go from dark to light the times in the light always last longer.

To my beautiful kids, the coolest most amazing spirited human beings, I am blessed you chose me to be your mum, know that I live and breathe, and will always live and breathe every day of my life for you, you are my purpose. My darling babies if you ever need to hear this, and my family, friends and anyone else who needs to hear this…

I am not alone in my experiences. YOU are not alone in your experiences.

I don't always have to do it by myself. YOU don't always have to do it by yourself.

I will always ask for help when I need it. YOU can always ask for help when you need it.

I am flying the flag of peace in my life. YOU can fly the flag of peace in your life.

I have learnt never to carry such turbulent inner turmoil alone. I have a voice and I can use it; it's much more detrimental to my being to keep shit internalised, and its way much easier to own my truth...EVEN when I'm scared shit to own it!

I pay attention to my soul now, the wise silent one, the one who doesn't judge or come from a place of anger or criticism, the one who only speaks from pure love with peace, kindness and grace. And if I'm having trouble hearing her, I either sit still and wait for the silence, or I seek help from my awesome wisdom council, because it's OK to ask for help and we're never truly alone.

I am not my mind or my thoughts,

I am not the emotions that grow from the thoughts,

I am the intense deepness that glides in the core of my being,

I am the silence.

[1] Gilbert, E. (2022). *Eat, Pray, Love: One Woman's Search for Everything Across Italy, India and Indonesia by Gilbert, Elizabeth (2007)*

Rooted in Gaia

Amaya Lupe

How fate changed and enriched me and my life purpose.

Seven decades ago I came to Earth in The Netherlands as an eight months child with certain 'physical shortcomings' to grow with...I was born with a heart issue and needed annual check-ups with a heart-specialist. Eighteen years old, I visited him for the last time. After the examination he convinced me I did not have to come back anymore which gave me an exploding happy feeling of freedom. I left the building head in 'the clouds' with a sunny sky above. A whole NEW life waiting for me, I embraced my healed heart.

As a little baby I all of a sudden was completely deaf for some time and at the age of four I told my mom I saw her twice; my left eye turned out to be nearly blind and to exercise the eye-muscles as much as possible my other eye had to be covered in support of the process. With this covered good eye I stumbled and fell upon everything which was on the floor, misjudging the distance. However, it also handed to me the possibility of 'looking with my inner eye' and in that way I learned to use my inner-sight, instead of, or and, both physical ones. This turned out to be convenient and safe to me.

Years later I realized I had seen my mom's aura, assuming then that everybody was able to see this in the way I did. But at four, with one eye covered I lost my natural balance and felt rather clumsy; I started believing there must be something very wrong with me and started hiding within, blocking inner sight for a long time.

My mom and I have always had a hard time to get along with each other. This made me feel very insecure. After a traumatic childhood I married to 'the wrong person', being convinced that this would change my life for the better. Somewhere inside a bell was ringing that this choice would probably bring me hardship. My father, whom I loved dearly, tried to make me see; I did not listen to the bell nor to my father; I wanted to leave home as soon as possible.

It didn't work out well; I took all my existing trauma with me into our relationship. We did not match at all. The way we felt and experienced life was not shared, understood nor heard by each other. Our expectations of what life is about and what inner feelings could tell were so different that I began to feel very unhappy and alone. This personal emotional situation increased with every year.

I wanted to understand and found out that my inner world was different from what many people experienced. Being a highly sensitive person it seemed that I could rely on my intuition. I learned my inner sight had returned to me. I began to feed this hunger-to-grow and visited people for hand-reading, psychic reading, card-spreads to hear what I already knew and did not want to believe. Angels and Guides came into my world as part of my life.

When my first child was born, I had a spine-issue. A good friend put me in touch with a doctor who specialized in the healing-art of the human body/mind and spirit. This man became one of my dearest friends, inspiring me spiritually which brought a big shift into my life. He encouraged me to unfold myself 'to never give up and to go for the Light'. This is printed in my heart.

Besides my marriage I started living my personal life which drove us apart even more. A common thread began to run through my development. Marking a list of different qualities and the personal awakening of my talents.

Having started with a degree in French, I became a dancer and also offered dance classes. I also joined a drawing-class with an amazing, gifted teacher and well-known Artist. I was over the moon to be in his class and to be able to awaken my so hidden creative gifts of that moment.

After five years I received a dream where I was connected to my daughter's spirit and felt she was about to be born. Ten months later a baby-girl was born. I loved being a devoted Mom of two and besides I continued my process of awakening opening a practice as a psychic reader. Dancing I still did with a semi-professional Dance Company, performing at the weekends. Although I felt like a juggler sometimes, keeping all balls in the air at the same moment, I also loved what I was experiencing and the way I was growing. The rollercoaster of my life rolled on until after another 4 years I had a similar spirit encounter in the Dreamtime. It was very clear that another baby soon was to be born in my life, which he did a year later.

The rollercoaster rolled on. When my third child was a year old I was admitted to the Royal Academy of The Hague for the 5-year evening training to become an interior architect. A wish from childhood came true. As a little girl I always was busy designing little furniture for my dollhouse and re-modelling the little rooms. Never 'playing with dolls'. I loved the study years of designing and creating intensely and became more confident of ME, more independent. On the day of my fortieth birthday I graduated and started my buro for architectural designing. My father died four months later. Four years later I divorced my husband and had to close down my buro since I fell seriously ill.

***

During my divorce I met somebody special and although he wasn't at all the reason my ex and I were splitting I knew right away that we would be a wonderful match and this is proven to be true. Over twenty-five years we are soulmates now who understand, support and love each other.

During healing time I saved all inside what I learned about various holistic ways, developing my skills at the same time. When I got into contact with a shamanic practitioner who was practicing shamanic healing-arts this was a revelation. It felt like coming Home. I 'remembered' this deep down and began to study and retrieve shamanic practicing. I started initiating Full- and New Moon Womencircles. While visiting my teachers in the Americas I retrieved some very important pieces of my Jigsaw puzzle. My private Shamanic Practice was born and I felt like a fish in the waters.

One of the Life-changing initiating events I recall was received during surgery and etched into my soul. During this operation I had a near-death experience and was told to go back because there was work for me to do on Earth. Recovering from the operation I began to discover that I had to create Healing Art. Not realizing in what way yet.

After a serious disagreement with my mother I felt so frustrated that I wanted to shift that energy into the positive. During the shamanic trainings I had embodied a strong focus in order to shift intention. I set mine to 'go to the beach with the purpose to collect a Bird's Wing' to use in my work. (Birdwings are used for special and various ceremonies and cleaning purposes). I hardly set three steps when I saw a Sea Gull's Wing standing right up in the sand. A whole wing! I gave thanks to the spirit world and the Mother Earth singing. Home again I cleaned the wing and put it on my Shamanic Altar.

At the end of that week I was drawn to the beach again with the focus to collect the other wing. My intention was still strong and I was sure this should be realized.

There had been a violent storm and while walking along the shore I noticed all kind of objects thrown on the beach by the wild waves. It was remarkable to notice some tiny bird wings, scattered around. The closer I looked, the more little wings I saw and I began to gather them, like picking beautiful flowers. This experience was truly overwhelming and blew my mind. I ended up holding a bunch of 24 of these little nature objects in my hands. Just about to turn back home something strongly caught my attention: the other Seagull's wing was waving on a wire in the wind.

Again I wanted to understand. Deeply grateful I went home and spread them all out to give thanks in Prayer; requesting to the spirit world 'why had they come to me?'

This was the message I received:

'You were the one to find these little wings. It is meant to 'create new life for their little 'bird spirits' by making artworks with these. Each art piece will heal the spirit of the birdies who had to offer their lives and have offered their wings to you now. Your work will bring Medicine and healing to Humanity as well.'
Gratitude was flowing through my body although I had no idea of how and in what way possible I could give form to what was requested.
It took me some months to get ready for this. Then things began to unfold: from all directions feathers started coming to me. First one by one and then I began to find all kind of feathers daily. From all Four Directions people began to save feathers for me. I got intensely inspired and started to create.

At first small framed pieces, then more free objects to use in shamanic practices like feather-tools to cleanse our etheric field and spaces where we live in, hair- and ear pieces, series of power shields, etc. I began to understand which feathers come from protected birds and therefore are not to be used in my work. I connected with the meaning of various feathers and the Medicine of birds. This is how my Native Art has been born some twenty years ago.

***

Besides being a photographer of Nature and creator of sacred art, I also offer my skills as a shamanic practitioner by offering various ceremonies for Mother Earth. For some decades I initiate women- and other circles and gatherings. I have embraced the Medicine teachings of the Thirteen archetypal Clan Mothers (Jamie Sams) [1][2]. Their stories have become my natural way of living. Giving thanks to the Mother

Earth, all abundance and colourful surroundings she offers to us daily.

As a little girl I was strongly drawn to Nature. Especially to trees and stones. They were my safety and the ones I shared my deepest inner thoughts with. Being beloved soul-companions they shared their unconditional love with me. Growing older the interaction with nature became deeper by taking pictures. The more I connected with them the more they invited me to photograph their image, showing to me their spirit. It could happen that one visible spirit being caught my attention at first and afterwards, more of these ones became visible on the image, manifesting themselves. I honor and cherish this incredible gift of our planetary relatives as an ultimate Gift of Life!

Again I was drawn to the trees in the summer of 2018 listening to a podcast with Clare Dubois[3], founder of an amazing worldwide organisation called TreeSisters. They globally offer many possibilities to (mainly) women to awakening and with the many projects they offer is taken care of the reforestation of our forests. Clare's words rocked my world and came right into my soul. I became a member of TreeSisters... where I still am today. Giving back to our beautiful planet by offering and sharing all gifts I have retrieved from Life in order to have many more trees to be planted.

And now I find myself here. Happy to offer my sharing to this beautiful book! Our beloved Mother Earth is changing dramatically. I am grateful for all challenges met and I believe in developing oneself is an infinite process. Besides; I am always curious what will unfold next.

[1] Sams, J. (1994a). *Earth Medicine: Ancestor's Ways of Harmony for Many Moons*
[2] Sams, J. (1994b). *The Thirteen Original Clan Mothers: Your Sacred Path to Discovering the Gifts, Talents, and Abilities of the Feminine Through the Ancient Teachings of the Sisterhood*
[3] Clare Dubois's podcast is part of this series *Encounters on Belonging, with Toko-pa.*

Sovereignty

Daphne Helvensteijn

"It is to belong to yourself; it is to feel strong, to be true, and to embody your integrity." - Bethany Webster

Again an angry man stood in front of me, screaming, directing his fiery energy at me in an attempt to burn me down. I couldn't look directly at him, so I looked at the ground. Meanwhile, I was searching for the chair with one hand, I needed to sit down. The continuous avalanche of fierce words made me so dizzy that I was unable to respond to his violence. I tried to listen, to the point where I couldn't even hear him anymore and a loud buzzing sound filled my head. The feeling that I had done something very bad completely took me over.

And at that moment I fainted.

There was another moment in my life like this when I was hit by an avalanche of angry words for doing something 'terribly wrong'.

Six years before that, I had immigrated to the United States to be with my American partner. Letting him immigrate to the Netherlands had turned out to be a fiasco, but after a long year of administrative wrangling, I was allowed to go to the States. We got married in Las Vegas and within three months I had the coveted green card in my pocket.

He had proposed to me the summer before, on a hill with the spectacular view of Barcelona. I felt the

128

moment coming all day and it made me quite nervous. And when it was suddenly there, a spontaneous 'no' escaped from my mouth. Without really thinking about it, I quickly corrected myself and said yes.

I said yes for so many reasons: because we had been together for quite some time but still lived separately, because we spent so much time and effort applying for my green card, because that in itself was a promise I had to keep because, well, who would say no to such an offer in such a sparkling city? I remember I was feeling like I wasn't worthy of my engagement ring, but had no idea where that came from.

That swallowed 'no' had to come back one day and that dreadful moment happened four years later. This time the no would stay. I sat on the bottom steps of the wooden stairs of our beautiful century-old house, trying to breathe after the explosion of emotions just seconds ago. My husband had grabbed my phone and without my knowledge read through my conversation with another man.

The anger that came at me paralyzed me completely. I couldn't find proper answers to the questions he asked in his harsh voice. There was a knot in my stomach, a buzzing silence in my head, and it was as if time stretched into a vacuum.

In that vacuum, a consciousness rose from my belly. Wasn't this what I wanted? Wasn't this a good reason to get out of here? Didn't it look like the universe had opened the door of my self-made prison saying, "fly my love, fly?"

My no in Barcelona had been hiding in a dark corner for years, but was actually a red flag. A sign on the wall of something I didn't know about at the time. And it was now standing there in that room, asking for attention: I was not happy at all with my relationship, with my partner, with where I was, not even with myself.

Within seconds I decided to leave. To leave everything behind, without knowing where to go. I just knew I didn't want this. Not anymore.

The feeling of 'not anymore' pushed me through the last three weeks of my stay in that big house that now felt only like an empty, dark crater. As if I still didn't believe my own decision, I decided to rent another house first. Then I thought about maybe volunteering in the area, but I ended up with the plane ticket back 'home'. I gave up and went back to the Netherlands empty-handed.

Back in Europe I started the Camino de Santiago. It was a painful and strange time in my life. Really I was physically unable to walk 900 kilometers, but I was pushed by my mind to complete it. I eventually landed at the zero point of the camino.

It was also the zero point of my life, the zero point of my psychological state.

There on the edge of the ocean, with a view on the great distance to that other life on the other side of that big water, I knew I really had to say goodbye to a living in the United States. I felt disoriented and lost, but there was also a little yes inside me that pulled me back. Back to my roots, back to the continent that lay behind me, back to Europe.

There on that edge I said yes to more time with my backpack. And a yes to a life in truth with myself. I wanted to get rid of this sense of victimhood and become responsible for my own life. I was done following others. I was done saying yes, when I actually felt a no.

But there was one thing I couldn't say yes to. And that was that big crater of guilt that I dragged behind me to every new place I went. I couldn't seem to get rid of it, I just couldn't get over the idea that I had overturned someone else's dream and brought his happy life to a full stop. I tried to avoid it and at some point I thought I was over it.

That was around the time when I thought my wandering existence was over, that I had found my roots and so I moved in with a man who rented me a room for a symbolic amount. But he turned out to have different expectations than I did and after a few months his patience exploded. Right in my face.

And that was when I fainted. Big time.

Afterwards I knew it was time to really look that guilt in the eye, to know what I was dealing with. I invited it for tea. I wanted to understand why I still felt guilty for something I had done years ago when I was clearly living such a better life now. I felt much happier, doing what I really wanted, and I knew I had left a life behind, that would, in the end, have taken the joy of life out of me.

It became clear to me that what I couldn't seem to forgive myself for was that I had played make believe, that I had spent a long time looking for all kinds of secret ways to get out of my marriage, that I let the tension build up and had done nothing to stop that.

I was, in my opinion, **a very bad girl**.

I don't know how many times I've dared to let that overwhelming thought enter my mind, but each time I found a new depth. I went on a quest and, like an onion, I peeled away layers and layers of my inner self, and like a flower the core opened little by little, allowing me to see more parts of the truth. And I discovered some interesting things there in the deep depths of myself.

I suddenly remembered that there were many more moments in my life when I felt like a Bad Girl: when I was afraid of a spider, when I came home five minutes later than I said I would. When I wanted to go to a bar and stay until at least 2 am or when I was 'already' having sex with my boyfriend after being in a relationship for three months. These are just some of the times when I did something that someone else didn't like me doing. And usually the reaction was great anger, overwhelming fear or devastating silence.

Because of this, during my upbringing, I slowly began to understand that I was responsible for all those emotions of others. I convinced myself that in order to keep the peace within the family, as well as within myself, I had to remove every bit of tension that might arise. After all, the fact that I had my own needs was what made them feel so tense, so I better behave and be a good girl. Therefore I kept quiet when I disagreed, resolved arguments between family members, came home right on time and didn't ask for the psychological help I needed.

And then, years later, I said a reassuring yes to a marriage proposal, whilst inside I screamed a no.

What I didn't know was that many women understand this. Many women feel the responsibility to keep the peace, to resolve the tension, to always be happy. I noticed that in this largely male-dominated world, it's often the woman who has the responsibility to keep that world going. And although I saw myself as a very modern woman, I also apparently felt responsible for my husband's well-being and for the success of our relationship.

Because emotions are the women's domain, and forming and maintaining relationships is our gift, we are also responsible for their success. However, when a relationship fails, it of course feels like it's our fault too.

Hence **my guilt**.

But I felt there was more. With all this knowledge, everything was not yet explained to me. After that little accident with me passing out, I decided to see a therapist to create a family constellation, because passing out is a very strong, but emotional reaction. The therapy was a weird moment. The woman delved right into the long-forgotten past of my female family line because, as she later said, some patterns are survival mechanisms that have been around for generations.

And my strategy was to constantly say yes to every offer a man made me. So we dug deep and we found it. We found the moment when my grandmother said yes to something she knew she had better say no to. But to keep the peace and protect herself and her family, she relented. She said yes to being pregnant again, against all medical advice.

She lived in a time when as a woman she was obliged to her husband and not to herself. She wasn't allowed to make decisions about her own body, her own health, or even her own life. She never had the courage to tell anyone exactly what happened in the bedroom and all her life she has kept silent about that real and inconvenient truth.

Saying yes, even though I felt a big no, and being silent, apparently all of this was ingrained in my DNA.

After that session, I felt like I was swimming in toxic water. Water that I had taken for granted all my life. I took it as normal, as it was, is and always will be. But it wasn't normal anymore and now I had to get rid of it. I didn't want to be the victim of this toxic behavior that hurt myself and others. I felt like I had to wash myself, over and over, inside and out. Years earlier, on that edge of the ocean, I promised myself to be honest and take responsibility for my own actions and my own life. And now it was time to be strong and do that.

And so I did.

To wash away all that toxicity, I decided to give myself all kinds of baths:

An acquaintance took me to a session with singing bowls. It stuck and I went back often, because those moments were one big bath of sound that washed away the pain in my bones.

A friend invited me to a three-hour dance session. I plunged into that pool of dancing bodies only to reappear after the last note had drifted away. From that day on, every month, I danced my anger away.

And a therapist prescribed me a daily bath in ice cold water. For a whole month I went swimming every evening, at one of the most beautiful places imaginable, in the cold fresh mountain water. There I rediscovered my own inner fire.

But the most healing was the bath of being alone. After work I went into the mountains alone for hours. By being alone, on mountain tops and in desolate valleys, relying on my intuition, knowledge and physical strength, I learned that being alone is not the same as loneliness. I found myself being the perfect company on those long walks.

And that opened up a whole other world for me, the world within myself. Deep inside the idea grew that I belonged to myself.

I am my own, not someone else's!

That one thought was the biggest change in my entire journey. It gave me a strong and powerful feeling. It meant that I was answerable only to myself. It meant that I increasingly chose what I really wanted, because at least I could explain that to myself.

I suddenly realized that no matter how angry my ex had been at me for breaking his heart, in that moment I only felt how I had constantly broken my own heart, how badly I had let myself down all these years.

I met my **sovereignty** and with it my own truths.

And finding my own truths made my yes and my no come more and more from a place of **authenticity**. By examining my own inner world, by connecting with my deeper core, I now know better what is good for me and what I no longer want to accept.

In other words, I'm starting to put myself first.

In doing so, I learn to set healthy boundaries between myself and the rest of the world. Because I'm no longer afraid of my world collapsing along with yours, I hear better what you want and what you desire, but without feeling the urge to ignore my desires. Without feeling the urge to change me for you. I can stand in your storm, but don't make it my drama.

That doesn't mean I feel like a super woman right now. Then I would ignore my own feelings, because often I still feel guilty, I feel out of balance, I feel fear. I can even catch myself asking my boyfriend first if he's okay with me going on a three-day trip in the mountains. But those are my feelings and by acknowledging them, finding out where they come from and then accepting them, I can finally take responsibility for what's mine and leave what's yours to you, without feeling like a bad girl.

During my process there was a very special moment when I could feel that crater of guilt being filled with love. It was as if hot water flowed into a lovely smelling bath. It was of pink light and it took the darkness out of my feelings. I sat down and immersed myself in that moment of absolute love.

Then I wondered who had done that. Had my ex finally forgiven me? Did the angels pour in their loving light? Or was it my connection to the eternal love of the universe?

Looking back now, I see that it could only have been MYSELF.

Sudden Loss and Hope

Dawn Foote

I am going to share with you a specific chapter from my life when over 2 years I experienced 3 sudden events. The sudden loss of our first expected child, the sudden loss of my dad and then my super healthy husband having a sudden cardiac arrest. Each resulted in a tsunami of emotions and feelings to process.

I am sharing the following so if anyone else has a loved one experience sudden loss or a sudden cardiac arrest they can read my experience, but with the knowledge that no circumstance has the same outcome. When my husband had his Sudden Cardiac Arrest (SCA) I was desperate to find other people who have been through something similar, searching for answers, hope and survival stories.

Sudden Loss

In 2013 I experienced the loss of our first expected child due to an ectopic pregnancy, which is when the foetus implants outside the womb. I was acutely aware of 'ectopic pregnancy' as my mum experienced loss due to an ectopic after my two older brothers were born. So when she fell pregnant with me it was unexpected, as after losing a fallopian tube my mum's chances of conceiving reduced significantly.

I had been diagnosed with Endometriosis after 7 years of symptoms which can affect fertility, so when I finally became pregnant after years of trying I was so happy, but I sensed something wasn't right. I went to the doctors after a positive pregnancy home test and he pulled out this cardboard wheel that showed the 'due date' - I said then, something doesn't feel right, he reassured me that 'feeling' is normal. I partly dismissed my feeling as being down to me always thinking I would struggle to conceive, which was a feeling & a belief I held since I was in my teens. I started having pains and went for a scan, they informed me it was an 'unlocated' pregnancy. I was placed in a room where I sobbed uncontrollably. I had to wait two weeks until I was booked into the hospital for them to investigate. During which time I hosted my friend's Hen Party, my emotions were all over the place but I sucked it up to ensure everyone had a good time. I was eventually admitted to hospital for an operation and an overnight stay. When I was wheeled through for anaesthetic I asked how I would know the outcome when I came round and they said if I had a scar on the front and either side it was likely they would have removed one of my tubes. When I woke from sedation, I slowly lifted the blanket and looked down, there was a scar on my left and in the centre. I was devastated & felt empty. They told me our baby was viable but had implanted in the wrong location. My husband, Simon and my parents had come to pick me up from the hospital later that afternoon. When I got home my dad sat with me holding my hand as I lay on the sofa, we just sat quietly together and that evening they drove back to Lincolnshire.

The following day my dad collapsed whilst playing golf. They kept him in for observation and then discharged him after 3 days giving him the all clear. He was happy to be home but later that evening he collapsed in the bathroom and I got a phone call at midnight from Cathy, my sister-in-law, to say I needed to come, now. I was still recovering from the operation and grieving our loss. We drove the 2 hours from Derby to Grimsby hospital, arriving in the early hours. When I arrived, my family was in the relatives' room. My aunty who was visiting from Canada said 'I am so sorry' - it was then I realised the reality of the situation...there was nothing more they could do to save my dad. Due to safety, as we had to drive to them, they had been advised not to tell me until I arrived. We waited another 2 hours whilst my eldest brother arrived who had travelled up from down south. Then my mum, eldest brother and I sat with my dad, Eric, holding his hand whilst they switched off his life support. He had suffered a catastrophic brain bleed, he was 64 years old.

Two days later we attended my friend's wedding, I figured my dad would have wanted me to have gone. I was there physically but emotionally I was running on vapers. My eldest brother and I spoke at my dad's funeral and shared many stories, from our childhood, holiday's and things that my dad did that made us laugh. Which were plenty. We also heard stories from old work colleagues, where we learnt some new and entertaining tales.

My dad was from Liverpool, Norris Green, he worked and studied hard, ending up at university where he went on to achieve a Doctorate in Physics. So he was Dr Eric Lockett but never insisted being called Dr. He loved to joke and mess around, he was always interested in what us kids were doing, how we were and above all was super proud of us all. Something he said often.

Three months later I hit an invisible wall, I couldn't think straight, couldn't focus, fatigued and felt flat. I started to wake multiple times in the night worrying that our dog wasn't breathing and having to check if he was. I decided at this point that I needed to speak to a professional counsellor. Which helped me through the grief.

Light and Hope

In December 2015 when out for a Christmas meal with close friends, my husband Simon and I were able to share the news that our first round of IVF, after failing to conceive after losing a tube, fibroids and having been diagnosed with endometriosis, we had been successful. I was pregnant. Oh…. the elation I felt was so joyous. We were telling some close friends early about the test being positive as if anything was to go wrong these friends would help hold us together, just as they had done before.

We were super happy at the prospect of being parents, nervous of course that the little bean would make it. A week later I had a small bleed and went for an early scan, to be told it was 'un-located' - geez not again! but my blood tests showed HCT levels rising in the following weeks and by the next scan the little heart beat was there. Phew, the relief! The next few months were bliss. We slopped off in March for my birthday to a couples retreat in Cornwall. Bump nicely growing, walks, great food, spa treatments and Cornish scones by the sea. We came back refreshed. By this time I was in my second trimester with good energy levels, life felt good, calm and super positive.

Sudden Shock

Friday 27th March 2015, a week after being back at work after the idyllic Cornish coastal trip. Simon had dashed out the house in the morning to go to a personal training session, he was training for a triathlon. He had run 6 marathons (New York, Berlin, Chicago, Tokyo and London twice) over the last 7 years and now was looking to give a triathlon a go. I had gone into the studio, and was chatting with one of the designers, who's birthday had been the day before. A call was transferred to me 'Hello Dawn, it's Emma, Neil's wife. Simon has collapsed, you need to come now...our postcode is….' - I scribbled it down on my pad.

I stood up and cried out – 'I need to go now, Simon has collapsed'. There was a hum of reassurance from the team 'he will be fine, it is probably a seizure of some sort'. One of my business partners drove me. I was verbalising my fears and thoughts, he was calm and giving me reassurance. It was a 15-minute drive and just as I arrived an ambulance came flying past and pulled onto the driveway. The back doors flung open and two paramedics ran from the vehicle. There was already another ambulance and a paramedic car there. I said 'this isn't good'. I walked up the drive and Simon's personal trainer, Neil, was stood outside. He was white. All he said was 'It's not good'.

I overheard the paramedics say 'The wife is here, she is pregnant, keep her out of sight'. They told me it was best if I wait in the hall and do not go in. I paced the hall and repeatedly said out loud 'He has to be okay' and that 'this can't happen now, he has to be okay'. I remember needing a wee and thinking I can't go for a wee whilst this is going on but the baby was leaning on my bladder, so I had to! Whilst in the toilet having what felt like the slowest wee ever. I pleaded. I pleaded so hard and asked the universe for him to be okay.

After a while they came into the hallway and said they were blue lighting him to A&E and for us to make our way there. I asked for an update and they replied 'We are still working on him and doing all we can'. As we drove there I called Simon's mum telling her to meet us there, she asked me if it was his heart? As there was family history, 6 months after Simon & I met in 2001 his dad, Jim had died from a heart condition aged 56, his mum had found him collapsed at home. I continued calling family, calling his sister, my mum and my brothers. All I could say was that Simon was very poorly, he'd collapsed and we were heading to Derby Royal Hospital.

When I arrived at A&E they asked me to go into a family room but I really didn't want to go in there, from my past experience that room is where you are told bad news. They managed to coax me in with the very British offer of a cup of tea, I recall asking if it could be decaf and the nurse who managed to locate a decaf tea bag. This normality created some grounding in a situation where my mind was spiralling. Eventually a doctor came in to speak to me. 'He is very very poorly, but we have an output, you can come see him for 1 minute'.

He had an output. His heart was beating. He was not dead. I was so relieved. I wasn't sure what lay ahead but I knew he wasn't dead and that was something I could work with. From this point forward I had a positive mind set, as the worst hadn't happened. His heart was beating. He was alive. There was hope.

I went into the emergency room and there were around 15 medics, machines, wires and tubes. I was able to kiss his head, his mum was able to too, and we told him we loved him and not to worry, everything would be okay. It was another 4 hours until we were able to see him in ICU. He was hooked up to all the machines and having these seizures. I look back now and feel for anyone who has had to go through a loved one being this severely ill during the pandemic & not being able to be with them. They advised it would be 48-72 hours before they attempted to take him off sedation. He had suffered a Sudden Cardiac Arrest (SCA), maybe caused by an electrical wiring issue which sent his heart into a fast rhythm, something that can happen to fit and healthy people. There have been a number of high profile cases of footballers collapsing on the pitch.

What became clear quite quickly was, the doctors were not worried about his heart. They had that back pumping and it was doing its job. The concern was the impact to his brain. As his heart had stopped its oxygen in the blood that pumps oxygen to the brain, so the worry turned to the extent of the impact of a hypoxic brain injury. From the moment he collapsed to the moment they were able to get his heart started again is referred to as 'downtime'. The longer your downtime, the worse your outlook. For every minute that they don't get you back if you haven't had CPR, then the chance of you surviving goes down by 7% per minute. If you have an out of hospital cardiac arrest your chance of survival is 8%. So he was already beating the odds. Thanks to the quick actions of his personal trainer who started CPR immediately and when the ambulance arrived a number of defib shocks were given. But his total downtime was 40 minutes. That's a significant time.

So they prepared me that although they got his heart pumping again, it was brain damage that was their primary concern. They said if he makes it, it is highly unlikely that he will be the same person that I married.

Journey of Recovery

I had been keeping a pregnancy journal and this then morphed into a journal documenting Simon's progress, so I could keep a track. Every day felt like a week!

Intensive Care Unit (ICU) - 5 weeks
March 27th 2015

Day 1 - 4 - Sedated and attempted to bring him round a number of times but he had seizures. He also got pneumonia on his chest, so was also fighting infection. I was with him at the hospital from 9am to 8 pm every day and was gathering as much information as I could from the nurses & consultants. Family & friends visited, giving us much needed love and support.

Day 5 - The day of the 20-week baby scan, whilst Simon laid sedated I headed downstairs at the hospital with my mum, Simon's mum and his sister - it was emotional to explain why Simon wasn't there but the scan showed our baby was doing well. Simon's CT brain scan results were back which showed changes to the brain but doctors advise that they have seen similar scans that people haven't come round and also seen people recover. I hold onto the hope of a positive outcome. We started discussing quite pragmatically what levels of brain injury we could manage and what that would mean. Even had someone at the hospital that did a survey asking if we had ramps and hoists in our house, to prepare for what modifications may be needed.

Day 6- Simon starts to be able to breath on his own so they look to take him off sedation, but he bit the tube and turned blue but showed one promising sign as he followed the nurse with his eyes as she walked around the bed.

Day 9 - After being on a waitlist, Simon got a slot for an operation to put a trecky in so he didn't have tubes in his mouth. He's taken off sedation and starts to come round. Slowly slowly, yawns and stretches, hand movement and a little bit of eye movement. We are watching closely, as they told us what to look out for in terms of what would be 'concerning'. Such as involuntary movements and seizures.

Day 10 - He does some hand squeezes, eye movement, moved head towards us. Doctors say they are waiting to see more signs of 'Simon'.

Day 11 - Simon was able to point at photo's, bopped his head to music that we played on the iPad and was able to be hoisted to sit in a chair for a bit. We noticed at night they were sedating him as he would wake up disoriented and try to get up & leave. I felt these drugs were affecting his recovery. The hospital was very understanding when I asked if we could have a rota of family/friends who stayed with him overnight. This helped hugely. The lads he went to school with would each take it in turns to stay overnight with him, so when he woke he saw a familiar face and settled better.

Day 12 - 24 - Simon remains in ICU - had a number of infections and setbacks but continued to make steady progress. He recognised some people that visited but others more recent in his life he didn't. I remember trying to show him the 20-week scan photo & he ended up confused thinking it was a scan of his tummy and that there was a baby in it...I had to laugh. He had no idea we were about to become parents, but I was just relieved he recognised me.

Day 25 - Discharged from ICU and moved to cardiac ward. Amazing progress.

Cardiac Rehab - 4 weeks

May 5th 2015 - He is moved to cardiac rehab where he spent 4 weeks. Lots of tests and scans to see if they could establish the cause. He also had a ICD defib fitted which is a device that monitors his heart and if it goes into an irregular rhythm paces him out of it and if that doesn't work shocks him. This was a relief to have in place. During his time in the cardiac rehab I was there every day from early until late, and became his carer. The nurses joked saying I could work there. It became clear that spaces in the neuro rehab facility had a wait list, so I took to researching what things I could do to help. Getting hold of primary school learning books, re-teaching him to tell the time, read, motor skills by bringing in games and LEGO. I created a scrapbook with memories of where he grew up, where he had lived, who his family were, his friends, his education, our wedding, holidays, his work and key life events. I had many happy memories to share but also had to retell him that my dad had died, our dog Brad had died. He cried. I wrote on post-it notes which I stuck around the room to remind him what day, month and year it was.

There was a clock on the wall and I asked him if he could say what time it was…he gave the complete wrong time but was very calm about it, he said 'how mad is that, I can't tell the time'. He would think a certain number but say another.

Neuro Rehab - 6 weeks

A place in the neuro rehab unit was finally secured, which he was in for 6 weeks. When he first arrived a nurse came in and said really slowly…'Hello. How are you?' - Simon replied and said, 'I'm alright, thanks mate'. The nurse looked visibly surprised & checked his notes. Sorry, are you Simon - I have on my notes that you had 40 minute downtime'. They were expecting him to be in a bad way.

He was very fortunate, due to him being so fit and his trainer performing CPR so quickly he was on the and his brain was slowly starting to rewire, reconnect & piece things back together. All sorts of rehab work followed and after 6 weeks he started to be able to come home at weekends. One of these weekends I took him to Mothercare with me to help choose a car seat. Poor guy. This makes your head hurt, without a brain injury! After 5 minutes of being in there, I could see he was so overwhelmed, sensory overload. He asked to be able to go somewhere quiet. The staff were great and found a quiet staff room with a drink to go sit down.

Coming home and becoming parents.

I had been so used to all the machines and doctors around, so coming home with just me was quite overwhelming, I felt really anxious. I would set up the baby monitor, so I could do things around the house but see that he was okay. It was also sensory overload for Simon, too many things, people, noises. If there were things left on the side, he would just put things in the bin. I would find things like books and candles just put in the bin. There was a lot of adjusting to do and it was about taking it steady and slowly. Something he was okay with to begin with, but then the slow pace of recovery he got increasingly frustrated by.

We both run our own businesses, I was fortunate to have business partners & a team that could hold the fort. Simon is an Architect and the circumstances there were more reliant on his imminent return. This became a growing and added pressure.

The due date was fast approaching and I was in nesting mode. We had an amazing raft of family and friends who helped…from raising funds for plants for the recently renovated garden, my mum staying with me, friends cooking meals, giving support, my brother fitting our kitchen and my mother-in-law helping to decorate the nursery.

My waters broke late one evening and I was able to drive to the hospital (Simon was unable to drive for at least 6 months after his SCA). We created a calm environment at the hospital and I ensured Simon was able to get rest too. Our daughter ended up arriving via C-section. I was borderline needing a blood transfusion and completely wacko but was sooo happy she was here, safe and well.

Adjusting to becoming new parents can be pretty overwhelming in normal circumstances. On top of this my protective instincts around our little family were on super hyper drive. I was utterly shattered, with pretty high anxiety levels worrying something bad was about to happen but I was being powered by an elation and joy that our family was here and together. We had A LOT to be grateful for.

The following 5 years are likely for another chapter but they were a mix of recovery, discovery, rediscovery, patience, frustration, anger, mis-communication, learning, reflection, appreciation, compassion and understanding.

Reflection & Perspective

I have spoken to others whose partners have had a sudden cardiac arrest, some that tragically didn't make it or that 3+ years on still remain in hospital care. I knew nothing about sudden cardiac arrests before it happened to Simon. I have learnt so much since, how it can happen to very fit people and how it is completely different to a heart attack. I would be quizzing all the consultants, cross referencing, seeking advice and information. I went from being his wife, to being his carer and then becoming a mother, wife and me again.

I encourage everyone to learn CPR – it's literally lifesaving, also to know where defibrillators are in the area you live, the sooner a shock is administered the better the chances not only of survival but also recovery. I encourage people to seek counselling and support when needed, on their own and also together as a couple. To cut yourself some slack and don't be too hard on yourself, I nearly broke myself whilst trying to hold everything around me together. The recovery journey is a long road.

This chapter is a chapter of my life. It doesn't define me but it has changed and shaped me. Speaking from my view it has shifted my outlook, my perspective, which in turn enabled me to refocus my business, it has tested our marriage, it has tested my resilience, made me both more fearful but also more grateful.

Our daughter Libby is now 6, and last weekend she went kayaking with her dad and I, along the canal. Sounds like a pretty normal family outing. But I write that and appreciate that every single ounce of that is flipping amazing!

Resources people might find useful:

Sudden Cardiac Arrest UK Facebook Group -
https://www.facebook.com/groups/SuddenCardiacArr
estUK/
Sudden Cardiac Arrest UK was set up to provide peer
support for survivors and others affected by the
survivors cardiac arrest and unfortunately are not
equipped or trained to deal with those bereaved by
an SCA.

If you are bereaved by an SCA it may be best if you
contact one of the appropriate organisations listed on
this website -
https://www.suddencardiacarrestuk.org/bereavement

Here you can download the Learn CPR App
https://www.redcross.org.uk/first-aid/first-aid-apps

Ectopic Miscarriage https://www.tommys.org/baby-
loss-support/ectopic-pregnancy-information-support

Endometriosis https://www.endometriosis-uk.org/

The Courage to Shine

Clare Dubois

The Courage to Shine

There was a time in every woman's life where we get to choose ourselves. For some of us it feels like fumbling in the dark, not ever really sure that there even is a 'self' in here somewhere. For others it's a slow surfacing, remembering and a claiming of what has always been sovereign. For others it's night and day, walking around a corner and nothing is ever the same again. The choice is clear, it's made, it's done.

For me it's a continuous spiral of getting lost and getting found, remembering what matters, putting one foot in front of the other and continuing to move forward, no matter how blind I'm feeling. It never stops requiring courage. It never stops unveiling more lies I believed and more truths waiting to be lived.

The courage to shine really is the courage to drop the crud that clogs up our light. It is not ours, it was never true, it serves nothing to keep carrying or believing it, it is not you!

If you hesitate.

If you long for that wild untamed river

To surge through your cells,

And for pleasure to choose itself

Over the temptation of far too safe,

Then wake up.

Those insidious fears if swallowed

Will see you bow your head

And dim your light,

When strutting naked

Through the streets of your own desire

Is the path of truth and permission

You long to embody.

If you're done with the pleasing

Over promising,

Yes'ing instead of no'ing,

Being the thing that works

Instead of the thing that you are,

Then wake up.

You are a miraculous

One of a kind for all of time

This you, this now

This moment of glory

Is waiting for you to turn within

To turn to yourself

And yell YES!

Unchain your power.

Fall into the river of love

That is the current of your own soul.

Why did you think

That there was ever anyone to impress?

That anyone other than yourself

Could conduct the orchestra

Of your own becoming

Or listen for the music encoded

Within the stratosphere of your own cells?

This life is not for begging or pretending,

It is for grabbing,

Like the love affair of ages

Savoured and sung utterly,

So that the very sweetness of existence

Can come to know itself

Fully met,

Fully known,

And fully lived,

As the miraculous

Expression of you.

Witch Time

I'm not sure that has ever been another time more catastrophic epigenetically for women, than the burning times. Almost 400 years of continuous fear mongering and cruelty, suspicion, separation, torture, shaming, betrayal and murder. Just for being woman. It doesn't bed thinking about, and yet for most western women, this lives in our bloodlines, our DNA and our ancestral memory.

It requires significant compassion for ourselves to really understand why it is that so many of us are held back by levels of fear that don't just whisper, they yell how much safer it is 'to stay small' rather than 'rock the boat.'

And, there is only so long a lie as great as 'women are evil' can stay bedded in consciousness before it gets spat out. As mum would say 'the truth will out'. The truth is coming, and the lie has had it's time.

Because the soul of women cannot be destroyed and we are rising.

You cannot take the witch

Out of the woman.

You cannot strip the soul

Out of the sky.

You cannot justify the countless reasons

That you did the things you did,

And we are past the point

Of needing to know why.

For a body cannot claim

What is immortal.

A story does not end

When breathing stops.

The resonance of life

That holds the mystery,

Carries everyone of us

You thought you lost.

For the witches are returning

And remembering

That the soul of women

Cannot be destroyed,

The awakening accelerating wildly,

Is the coming home

To potency denied.

Because Gaia in her urgency is calling

Because life knows everything is on the line

Because evolution calls us to remembering

Who we are

And what lives through us

When we thrive.

So the melody of womanhood

Is rising

The drum of our awakened heart

Is loud

The knowing that we're here to serve

Is healing

The path ahead is one

Of naked love.

So my sisters we are here to raise the dead.

To resurrect outrageous truth and power

To understand that those that lived within us

Still bring the magic, the knowing and the fire.

For alchemy is happening to and through us

As our blood unlocks the keys to natures codes

And our femininity is charged with holding

The restoration of the sacred natural world.

How do I know

I wrote this poem as a message to myself to remind me that the only voice I need listen to is that of my own soul. That goes for all of us. How can anyone ever know what is true for our own soul, when they do not fully understand the nature of us, the journey of our incarnation, the learnings that we came for, the love that we are capable of and the difficulties that we need in order to grow?

Do we want others to define us, or do we want to define ourselves? And if the latter, is there any useful limit on wild beauty?

How do I know

Who I am

When all I have been taught

Is who to be

According to rules

That belong to a past

That believed in the domination

Of nature

As a path to power.

How do I know

Who to be

When the judgment that gets thrown

Arises from a fear so old

That no one even knows

Why it's wrong

To shine

Or show pleasure

As a woman

Why would I stay

Cooped up in a cage

Of shoulds and oughts

When this body

Is crafted from moonlight

And fire

And the deeper river

Of ancient knowing

Guides my every felt sense

Of what it means

To be a woman

So I stand

Shameless bright

My heart open wide

Wild crafted pleasure

And mountainous might

I define myself

As I set myself free

And I laugh out loud

As I birth a new me

For all women.

Memoirs of a Menopause

Liz Clayton-Jones

She sat on the cold iron garden seat cradling her mug of now tepid coffee, her back to the patio doors, facing out into the tangled cottage garden. Tears quietly rolled down her face.

"I don't know how to do my life anymore…" she whispered to the world.

A sob choked through her; her shoulders heaved.

She quickly exaggerated the movement into a shrug, should anyone walking into the living room behind her have spotted the movement.

Cup in hand, she rose slowly to her feet and made them walk her down the length of the garden; just a normal morning for a normal working wife and mother, checking out nature's overnight effect and breathing in the air before the working day started in earnest.

At the bottom of the garden she quickly wiped her face, drew in a deep breath, mentally shook herself and turned, striding purposefully back up towards the house.
Things to do.
People needing her.
She, needing to find an element of control to her day, in the life that slowly appeared to be unravelling.

***

Looking back, this feeling of loss, being lost, has been building for a couple of years.

She is known as an "on-it" achiever who deftly juggles family and work. The impression of deftness is one she covets as inside she often feels that she is letting both sides down. But she consoles herself with the story that this is the "normal" guilt of a working mother, always split between the two roles. She takes comfort in reflecting on the strong work ethic and pride in purpose she is passing to her children, and the knowledge that the income is essential.

Her love for her daughter, her stepsons and her husband is deep and unconditional. She is grateful for this second chance at partnership, loves how the two families have combined, and works hard to meet the various needs of those in her care. They have what she feels is a good life.

At work she prides herself on her ability to grasp ideas quickly, to connect with people easily and is seen as someone who always exceeds expectations. She has the odd battle with imposter syndrome but, broadly speaking, she just rolls up her sleeves and gets to it. Work defines her. Her identity is inseparable from it.

But slowly, inexorably, she is experiencing a change; a change that is rocking her foundations; knocking the wind from her sails.

Despite no significant shift in diet or exercise her weight is creeping up. She's never been confident in her appearance, so this is not only perplexing but very unwelcome. She has started to wear over-shirts and jackets to work; has started undressing in darkness.

Her skin is worse than when she was a teenager. Compounded with the weight gain she is more and more self-conscious. She's spending a fortune on special make-up and is swallowing prescription meds so strong that she must take a liver function test every few months.

She has started to drop some of those juggling balls.
Struggling to think straight.
Struggling to think sharp.
She has started to have terrors about early onset dementia, real horrors at the memory of how her grandmother was stolen by Alzheimer's. But giving voice to those fears makes her sound absurd. Her husband and daughter, bored of the repetition, merely suggest she might be tired.

And she is exhausted a lot of the time.

Her internal thermometer is all over the place and it is keeping her awake most nights, tossing and turning, her feet seeking out the cooler corners of the sheets, kicking off the duvet even though the windows are thrown wide. Her husband has resorted to a double quilt on his side of the bed to keep warm; he touches her skin and says it feels cold…but inside she feels aflame; she can't understand how she isn't visibly on fire.

Performance at work has suddenly become a battle to prove herself to her boss, to her colleagues, to herself. Four hours of restless sleep a night is taking its toll. Thinking is done through layers of internal cotton wool. Her to-do list is winning; she's missed appointments, overlooked deadlines. In a critical meeting the other day she completely forgot what she was saying, and momentarily was not even sure she knew what meeting she was in.
The internal panic was piercing, painful, pounding.

She's out of sorts with people.
And she's out of sorts with herself.

She cringes when she thinks of the times that she
has been short with the children.
And her love... she suddenly can't bear for him to
touch her. She used to love the way he would come
up behind her in the kitchen and put his arms around
her; now it's unwelcome but she can't explain
why. She tries not to stiffen but it feels like her nerves
are on the outside.
And why does he think sex can fix everything? She's
lost the desire, and he laughs at the cliche if she says
she has a headache… but a lot of the time lately she
really does. And when she does grin and bear it, it
hurts… and she knows it's starting to bother him.

She's rapidly losing her sense of self.
Where has that confident achiever-super-woman
gone?
Who is she now?

If she can't do work, and she can't do home, what is
the point of her?

***

This is, of course, my story.

It is, of course, the menopause.

I know now, through years of lived experience and
research, that many women go through all of this and
more. But we aren't aware, we don't share. It can feel
like an ending, something to be ashamed of – and yet
it is as natural as life.

I am sharing this with you as I don't want any woman, or person assigned female at birth, to reach this juncture of life unready and to bear it feeling alone.

This stage in our lives, this bookend to puberty, is something every woman will go through, but we have the opportunity to grab it and see it as a metamorphosis: our transition to something more; a transformation to the wise women and shaman of ancient cultures.

It took me too long to see this opportunity; too much misdiagnosis, too much fear – just too much. So, walk alongside me through my story, be ready to find your opportunity for transformation!

***

The day I sobbed that I didn't know how to do life anymore was a turning point for me.

I am very fortunate in that I am, at heart, a scientist, and at this point in my life I was embedded in a Research & Development environment. Somehow, I could sense that the feeling I was feeling wasn't "real" but another symptom of whatever it was my body was doing. So, I set about some research.

Visits to the GP at this point had been non-committal in terms of diagnosis. Depression and chronic fatigue had been mentioned but neither felt right to either me or my husband, so I batted away drugs. Eventually, however, a push for blood tests revealed I was both low on thyroxin and low on oestrogen… this was menopause.

Now I needed to know EVERYTHING.

I discovered there are thought to be thirty-four "common" symptoms. Two websites suggested upwards of forty. Another mentioned that oestrogen has over three hundred functions in the body. No wonder then, that your body goes haywire when it can no longer make enough.

I discovered that, while most women experience the start of this natural four-to-ten-year journey around the age of forty-five, as many as one in a hundred start before they're forty, and one in a thousand even earlier than that. In addition, women who have certain gynaecological conditions and surgery, and those taking certain drugs for cancers, can be catapulted into menopause as a result.

In addition, anyone assigned female at birth can go through it. I can't begin to imagine what it feels like to spend most of your life seeking to be accepted and identified as a different gender to your birth-assignment, only to find that your body has other ideas.

I discovered that ninety percent of women will suffer from debilitating symptoms; that forty percent feel they can't manage their work; that twelve percent of women quit work as they feel there is no way to juggle work AND menopause.

And I discovered that I was just a little bit indignant about that.

My next move was to SHARE.

My first conversation was with my Mum. At this point she was nearing eighty. At the time that she was experiencing the very worst of her menopause I was living away from home so didn't "see" her. We certainly didn't talk about it then.

But our "now" conversation showed me another impact; one tied into the very fabric of how our family had evolved. The uncomfortable truth is that, without understanding and support, relationships unravel.

My parents were a military couple. They had married in their early twenties; Mum a young teacher, Dad a dashing flyboy in the Royal Air Force. Three children and many countries and house-moves later, they were looking forward to the early retirement that military service brings. But cracks started to show in their connection. Mum was short-tempered; Dad was intolerant of her tiredness, her lack of energy. There were other impacts too. Mum saw a doctor, mentioned menopause, requested help. An older, male, military doctor told her to pull her socks up. Dad, perhaps stereotypically, sought solace in a younger woman. Twenty-seven years of marriage, over. My Mum still blames a great deal of this outcome on untreated, unsupported menopause that she just didn't feel able to discuss.
My indignance rose a notch or two.

I discovered the saddest fact.
In the UK, the highest demographic for female suicide is between the ages of 51 and 54.
Tell me that's pure coincidence.
I sat back and remembered that day in my garden.
I could see it.

Now I'm not just indignant.

***

We find our missions in extraordinary places.

As I neared the end of a corporate career spanning over three decades, I expected my mission to be about people and teams; this is, after all, where I had spent the largest part of my career. I felt this was my purpose (certain remarkable women are chuckling reading this… a knowing chuckle).

While I had been undergoing my own journey with the rollercoaster that is menopause, I had been coaching some women in my organization who were at a similar life-stage. They had one thing in common; they didn't want anyone else at work to know. They felt they would be judged and found wanting, blocked from progression. They were fearful that drops in performance would lead to loss of status, loss of opportunity, loss of bonus. They perceived that the women who were in leadership positions in the business were in the "lucky ten percent" of those with no symptoms; that if they admitted to symptoms any hopes of leadership would be dashed. They were all in "fake it to make it" mode, convinced that if they mentioned the M word they would no longer be taken seriously.

At this point I knew I had to be the one to speak up and speak out.

I set up an internal webinar, found some additional support, shared the invitation out into the business expecting a handful of curious women to join.

Almost one hundred and fifty people joined. All ages; not just women.

They came to listen to my story; they came to understand what was happening to themselves; they came to understand what was happening to their wives, their mothers, their sisters, their colleagues. Sharing my story unlocked something. Other women took up the call; shared their stories about their menopause, early menopause, menopause after surgery, after cancer.

Men wrote to me afterwards sharing their agony of not knowing how to approach their wives, avoiding dealing with it so successfully they had breakdowns of their own.

Women who were lost; men who were lost.

And now they could share. And through sharing they could support each other; they could feel less alone.

Powerful things happen when you speak your story into the world.

Some months later I was reflecting on my mission. The power of the sharing and the indignation in the way this life-stage was landing with so many people inspired me to DO SOMETHING. The scientific stage of metamorphosis came to mind. The chrysalis form of an insect is not very attractive but look what happens inside it! Menopause may not be a very attractive phase of our lives, but what if we could literally transform, and emerge into this later phase of our lives with a new way of being.

Ancient cultures revered their elder women. This is the time in our lives where we can step into our wisdom, our knowledge, our experience, our power.

The transformation of course starts with me.

Acknowledging that being in the throes of this life-stage can make someone feel "less than" (and loving a bit of science), my focus is on experimentation. As R Buckminster Fuller said, there are no failed experiments, only unexpected outcomes! So, transformation is about experimenting; selecting a path, "hypothesizing" what it may bring, trying it out… and learning from it. Growing our wisdom ever further.

I have selected various teachers to guide me through my transformation. Some know who they are. Some don't; their wise written words triggering thought and action and experiments. Some have arrived unexpectedly. They are all welcome, indispensable, invaluable.

I'm still on my journey but I hope that by walking alongside me for a little of it, you are ready to start your experimentation when the time comes; ready to share, ready to become "even more than"…

Perception of Perfection

Donna Hicklin

Paralysed, staring in the mirror. My heart is racing, I can feel the blood pulsing through every vein in my body. I have stopped breathing for a few seconds now, and my hands start to shake. As tears then fill my wide, frightened eyes, I wonder...will I ever feel normal?

Like many other people, I have struggled with my confidence. I suppose, who hasn't on some level, right?

For me, until more recently, I have never truly felt good enough and if I'm being completely honest, it's still a work in progress.

I was a perfect little girl you see, loved and adored by parents, family and all who met me. Golden ringlets and a big smile. I certainly earned the nickname 'Smiler' and wore it proudly like a badge. I really could do no wrong and was (apparently) never naughty. The only time I remember doing something 'bad' was when I was about three. My nemesis brother, who would do his best to torture me in one way or another, gave me a stone and kept on and on at me to throw it at the TV...and so eventually, you guessed it...I did! I couldn't believe it when it hit the TV and BANG, the screen smashed into a million pieces everywhere in the lounge. My poor parents! Anyway, other than that, I was basically a little princess in pink. That's great isn't it? I'm not so sure…

Being so perfect in others' eyes is a hard act to keep up. Over the years, anything anyone said to me that was negative in the slightest, would feel like an attack and would make me feel unworthy and not good enough. I feared that my perfect persona had been broken and shattered, just like the TV. I am sure I have so often taken comments and situations way more to heart than I should have. On the other hand, anything positive made me feel safe and loved. I must have thought subconsciously (as I certainly wasn't told this) that I needed to be perfect to be loved and to keep everyone happy. Fortunately I now realize, this was so wrong.

At the age of 14 I had the shock of my life. My grandad, who I loved so much, took his own life. This was my first experience of mental health issues. To me, he was such a fun grandad and I just thought he had been a little bit poorly. I had no awareness about depression and don't know if I had ever heard about anyone taking their own life before. I couldn't understand what on earth had happened and why. It was utterly devastating. As a family, we all healed to different degrees and in the best ways that we could. It left me with that aching feeling though, of what was wrong with him or his life, or something around him to cause this. Or to flip that around, what was not perfect to cause this? If everything had been perfect, this would not have happened...right?

I don't know if my Grandad's death contributed to the next turn in my journey or not, but later in my teen years, I suffered with an eating disorder. I still remember all the tricks. Hiding food, pretending I'd already eaten, quietly being sick and exercising in my bedroom. I just wanted to fit in; I wanted to be pretty; I wanted to be liked; I wanted to be PERFECT. I didn't want to be a turtle like I was told at school (this was in

171

reference to my petite frame making my school bag look like a big turtle shell). Okay, you can laugh, it is funny to me now. I didn't like how I looked. I was obsessed with the thought that I was too fat and needed to lose weight. The 'tire' around my belly (you know that roll of fat that you get when you sit down), 'shouldn't' have been there. I used to visualize cutting it off with a knife or scissors somehow. Shocking, I know. Thank goodness I never tried. Controlling my eating gave me an element of control in my life where I probably felt I had none. After some time, at around 16, and after my mum found out about my eating problems, I realized I needed and wanted help. Unfortunately the doctors weren't able to offer that. I believe that they didn't really try as I wasn't ill enough to them. The good thing was though, that I knew now that I was ill, and luckily knew my eating habits were not healthy and would end badly if they continued. That realization helped me to want to change.

I turned 16 and couldn't wait to leave school and go to college as I knew that I wanted to study beauty therapy. This is where I began my healing journey. I took some extra classes in holistic therapies and was hooked. I learnt how holistic therapies can help people to feel better physically, emotionally and spiritually. I was so interested in how I could help others and myself too. So, alongside my beauty course I started to do additional training in everything I could related to holistic therapy, starting with aromatherapy massage and ear candling. I then continued on to learn reflexology, reiki, crystal healing and shamanic techniques.

While studying, I met my first boyfriend Rich (who years later became, and still is, my husband). Life definitely changed for the better. I felt the happiest I ever remembered being. I became healthier, I got on top of my eating problems and I did well at college. I started work as a manager at a brand new salon. I let the need for perfection drop for a while and I felt so much better. This was a whole new side of me. Support from Rich, my parents and new friends who I actually opened up to, together with exploring holistic therapies, all gave me a boost.

I worked at the salon for about 11 years and everything was fairly going well. There were still challenges over the years however and a few stressful times gave me my first real experiences of anxiety and panic attacks. I remember quite clearly my very first panic attack. There had been a very unsettling series of events that had happened between myself and a client at the salon. Someone who had witnessed this brought it up with me a few weeks later to check I was okay. I replied to her comment in quite a calm way but soon started to have the most weird feelings in my body. My heart started thumping, and my arms and hands suddenly started shaking uncontrollably, even though I thought I felt fairly calm. I quickly made my excuses and dashed into the other room feeling confused. I felt a little unsettled by her bringing it up, but my physical reaction suggested I was much more upset than I had realized. I remember feeling shocked and concerned, then intrigued that my body could react so profoundly to an emotion so locked away that I didn't even know it was there. I managed to calm my body down after a while but this seemed to be the start of my anxiety journey.

Eventually a situation at the salon forced my decision to leave and start my own therapy business. I am so grateful this happened, as otherwise I would never have taken the leap.

Starting my own business was a fantastic opportunity but this is when perfectionism kicked back in big time. The pressure I put on myself to do well was so strong that I didn't even really try. "If you actually try and fail then you really are a complete failure" said my inner voice. I felt that if I really put myself out there and it didn't work then I truly would be admitting to the world that "I am just not good enough". So I just plodded along for around eight years doing ok but not doing really well either. I was just playing in the safe zone saving myself the trauma of being a failure.

During the first years of running my business, both myself and Rich had several health scares too. I always coped strangely well during these times, even when I thought I would actually lose my soul mate. I tapped into an inner strength I did not know I had. When things were better health wise, anxiety really kicked back in. It was always there lurking and waiting for a weakness. It's like a dark cloud hovering and waiting to pour a whole load of rain down on your head when you least expect it. Even when I didn't realize I was anxious, I was on edge with the slightest thing and probably quite a hard person to live with at times. The pressure I put on myself to be happy and be the person I thought everyone wanted me to be was overwhelming, especially as I had been shown so clearly how short life could turn out to be. "I must be happy, I must have everything all sorted and in order, I must… I must…" I didn't realize that at the time but now looking back it is quite clear.

I find anxiety such a sneaky little monster dressed up in different disguises. It's like going out on Halloween; which monster will I see next. It comes in so many forms which makes it easy to go unnoticed and not dealt with. Many people don't realize that what they are feeling is in fact anxiety. Gosh, over the years my anxiety has taken so many forms: palpitations, chest pain, shaking hands, shortness of breath, crying, sleepless nights, agitation, anger, worry over the slightest thing, overthinking, hopelessness and foreboding. One that was more of a shock to me was physical tics. I had seen people with Tourette Syndrome have tics but had no idea they can simply be caused by anxiety.

Now, for my biggest, most vulnerable share of my journey so far... let me take you back to the first paragraph.

Paralysed, staring in the mirror. My heart is racing, I can feel the blood pulsing through every vein in my body. I have stopped breathing for a few seconds now, and my hands start to shake. As tears then fill my wide, frightened eyes, I wonder...will I ever feel normal?

What was happening? Was it a panic attack? Yes, but why was it happening? It was the result of seeing my reflection in the mirror. This wasn't because I thought I was too fat like earlier years. It's as if my self-consciousness morphed into another form. I had beaten the 'fat thoughts' so the anxiety needed something else to feed off. It was the slightest flaw or imperfection that would set it off, and to me that thing was all I could see when I looked in the mirror. Those 'flaws' would consume me. I would panic, stare in the mirror time after time checking if whatever the flaw I had spotted that day had got worse. I would constantly obsess about how to fix these problems and how or why they were there, as they 'shouldn't' be! I could go from one room to the next, checking in different lights and angles. It was utter torture. Then other days, I would avoid all reflective surfaces completely to the point of diverting my eyes when I walked near a car in case I caught sight of myself. I was told that this is called body dysmorphia and realizing that how I felt was actually a thing and not just me, helped. Knowing it had a name meant that there are other people out there feeling the same way and that gave me a little more power. This does not mean that I identified with this 'condition'; It just gave me the power and strength to know that I AM NOT ALONE. It is not something that I 'have'. It isn't me, it is an accumulation of false thoughts, beliefs and bucket-loads of fear.

I want you to know that all the feelings you are having, whether they are like mine or completely different, I guarantee you, many other people are having those same thoughts and feelings as you too. That is why I wanted to write this. No matter who you are or what you are feeling, I want you to know from my heart to yours that YOU ARE NOT ALONE either.

All these feelings and experiences have kept me on my journey of self-discovery and finding more ways to help myself and others. Helping people is what I love. If I can make a difference to someone's life, that simply lights me up, so in a way my experiences have been a gift to enable me to help others.

Sometimes, even when things seem to be working out for people on the surface, it doesn't mean there isn't deep pain underneath. This is the same for each of us. So take time to look beyond what you see on the outside and don't judge, as we never know what others are feeling. I still occasionally keep that same smile on my face that I had as a child in front of others, no matter what is happening as this is my mask. I have however learnt to be more open and vulnerable. Deep down my own hard-wired pressure for perfection has been draining and so detrimental for most of my life. I think, with feelings like fear and unworthiness, it comes down to our identity and who we think we are. We all have an identity and, for the most part, this identity is probably wrong. It is something that has been ingrained in us since birth, through family, friends, teachers, carers and even people we have brief interactions with.

How do people treat you? What do they say to you? What false thoughts and beliefs are being or have been given to you? This all creates an image of who we think we are or who we should be. For some of us, we feel comfortable staying within those lines of expectation. It is a hard spell to break, but recognising it is the first step. The inner programming in my mind has been that I need to be perfect, which consists of being sweet, pretty, petite and clever, but life just doesn't work that way. No-one can stay looking or acting a certain way forever. I now know so deeply that perfection is unattainable. The sooner you feel that too and let go of the pressure to achieve it, the sooner you can start to live a more exciting, fulfilling life. I can now happily say that I try to push myself each day to feel the fear and do it anyway in my life and business. Standing still is not an option for me anymore. I deserve to be happy and so do you. We are just humans on a journey, trying to do our best. We should be changing, experiencing and expanding. Let's do that together, perfectly imperfect and support each other on our amazing, and yes a little bit scary, journeys.

Life As Prayer Flags

Jennifer Comeau

These poems and writings are like the prayer flags that stretch across a span of forest garden on the land where my home sits (not "my land", it is sovereign to the Abenaki people). It's an area I call the fairy garden, where a Dreaming Tree swing suspends from a kind branch of Grandfather Oak, lifting and swaying in the breezes, and where I go to make sense of my life's journey, seeking nature and medicine from invisible realms.

April in Connemara

On a day when winds are raw,

rains insist

on their priority,

and fog is playing stingy

with the view

don't climb Diamond Hill in some

stubborn display of endurance.

No panorama rewards your foolishness.

Go instead to the trail

entitled, "Nature."

Be a humble guest in the home

of Beech, Ash, and Alder broadleaves

who baptize you

with holy water from

ancient limbs.

Let your reverent boots meander

past tiny patches of yellow green

wolf's milk, lone butterwort,

lemon primroses, and

hillsides of shiny, wild garlic.

Quiet your mind and

listen to skylarks and song thrushes –

descants amid falling-water melodies.

Sink into the mossy, feminine landscape

and feel her reassurances.

The day will come when

bright skies invite an ascent

to the sweeping views

of Connemara's bens and bogs.

Until then,

drink in the embrace

of her lush woods.

I was on a month-long solo sojourn in Western Ireland – no itinerary, no one to tell me what to do or where to go. Still, I found myself wanting to "get it right" – a pattern in my life. Here, where there were no rules and no one to please, I had fallen into the trap of *pleasing*. Pleasing who? Carrying the deep programming of domination and conquer that is so pervasive in our culture, I thought I *must* summit Diamond Hill. Catching myself in this age-old pattern, I surrendered to the rains and the mist, and instead, wandered through the lush, feminine, valley trail.

Dirty Dishes

Sometimes the gunky cheese board

and oily salad bowl

    [can]

remain in the sink

alongside the soaking fry pan

because a wild

dream-filled sleep

seems the better

devotion.

Sometimes the empty quiche plate

and crumb-filled cutting board

    [can]

join the pile

because a breakfast

picnic of reheated leftovers

seems imperative —

down Land's End, overlooking

Cape Porpoise harbor

sitting on the tailgate of

a vintage F-150 pickup;

dog whining for handouts,

thermos of coffee steaming

into the air.

Sometimes the soapy sponge

and lemon-scented water

    [can]

glide across the cheeseboard and fry pan

a meditation, not obligation, because

fantastical night capers linger

in your aura,

and you are full

of seagull cry and salt wind.

Your blood now ripples

of shoreline over stone,

and the sun shines out of your eyes.

Each New Year's morning, in the early dawn, I find myself writing a poem. This one began on the eve of a new year in 2020, and then played itself out for the day. I found myself refusing to "do the customary thing" in washing dinner dishes. Instead, I gave myself permission to allow my own dreaming to guide my actions, and the dishes languished until the end of New Year's Day. Who cared? No one. Especially not my joy-filled heart. And now I realize the experience was a harbinger of a year filled with *un-customary things* – 2020.

Storm

Dark clouds kiss

the sky,

lay themselves down like a vixen waiting

to be ravaged.

Winds aloft are warm

like breath, but here

where I stand, it's frozen.

Tiny, iced ball-bearings pelt

the earth and leave

striations of white

against my window.

Who gives a storm

a name as if it's been invited

to tea?

For this unwelcome

guest I have infantries

of resistance and snipers

in the trees.

Behind the wild sky our cheeky

planet eclipses a full wolf

moon, and in the blackness

cosmic forces howl.

I feel, rather than hear,

their impact. I know

their intent.

My soldiers

are weary; urge me to stop

the war. I lay down

my arms.

N'oreaster winds blow

like a bellows on

the embers of

my heart.

I wrote this poem during a time when I realized the brutal winter N'oreaster I was witnessing precisely mirrored the storm playing itself out in me. Mythologist Sharon Blackie writes about being *in good heart.* Is the land where your home resides *in good heart*? Do you walk through the world *in good heart*? Saboteur thoughts had been at war with my better angels. How uncanny and perfect, really, that the outer climate reflects the inner climate. I realized then, it was time for another layer of healing.

Sometimes It's Hard

Sometimes it's hard to see where the ocean ends

and the sky begins.

Sometimes it's hard to find

the impulse toward compassion

from my wounded shards.

185

But I promise you,

my heart knows. She says: give up the need

to be right. Be kind instead.

Our souls know what to do. Think of the wild-eyed

and expansive child you once were

before the thousand bruises calloused you.

Befriend her again. Welcome her

back into your heart

and watch a brilliant sun

reappear from behind

platinum clouds

and a rainbow arch itself

across the sea.

I wrote this poem as I looked across our Maine seacoast on a gray-on-gray day. I was weary from a full-out effort to bring awareness to Earth's plight, from attempts to inspire a shift in consciousness toward a more beautiful, equitable, and balanced world, and from bearing witness to so much loss and devastation. I needed to reclaim the girl with an innocent and ever-hopeful heart.

The Woods at Timber Point

Yesterday

with a breeze like assurance from a gentle god

and skies as fair as my eyes

I walked

through her woods.

I worked hard to slow my pace,

holding a question.

I searched for signs --

aware that each step

whether on crushed stone

or wood chips

landed

like an assault

on her solitary loveliness.

Today

with fog draping the coast

in a sudden mood swing

and winds extinguished like a candle,

I tip-toed,

slow, and quiet

through her woods

intent upon only this:

With each shift of my gaze -- a

sinking, deepening, honoring

of this holy place

and the wisdom I had so desperately sought —

revealed itself

everywhere.

In this poem, I write about the difference between "trying too hard" to find answers, and letting come what comes with a grateful heart. When I give up the illusion that I have control of anything, the gifts, messages, and insights appear.

Bear and Saint Brigit

Kildare, Ireland. Standing in front of the well attributed to Goddess Saint Brigit, our guide said, "Give your sorrows to Brigit's holy well." I realized I had a sorrow I hadn't written about yet. It had been two years, and the grief I carried wanted release at long last. I share this rather difficult piece to honor Bear, who suffers at human's hands, and Bear, who nevertheless, comes to me in my dreams, bringing me healing medicine.

Kildare, Ireland. 2016.

I stood in a circle with other women sojourners at Goddess Saint Brigit's well, the Celtic triple goddess of midwifery, smithcraft, and poetry. Built millennia ago by local clansmen, a three-foot rock wall surrounds clear, artesian water. Once women and girls came to fill their wooden buckets for supper, sometimes pausing to dip a scrap of fabric into its healing essence before tying the "clootie" onto a nearby whitethorn – their ailments or worries offered up to the goddess.

At this pilgrimage place, we conducted a ceremony for water, the essence of all life. Afterward, our guide invited us to release our sorrows into the waters of Goddess Saint Brigit's holy well." I stared into the well's mysterious depths, rolling the word *sorrows*

189

over and over in my mind. Then, like a sprung leak, the pain I'd stuffed away gushed out of me.

Two Years Prior: Kennebunkport, Maine.

A great battle waged. It was called "Citizen's Initiative Question 1." *Do you support a ban on all trapping, baiting, and hounding of black bears in the State of Maine?*

YES!

Voting night. 9:30 PM. The moon was on the wane. District after district reported its votes; smaller, rural districts first. Initial results were discouraging: 51% no; 49% yes. I groaned, but nonetheless maintained optimism. *Of course*, I think. *The "No's" have the edge up north. It's hunting country.*

"Wait," I chanted to my husband, John. "Wait for Portland." *Wait*, I told myself, remembering the driveways I'd walked, the wooden steps to back doors I'd climbed, or the stone walkways to front doors I trudged. Sometimes on a Saturday morning or sometimes on a Sunday afternoon. Hesitant. *There's a Patriot's Game. At least they'll be home. I'll go at half-time.* Hesitant. *I hate this. Breathe, Jenny. It's for the bears. Act like you're already good friends.*

A door opened, and there stood an old lady in a droopy and stained woollen sweater or a professional-looking man tinkering with something in his hands, or a frowning mother with boisterous children in tow, or a twenty-something in dreadlocks or – *shit*! – a big burly man in hunting cap and camouflage.

"Hello, my name is Jenny and I'm a neighbor of yours." I stretched the truth of "neighbor" some thirty miles, hoping they wouldn't ask where I lived. "I wonder whether you've heard about Question 1 on the ballot for November 6th?"

Old lady: "Question 1? No dear. Come in and have some tea. It's chilly outside."

Professional-looking man: "Yes, and I've already made my decision." Slam.

Young mother: "It's so horribly cruel, isn't it? Do you have an extra 'Yes on 1' sign? I'll put it on my lawn."

Twenty-something: "Uh. No, I'm not sure …I don't …I don't pay attention to politics, ya know?"

Burly man in camo: "Fuck you! Get the fuck outta here and go back to where you came from!" Slam!

"Thank you," my tiny voice answered after the hunter spewed his venom. My lip quivered. Shivering in a chilly wind, I returned to my car, willing myself not to cry.

It mattered so very much to me, this campaign. Initiated by a friend who had spent decades combatting the mistreatment of animals, when she asked me to join her, I said yes. I then received the most brutal of educations on how the odds were stacked against bears' survival by greedy trophy hunters. Unconscionable! To leave huge masses of donuts – super high caloric candy – in the same place day after day as bears sought to fatten up for winter was to habituate them to one spot. They became helpless, easy targets for some out-of-towner who'd paid thousands of dollars for a guide to guarantee a kill within four hours. Just to brag about the bear skin rug in his man cave!

The more I learned, the more my outrage simmered. Hoping to shift mindsets, I organized an event with, Benjamin Kilham, who has dedicated his life to rehabilitating orphan bear cubs whose mothers have been killed by hunters. From his book, "Out on a Limb: What Black Bears Have Taught Me about Intelligence and Intuition," I learned about the extraordinary language of bears, their society and social code. It motivated me even more, and I became obsessed with the campaign. But I sought guidance because the fight was lethal, and I wasn't sure I had what it took. An I-Ching divination revealed that in contrast to my natural proclivity to be a spokesperson, my role in the campaign was, "humble tasks," not "leader." A part of me breathed a sigh of relief, but also wondered why. Thus, besides door-knocking, I made phone calls, endless robo-calls that disguised my real phone number with another "207" number. I cringed when I heard, "Can't you people leave us alone?" or, "It's supper time. Do you have to call at supper time?" or, "Remove me from your list!"

At a town hall meeting with my devoted friend, I heard sniggers as she tried to answer a question during the so-called fair Q&A panel. "Shhhh!" I said at first, feeling like a schoolmarm. The intensity in the room amped up as a TV camera panned from the overly made-up male moderator to the guest panelists, stopping from time to time to zoom in on uniformed Inland Fisheries and Wildlife personnel who were squarely in the "No on 1" camp because of the monetary riches they gained from trophy hunters.

When the jeers continued, I turned around, looked a 75-year-old man who should have known better manners in the eye and said, "SHUT. UP!"

A young woman sporting a camo jacket and orange hat shoved me from her chair next to mine when I protested the moderator allowing the same "No on 1" guy to ask a second question, while the rest of us "Yes on 1's" hadn't had the opportunity for our first question.

At that physical contact, something arose in me, its dark energy like a burning, twisting thing. I turned to her. I read her name tag. From low in my throat I said, "Don't. Touch me. Jassie Bowman of Gardiner, Maine." My eyes spit hatred. My eyes promised I would hunt her down where she lived. Surprised, a flash of fear showed in her eyes. She moved away from me.

When it was over, I walked to my car, shaken. *I am becoming like them. I am turning into a machine that disregards life.* The experience pierced me and left me in shock at how the "other side" was reflected in me. Inwardly, I protested. I was not possessed of the same brutal mindset that allowed a person to send a pack of dogs heedlessly and without consideration for their own safety through the woods after a panicked Mama bear and her cubs.

Miles and miles Mama bear runs blindly, no idea where her cubs have gone, until, at last, terrorized and exhausted, she lunges up a tree, and climbs and climbs to an escape not possible; dogs bellowing below, and then watches a man approach. Then another, whose elbow jabs into the first man's side, "Tops a thousand, I'd say. Told you, I'd get you one, Doc." And then: BAM! Oblivion. A life, gone.

Voting night. 11:00PM. The City of Portland's results came in, and I stared at the screen as if my eyes betrayed me. Final result: 51% no; 49% yes. We had lost our bid to stop the suffering of bears at the hands of human trophy-hunters.

I learned that night about keening. I learned about pain like a flaming lance through the gut that made me stagger down my darkened wooden steps into bitter cold, eyes unseeing, face contorted with soundless shock and rage and grief.

I learned about keening as I stumbled toward my Saint Francis statue and fell to the hoar-frosted ground, grasping at grasses and rocking forward and backward on my haunches, desperate to be cradled. *I'm sorry, I'm sorry, I'm sorry, I'm sorry*, I said to Bear Spirit – over and over and over, my mind spinning its endless permutations and implications at the news.

And then I screamed – animal screams – like the screams I saw on those last terrible commercials – a bear caught in a leg trap for four and twenty hours now receiving the point-blank gunshot – not to the head because she thrashed too much in her leg trap. To the body. The scream of agony.

I learned about keening, when the last remaining fraction of my rational mind observed my own madness and wondered if I would ever return from that jagged precipice of grief. Ever. And if so, what would remain?

One Month Later: Kennebunkport, Maine.

I organized a shamanic journey to Spirit of Bear. Members of our campaign gathered around the drum of healer shaman, Comma Williams. *Thump thump thump thump thump*, she began, and the ancient call of the drum invited us to other realms. Each in our own way, we asked for meaning-making, guidance, and forgiveness.

The message I received was startlingly clear: *We, Bear, do not look upon you Humans with rancor. We understand you are like young children who are learning lessons about the sanctity of life. We seek from you acknowledgement and honoring before you kill. This is reciprocity.*

2015: Kennebunkport, Maine.

Two months after the bear campaign, on New Year's morning, I awoke from a dream. In it, my community was being visited by a family of huge black bears whose leader spoke in a language I understood though it was not my own. They seemed from another time. *Ancestors!* Some people were afraid of them, of their strength. I was not afraid. I was drawn to their leader. I called him, "Grandfather." I wanted to be near him, to learn that which must be learned.

High in a mountain-top chalet, we overlooked a field surrounded by nearby woods. In the field, a sea of people had lined up in rows facing the chalet moving in a kind of mantra-salutation. Starting on their haunches, they raised themselves to kneeling and opened their arms out wide, all the while chanting something at once ancient and powerful. It felt loving.

I wanted to learn the chant and the salutation. I turned to Grandfather Bear, who had become gray. I sensed he would soon depart us. I asked him to teach me the mantra. He began instructing me on the first three words, foreign and clumsy on my tongue. Only one word stuck with me – amuelpfth.

"Amuelpfth," I said. "Amuelpfth." It felt like a conjuring spell – calling into being something that had once been hidden or cast away.

I became aware that Grandfather Bear was readying to leave us. He looked at me and at my hair. He was playing with a very long strand of his own gray fur that came from his belly. I watched as he unspooled the strand. *How long it is*, I thought. Longer than an ordinary part of his coat. He reached out and wound the strand around my head. He said, "This will help." I looked into Bear's eyes. As I did so, I felt the strand on my head growing into a turban, pulsing with energy. While dreaming, I was lucid enough to physically feel a luminous, vibrating sensation on my crown. Half-awake, half asleep, I realized it was a mighty gift I had been given by Bear Spirit.

2016: Kildare, Ireland.

"Give your sorrows to Brigit's holy well."

My grief was heavy, like a standing stone at Uragh. It threatened to send me to that place of oblivion I'd experienced two years prior. I dropped to my knees and made a low, moaning plea to St. Brigit.

Bear Spirit emerged out of the well as though medicine for my grief. I remembered my dream. I sat on my haunches the way the dream showed me. I gave salutations to my Bear kin. I raised myself to kneeling, opened my arms out wide and said the word I remember from the dream, "Amuelpfth. Amuelpfth." I said it over and over. I remembered his simple words, "This will help," as he wrapped the strand of fur around my head. My seventh chakra tingled. The medicine ancestor Bear had given me reappeared in far-off Eire land, home of my own ancestors.

Today: Kennebunkport, Maine.

In the seven years that have passed since I pulled myself back from that lunatic-knife-edge and accepted with deep gratitude the gift from Grandfather Bear, I seek a different way to change hearts and minds. The way of Saint Francis and Goddess Saint Brigid. The way of inspiration. I acknowledge that it is worthy enough to be a voice for the voiceless, a convener, an artist, and a storyteller, who seeks another way into the war-torn hearts of mankind.

What happened to the fierce, warrior-like stance that I'd taken on Question 1? I've burned my bloody warrior robes. Donning them without a protection practice to transmute the negative energies had brought out the evil in me. Our culture hero-worships Warrior, and at times I feel "less than" because I cannot find the "thing" in me to survive such ferocity. I've worked hard to release my guilt for not being a warrior against a system that would destroy me or make me into its image. Still, it lingers.

In a recent Humanity Rising program, *Relational Leadership: Conveying and Elevating Indigenous Wisdom*, Lewis Cardinal, a Woodland Cree from Alberta said, "The ancestors are saying, 'How come you aren't asking us for help?'" Again, the words from Ancestor Bear floated into my awareness, *This will help.* Despite my altars and my chants, my embodying sacred circles and my work in climate justice, sometimes I forget to ask the ancestors for help. *I forget?* I ask myself. How deep *is* this colonial programming? These days, the darkness is so dark, there can be no forgetting.

Here in Maine, on the lands that carry Abenaki stories and spirit, I place some drops from the small vial of water I collected at Brigit's well onto a scrap of fabric, carry my clootie outside and tie it to a lone hawthorn. I leave an offering of bird seed and honey. I say, "Ancestors, I know the power is not lost, I am.[1] Teach me the mother tongue. Help me to re-member the *Mother's tongue.*"

Coda:

Long ago, in the days of balance, all beings spoke a single language – The Once-and-Only Language – a felt sense, with an exchange of meaning from inside the heart. All beings lived side by side. None had eminence. Each served the whole, yielding to a deeper connectedness within The World Tree. Thus, there existed a reciprocal exchange. In those days for example, a human hunter, before setting bow to quiver, might have asked the spirit of the bear to give his life so that he, the human, might live. It was also possible that the bear might have asked the spirit of the hunter to give his life instead, for the sake of her cubs. In this way, the deepest possible collaboration existed between all beings. There was no trickery or mistrust because spirits were in cooperation. Once this way existed with all beings.

This kinship with all of nature is still possible. Each human is being called to re-braid the cords of connection with nature and all beings. This is the time for remembering The Once-and-Only Language.[2]

[1] Apela Colorado, from Iroquois and Gaulic nations, author of the book, *Woman Between the Worlds*, describing wisdom from a Sioux elder.

[2] From, A MOON IN ALL THINGS, a historical novel-manuscript written by Jennifer Comeau.

Let Nature Be Our Guide

Ellen Dee Davidson

I'm in a large, white conference room in Africa. People sit around a table, looking for ways to create a peaceful healthy world, but I'm not with them. Instead I'm staring at an enormous gold-green snake slithering across the floor. Somehow, in the dream, I know the snake has many of the answers we seek.

Waking, the ancient redwood trees call me. They've been calling me for over a decade. This summer, I spent sixty nights camped out beneath their boughs, listening to their secret whispers and basking in the primeval magic gifted from trees thousands of years old in forests that have stood intact for millions. Somehow, here amidst the waist-high ferns, the musical creeks and calling birds, I come home to the old knowing and deep women's wisdom that is ours.

Sitting with the trees, nestled in their shallow roots, resting against rough bark, inhaling the almost cedar smell, fresh and redolent with life, I begin to receive. Sometimes it's a vision, things yet to come, things that could be, our world restored to leafy growing green, our hearts healed from generations of trauma. Sometimes it's a sound. The trees hum. I've taken people to the forest and when my friends are still, they also hear the hum. It's not always the same tone. Sometimes the hum is deep and sonorous, almost hypnotic, guiding us into trance. Sometimes it's a sweet high note carrying us on a river of sound. Sometimes we hum along, and we sing ourselves into deeper resonance with the trees.

Then my skin begins to tingle. There's more aliveness in my cells. Everything becomes fresh and new. I look with the eyes of a child, as if I've never seen this before, even though I've been coming every few days for over eleven years now. But I can't possibly keep this glorious beauty in my mind: shafts of light streaming down like gateways to higher realms, beetles and banana slugs making their way across the rust-colored forest floor, and the leaves on the maples shining translucently with new growth. Doves coo, Crows caw, and Steller's Jays tap-tap-tap holes in the bark. I'm amazed by the fern matts growing on the trunks of trees.

Caught in the crevices and crotches of redwood branches, bark and needles decompose into humus soil where dangling epiphytes create hanging gardens of lush ferns. These fern matts hold water like a sponge, moderating temperatures so that days are cooler and nights warmer, creating a home for creatures sensitive to drying out like molluscs, segmented worms and salamanders.

Sitting beneath Violet Tree, I notice a gentle sensation nudging the back of my heart. The tree reaches out to me with her soothing presence. We come into a slow rhythm and my breath becomes so fine it almost feels like I'm not breathing at all. My skin sinks into her bark, her bark enfolds my skin, and I feel myself, tree and me, me and tree. From this place of communion, I realize that the tree is asking something. Her request comes more as knowing than in words or vision: the redwood wants me to speak for her, to speak to the humans. She's not asking me to write this time, although a few years ago the trees did guide me to write a book about my forest adventures, *Wild Path to the Sacred Heart* [1]. This time she wants me to actually use my voice, to speak.

I have no idea how I will do what the tree has asked. Stopping to taste a glistening orange salmonberry, I think about how I don't really have any connections to get my voice out in the world.

The next day, a Tree Sister friend asks me if I want to speak at a Humanity Rising Conference. I reply, "Yes." My sharing is short, maybe eight minutes, and I don't know what I'm going to say in advance. When the words, "Let nature be our guide," come out of my mouth, I realize that this is the message the tree wants to share.

After the presentation, I'm back in the forest as usual. My heart is light as I make my way to beloved Violet Tree. No one is on this ridge and I sit for two hours, feeling a sense of satisfaction from the tree as if she somehow knows that I did speak as she asked. I'm invited to more Humanity Rising events, but my desire to sit at the round table of my dream with humans looking to each other for solutions has evaporated. Now my eyes are back on the green-gold snake that represented wild nature. What will nature teach me if I go to the forest and listen?

For months, nothing much seems to happen. After my years of visions, many of which came true, I'm kind of surprised that things are so quiet. I just breathe and relax, being with the redwoods. One day, I am told that my system is being rewired. I'm not sure what this means. What system? My energy system or my nervous system? I don't receive an answer other than my deepening love affair with the redwoods: Summer Tree, Star Tree, Violet Tree, Ancestor Tree, Spiral Tree, and Grandmother Dragon Tree reach out, coming to me in my dreams, in meditations, in heart's desire to be with them, and I go and go and go. One tree borders my backyard, but the other old growth redwoods are a fifty-minute drive past blue lagoons and coastal cliffs.

Sometimes I think I should be doing something real with my life. Something other humans understand and value. My husband and friends laugh at me. Even a meditation teacher tells me I might not always need to be with the trees. People tell me that I don't have to actually go to receive this energy; I can connect to the field. Maybe, but I don't believe it. There's a difference with embodied love, with actually being immersed in the forest. Memory, imagination, energetic connection are not the same as this tantric love affair I'm having with the trees. My whole body is opening in a sensual way. There's nowhere else I want to be, even without the visions.

The only thing that's been happening lately is this knowing that I'm being rewired. This makes no sense...until the falls begin.

I'm hiking up the creek behind my house when I trip on a slippery bridge and fall, head and shoulders first, down towards some sharp rocks five feet below.There's no time to do anything. My body takes over. In a split second that slows and stretches into something long and timeless, my body twists and does a half-flip so that I land on my feet like a cat. I've never been particularly coordinated and I can't believe what just happened. This was a feat worthy of a gymnast!

Marvelling, I go home wondering how my body did that. Normally I don't fall much, but in the next few months I have four more falls with equally miraculous outcomes. That's when it hits me and I remember what I was told at the trees about being rewired.

Have the falls been to show me I've been rewired to some sort of greater physical coherence? I know being in the forest is powerful. Spending so much time in the woods healed me from fibromyalgia and I am left wondering how else might wild nature heal and teach us if we spent more time immersed in Her?

I'm still pondering this when I take off to camp alone for five days on a river in the redwoods. Being in the woods is such refuge and healing balm for my traumatized soul. These last two years have heaped it on with Covid and the climate crisis. I know people whose homes have burned down, and many others who've spent the summer with bags packed for evacuation. The air has been toxic, and even here on the coast there were days I did not go outside. Normally, when I'm having a hard time, some of my friends are doing great and I can lean on them a little, and vice versa. Lately, everyone is dealing with so much. I'm grateful for the trees that have been saved and are still here, saving me.

But even the old trees feel a bit weary. Only forty to eighty miles away, the fires have raged for months. Fronds on the redwoods are brown tipped from thirst. Snorkelling in the river, I see a few crawdads but no fish. The water is warm and bright green algae blooms. We need rain.

So I'm happy when, curled up in my tent, I hear the patter-plash begin. It continues for hours, plunk-plunk split-splat, coming down harder and harder until it pounds on my tent and I wonder if the thin fabric will hold up for the night. There are rivulets on the inside edges of my tent. Huddled into a tiny ball in the center of my mat, I close my eyes and go back to sleep, hoping for the best.

When I awaken, the rain has slowed to a gentle drizzle. I can't wait to hike. As I walk past bright shiny huckleberry bushes, glistening green with moisture, and make my way around bubbly puddles, I let go of everything in the beauty of the moment. The trees are singing joy. Everything smells fresh and feels alive. Careful not to trip on the slippery roots that crisscross the muddy trail, I make my way to the waterfall. It's roaring! Nearby I find twin giant trees and sit on the duff where they join at the base.

There's a hush, a waiting pause, as I begin to listen to the voice of nature. She's subtle and enters in viscerally through my body, growing into extended awareness connecting me with little energetic filaments, like roots, to this holy place on Mother Earth. Slowly, I go beyond the boundaries of my separate self and understand that nature is offering to be our guide in restoring ourselves and our world. All we have to do is listen.

Our world is noisy now, neon blaring and clamoring for our attention, so that sometimes it is hard to hear the quiet voices of our deep selves and of wild nature. But these are the soft voices, the shy tender voices, the deeply feminine voices that can show us another way to be in harmony with ourselves, each other and the natural world.

Sharing some of the ways the forest is teaching me to listen more deeply; I invite you to begin with yourself. Notice where you are physically in space, and find a comfortable spot to settle. Breathe. Welcome the intimacy of air. Drink a glass of water. Feel her holy consciousness mingle with your own fluid body. Place gentle fingers on your crown and touch your head, inviting in the crystalline light radiance of your being. Continue stroking, neck, shoulders, arms, wrists, fingers, belly and back, down the pelvis and thighs to

209

your feet, so close to the ground. Give attention to the nature around you. She's always present because we are made of her and cannot live without her water, air, light and earth. If you do not have access to enough wild nature, surround yourself with houseplants, plant thoughtfully-placed trees or donate to organizations who do, and maybe even join neighbors in finding vacant lots and growing community gardens in the hearts of cities, as has been done in places like Harlem, New York. As we restore our world, we are healing and restoring ourselves.

If you're by a tree, feel the heart connection flowing between you. Be rocked and held in her arboreal grace. Gaia's dreams, visions, and holistic knowing will seep into you in myriad untold ways. This may spontaneously show up in daily life, as the rewiring of my own body did when I fell. Nature awakens instinctual grace.

If it's possible, find wilderness close to home. Spend time in parks and national forests. Be with meadows, creeks, forests, mountains, beaches and deserts. Visit the same places over and over again until you get to know each other well and an energetic intimacy is formed. Feel the caress of trees, rivers, rocks, and soil against your skin, mindful that they are touched by you as well. Our presence with unspoiled landscapes enhances interaction so that nature intelligence comes more strongly into our physical, mental, emotional and spiritual bodies. We receive on multiple levels, and the energetic embrace comes in both consciously and unconsciously. There's always more happening than we know. Here, we touch the mystery at Gaia's wild heart. As you allow nature to have her way with you, your heart may feel open and warm, like it does when falling in love or holding a baby. Soft. Melting. Or perhaps there's a tantalizing smell, a fresh idea, an image, or a sensation. Trust that whatever comes is just right. There's no need to try, to preconceive, or effort to create a certain experience; this is about making ourselves available, getting really quiet, softening, opening, allowing and receiving.

When we pause and pay attention to the beckoning beauty of nature, becoming more fully present, we open to whole-body listening, which is a sensuous state that awakens our animal bodies. We may feel ourselves like a cat, sensing all the subtle currents in the surrounding atmosphere. Or our ears may be pricked and sensitive like a deer, ready to startle. In all the ways our animal body comes alive, know that this is our heritage, our birthright, as fellow wild creatures living within the body of Earth. As we continue to listen, growing in our ability to perceive more consciously the constant communication of wild nature within and without, we may discover she is a portal into the infinite whole. From this holy whole, nature will guide us in ways we cannot yet imagine.

[1] Davidson, E. D. (2019). *Wild Path to the Sacred Heart*. Star Tree Press.

My Strength

Lale Wilson

Our little girl is just over two years old. We waited so long before she came. Our fertility journey was long, complicated and had so many setbacks and I could never have predicted the script.

I recently had a revelation; I had heard these words from so many people but they were just words. "You are so strong". One day, quite recently, I eventually felt it. The realisation of my strength hit me hard, for the first time in a very long time I felt happy. I felt light, giddy and warm in my stomach. I felt proud. I felt my wisdom. I FELT STRONG.

My Story

"What are you waiting for guys?"

"When are the babies coming?"

"Your babies will be gorgeous!"

"Well you have the big house now…so you need to get on with it."

"Is he shooting blanks?"

"Your biological clock is ticking."

"You never wanted kids did you?"

"You know, in Russia you can even select the eye colour for IVF treatment."

These were just some of the comments my husband and I had learned to become resilient to. We had well-rehearsed responses for each and every one of them.

Nobody ever asked how we were doing or if everything was OK. So taboo right? I figured that people are just not programmed to consider the challenges. Just assuming that getting pregnant is such a natural and definite thing.

But for some of us, it really isn't.

Why am I writing about this? Because the society we find ourselves in has made it impossible to normalise infertility, IVF, miscarriage, baby loss, and the endless list of fertility issues. Our miracle daughter is just over two years old and I still battle with the psychological trauma and emotions I experienced throughout our fertility journey.

I had wasted so much time; I feel that now having experienced this journey. Mainly due to initially being in complete denial about our situation, then deep down in my gut, I knew something wasn't right but I was too scared to find out what it was. It was September 2016, a month before my 40th birthday that it hit me. It was time we went to see a doctor.

We had been trying for a baby for years. I had been off the pill for a number of years, peeing on ovulation sticks every month, tracking my cycle on two apps just in case one was out of sync. Nothing worked. I lost count how many times I wished that I was pregnant after we made love or when a period was due. Sadly, each time my periods came like clockwork. Every month we shared the same disappointment. It was the same each month. I would be so sad, sometimes cry and listen to my sweet husband's words "oh baby, don't worry". It was heart-breaking. I had never imagined how challenging this was going to be.

In our close friendship circle, most couples had children. Every time someone announced their pregnancy, my husband and I experienced a roller coaster of emotions. Sometimes we would just shrug it off and promise each other that our time would come and at other times we would hold each other tight and cry with real pain. One of us was always consoling the other. Hearing a friend or loved one announcing that they were pregnant should have been a joyous time and a call for celebration but, to be brutally honest, I think we hated them for it, at least for a little while anyway. It is one of the hardest things in the world to stage how happy you are for someone in that celebratory moment whilst inside you are crumbling and your heart is in a million pieces. It just wasn't fair. Why not us?

One of my most painful memories is when I was out for a bike ride one morning and I came across a man with his little girl teaching her how to ride her bike. I would never be able to give that moment to my husband. I cried hysterically in the middle of the woodland until I was able to compose myself and park those feelings. Then I got back on the saddle and rode home.

We initially went to the NHS but for a number of contributing factors very quickly parked that option. There wasn't really much time to wait for referrals, so we decided to go for private treatment

Blood tests were done and I had some scans. All my husband needed to do was to provide a semen sample.

The results were worse than we expected. I had a very low egg reserve. I had a very large fibroid (non cancerous growth) which was sitting on the outside of my uterus causing heavy, painful periods. My husband had a low sperm count.

Could this get any worse? Actually YES and it did…

After a second, third and fourth opinion it was clear that IVF was our only hope. We found this so frightening. We were scared, apprehensive and I remember feeling angry too. Why was this becoming so hard?

We talked about other options, surrogacy, adoption, but all I desperately wanted was to be pregnant. To watch my tummy grow our little human. To feel our baby move and kick. To see my husband's face light up and eyes glaze when he placed his hand on my bump.

The clinics we went to were not very empathetic. It felt like we were just a number. To add salt to the wound, we were also paying to be processed like this.

At the time my husband and I didn't talk about this surreal nightmare to anyone. Why? Because the society we live in makes it almost impossible to talk about this topic. Couples experience the turmoil and most keep it inside a close circle. I do not believe there is enough support out there, and there certainly aren't enough people talking about it. I know that if it was normalised then we would have been better mentally prepared for the ride.

We chose a clinic in North Cyprus where success rates were extremely high and the cost was around a third of UK prices. It was a no brainer for us as I have a lot of family out there. I would be able to stay with family and start the treatment. The doctors had their concerns about the fibroid as this could not only cause issues during pregnancy (bleeding and pain) but also could hinder a natural birth. We were willing to take the risk.

It all happened very quickly and we made the decision that I would go first and start the drugs and my husband would come for the second stage, as this was going to take more than a week or two.

The drugs and injections were full on, and whilst there were no side effects, I was in complete turmoil. I was away from my husband having treatment for something which was so important to both of us, but I was doing it all alone. My family was amazing. I stayed with my aunt, and both she and my uncle made sure I wasn't alone; they were there with me every step of the way. For those two weeks my aunt (who hates needles) stood by me or put a comforting hand on my shoulder whilst I jabbed away. Some days it was like a military operation and I just did it with no emotion. My abdomen was pricked three to four times a day. Some days I cried and cried "Why me?".

Fortunately, I had responded well to the fertility drugs. My husband flew in for the next stage as we required his sperm sample and all that would be left was egg retrieval.

They were able to collect eight eggs however only six of these were viable. There was nothing more for us to do for a few days as the lab was now working their magic. We were sent home and promised update calls on fertilisation.

The next morning we got the call from the clinic to let us know that only five of the eggs had made it but three of those were of a good quality. This was disappointing, however we tried to remain as positive as possible. In two days' time those eggs would be embryos and after transfer day we would cross our fingers! I was actually starting to get excited. It all started to feel real. I would imagine what it would be like for us to be pregnant and then what it would be like to have a baby in our lives. We prayed so hard for this.

My husband had to fly home for work. On the way back from taking him to the airport I had a call from my doctor asking me to go in for some scans. I assumed this was normal, just tests prior to the final procedure. How wrong I was.

It turned out that at egg collection it was noticed there was something abnormal about my uterus and the scan confirmed it. It was something I had been born with and no one picked up. The chances of us conceiving naturally or having a viable pregnancy were near impossible. How had all of our doctors in the UK missed all of this? I was broken.

My husband was on a plane so I couldn't even call him to let him know what had just happened.

My fertility doctor was not willing to risk anything until I underwent surgery. He explained that I needed two procedures, one to remove the fibroid and the other to repair my uterus. Recovery, I was told, would be relatively short, a couple of weeks of discomfort and once I had recovered I could go back to Cyprus and continue with my treatment.

We didn't really have any choice at this point. All of our trust was with this clinic and I knew that I couldn't really delay it as we were up against my biological clock. Our embryos went on ice and within a few days

I found myself back in the UK and back at work with nothing to show for the last four weeks. I had been away and it was almost like nothing had happened.

I had so many thoughts, mainly around the negligence of some of the most reputable medics in London's Harley Street. From being told "don't worry, you can still get pregnant with a fibroid so go have your IVF" to now needing major surgery. We were stuck between a rock and a hard place. Did we start a formal complaint for negligence and waste our time and money? Or did we just get booked in for the op? We chose the latter.

I was booked in within a matter of weeks.

I was optimistic about my operation and dealt with it in true Lale fashion. Like a military operation, no emotion. "So many women go through these things," I thought, "suck it up and get on with it". Yet deep inside I was broken but couldn't let that surface.

On the morning of the operation my consultant came into the room to see me before I was called down. He assured me that the surgery would take no more than an hour and twenty minutes. There was going to be a small incision in my lower abdomen for the fibroid and as discussed he would go in vaginally to repair the septum.

My surgery took almost 5 hours.

The fibroid was the size of a melon and the uterus repair was a lot more complicated than he had assumed. Not such a small incision after all. I had been cut right across and wider than my bikini line from one end to the other, impossible to hide the scar.

My recovery took months. I had lost every muscle in my abdomen. My husband was my rock. I am so very thankful, and he helped me with pretty much everything as I was in excruciating pain every time I moved. You lose all of your dignity once you have surgery like this. How did I get here?

I injected myself with blood thinners for a while and was on a lot of meds.

I don't really know how the next few months went by. I do remember some pregnancy announcements and how my husband and I struggled with our emotions. Struggled not to be resentful. By this stage it was so hard to be positive.

This surgery and all the scars didn't mean that there was any guarantee for us. We just tried to get on with life and waited for our doctor to confirm my full recovery.

Almost a year to the day after the operation, I was back on a plane heading back to Cyprus to start where we had left off. They scanned me and all looked well. They advised that all three of the embryos were being transferred to give us the best chance, any less and we would risk everything. Were we ready?

Would this mean triplets? Do they even make buggies for triplets? We really hadn't thought about this. The main focus was always to have a child but I was now having sudden anxiety about a possible three! I don't think I slept much that night.

The day of the transfer came and I was a complete mess. I was anxious, scared and lightheaded. I felt weak in my body. I really needed my husband there and even though I thought I had this, I was absolutely crapping myself. We spoke a few times on the phone until it was time for me to go to the clinic.

Whilst I was waiting to go in, the phone didn't stop. Dad called first. I just cried and cried to him that I was scared, working myself up more and more. I struggled with anxiety anyway so this was just making my heart pound.

The doctor popped his head in and we were minutes away from me being taken into theatre. My nurse came in the room with a wheelchair and off we went. I had been in and out of this clinic so many times, it was pretty standard and not the plushest, however when the lift door opened to the floor where the theatre was I thought I was in the year 3000. It was like a snap from a sci-fi movie, all bright white walls and floors. I was wheeled close to the operating table and asked to hop on. Everyone introduced themselves and my doctor was there too. There was a screen attached to the ultrasound so we would all be able to watch the transfer as it took place.

The embryologist came in with a clipboard and asked me to identify myself. He then turned to my doctor and said "three out of the four are viable and two of them are of an exceptional grade". My doctor looked at me and explained that they would go ahead with all three. The rest was a blur.

I had mixed emotions. I was very happy that we had come so far and also had a slight fear of what the result would be. My wonderful, caring husband checked in all the time and the loving support from my family out there really made a difference. An IVF journey is a rollercoaster of emotions so having that warmth around me helped so much.

The dreaded two week wait went quickly. Finally, my husband flew out to join me. This was a huge weight lifted as I could feel safe now and share the next stage of the journey. We managed to squeeze in a couple of dinners before test day.

On the morning of test day, my bloods were taken and then there was a half an hour of butterflies in my stomach waiting for the results. I remember we were sitting in the row of seats opposite the stairs. We were holding hands and I was gripping his fingers so tight with my clammy hand. Two of our nurses were walking up the stairs towards where we were sitting with a piece of paper in their hand and they were speaking to us, smiling at us. I heard them but couldn't process one word. I turned to my husband, who was smiling and loudly saying "thank you", and asked him "is it positive?". He said "it's positive baby!" and then the tears of joy came. We were taken into a consulting room where both of the doctors who had treated me were waiting to congratulate us. Their job was done; we were pregnant! We flew home two days later.

We travelled home loaded with drugs. For the next three months, I injected, swallowed pills, inserted vaginal gel and watched everything I ate. The anxiety was 24 hours a day and until I had my 12 week scan I couldn't rest.

I had a scare two weeks after we got home. Bright red blood in my underwear, in the toilet on the tissue. It couldn't be! My husband rushed home and we went to A&E. After a couple of hours we were seen and when we explained that this was an IVF pregnancy post extensive surgery, we were told to come back in the morning where all scans would take place. It was the longest night. We didn't sleep, holding each other tight as we both knew this could be the end of our miracle. We were up early and straight back to the hospital the next morning.

The scan was a positive result. The consultant pointed out a little shape and turned up the volume, we could hear our baby's heartbeat. There was definitely a baby! The bleeding was a false alarm but also a blessing in disguise. We heard our baby's heartbeat!

This is my story. I chose to share it because the trauma is still with me. I haven't forgotten. I still get uncomfortable and sad when I hear about pregnancy announcements. Second babies, third babies - I feel the same as I did before our little girl came. I am aware that I/we are more protective of our daughter, in some people's eyes extreme. To become a parent is not a natural thing for some. We take it for granted that becoming a parent is a natural thing. Not for everyone. For some, it is a privilege, a blessing and in our case a miracle. We feel extremely lucky.

I wish I spoke more about it at the time instead of silently living this nightmare with my husband. I don't think I have ever come to terms with it, because every day I look at my child, and I still feel like it's a dream. I want to be the best that I can be. She chose us to be her parents so we need to be the best parents that we can be.

For anyone reading this who is in the same situation. Talk. Talk to your close friends or family, anyone you feel safe and at ease with. There are many groups you can join, counsellors who can help you manage your thoughts, feelings and frustrations. Don't do it alone.

You are not alone.

I was ashamed of being labelled. Scared that people would see me as a failure and damaged. If you have been on any fertility journey you can comprehend the pain, despair and desperation. If you haven't, maybe pause and think again on why that friend says she doesn't want kids. Sometimes it isn't all it seems on the outside. We all have a story.

The realisation came a couple of weeks ago. Our little girl is now a toddler, 2 years old. Sometimes when I think back to where it all began with the clinics, medics and drugs, I really struggle to place myself back there. It is still raw. It is still dark. I have not forgotten how it felt for us as a couple. The emotions that only those who have been through it will ever understand.

All the poking, prodding, bleeding. The injections, the pills, the suppositories and the pain both mental and physical were worth it. I would do it all again for her. I am stronger than I ever thought I could be and for that I am thankful.

Even though it was hell at times, we have been blessed and for us, we have our miracle.

I recently took a short trip back to Cyprus. It was a trip I was unable to make sooner due to the pandemic. I went to say my goodbyes to my father who we lost very unexpectedly. Sadly, the pandemic made it impossible to go to the funeral. This trip enabled me to have some closure and feel peace when I sat by dad's graveside. I reminded myself of how proud he was of my achievements and realised that I need to also be proud of myself.

So now, every day I remind myself of our journey, I remind myself of those words, "You are so strong". It has taken a while but finally, I now feel it deep down in my gut.

I AM STRONG.

Shifting the perception

This is the short story
of a woman shifting
her perception
about nature.

by Isabelle Blum

By Isabelle Blum

PART ONE
All is linear

There was a woman who wanted to know everything about nature.
So she went to university to study environmental sciences.
She was a very serious student.

After many years of studying biology, chemistry, physics, mathematics,
politics and economics she knew many formulas, figures, facts and numbers.
The natural world was mapped out as quite a linear functional system.

PART TWO
Some things are hidden

The woman went out into the world.
She explored and studied nature
with all her knowledge.
Trees, soil, plants and animals
were under accurate observation.

But in all her studies and observations
some things didn't match the data.
Some things were hidden.
Not explainable, not linear.

By Isabelle Blum

PART THREE
Everything goes in a cycle

The woman continued her studies. One day she realised a fundamental truth.
Everything in nature goes in cycles. Nothing is linear like she had learned.
She then reflected upon her own existence.
Her life and her inevitable death.

She moved around and did many cartwheels.
By turning the world upside down
she fully realized the cyclicity of her
being and all other beings.

PART FOUR
The fractal nature

With further observation of nature and her own being, the woman went deeper into the structure of everything. Over time she detected something quite amazing.

There was similarity everywhere.
The fractal geometry of the universe and all living and non living things was revealed to her.
The penny dropped ...
Nature was not linear.
It was all over the place.
The same at different scales.
Similar and yet unique.
A wondrous world of unified difference.

229

Mush

Sarah-Anne Forteith

You've come to this book looking for wisdom… unfortunately I'm not sure I have any truly worthy of print. What I do have is a collection of thoughts, feelings and notions. Little bits and pieces that I've gathered and cultivated as I've moved through life rather clumsily.

When I say clumsily, I *mean* clumsily.

I've somehow naturally avoided every straight path laid before me in life and instead found my way through convoluted, twisting roads, serendipitous discoveries and narrowly survived disasters.

I'm not a *well-put-together* woman. I'm not the type of person others will gasp at in awe while wondering, *just how does she do it all?* More likely they will roll their eyes and be glad they don't have to deal with me for long. I'm not neat, or well organized. My wardrobe doesn't inspire jealousy or delight and I'm not a particularly high achiever. Hell, I'm not even very hygienic. Where some women give off the air of effortlessness, you can palpably feel the effort seeping from me as I desperately try my best to keep up with my peers. I seem to always say precisely the wrong thing, I'm chronically late, chock full of too many emotions and this is just skimming the surface of my awkwardness.

For decades I thought this was just a personality trait. That I was just *quirky* and *scatter brained*, that I was maybe a little thick. This made sense to me of course, because it was what I had always been taught. I was constantly told by the adults, authority figures and media in my life that I just needed to apply myself more, to pay more attention, to wait my turn, to try harder, to slow down, and listen more etc etc. If I could just do these simple things then I would excel how the world wanted me to. It's taken me decades to learn that all this was wrong and that I was being set up to fail in a system that simply wasn't built for a brain like mine.

Earlier this year, after years of appalling mental health, months of waiting lists, endless filling in of forms and multiple assessments I learned that I was Neurodivergent - Attention Deficit Hyperactivity Disorder (ADHD) to give my precise diagnosis. Now I should warn you, if you are expecting to read through a beautifully profound account of how I came to terms with my diagnosis, defeated my challenges and emerged on the other side a fully formed butterfly of success and acceptance, you will be greatly disappointed. This is not a sanitised and neat piece of writing because I am simply not those things. What I am, is slowly coming to terms with myself. I am re-examining my life through a new lens and gradually relearning who I am.

What I am is mush.

I am smack in the middle of that point of transformation where the caterpillar has dissolved into something unrecognisable inside the chrysalis in order to remake itself anew. I'm the unseemly, icky, mushy part of the process that people like to pretend they don't see.

I am mush that has been newly diagnosed with ADHD.

Apparently, I'm a rather textbook case. A chronic daydreamer all my life, who hyper fixates on certain tasks and interests yet is painfully unable to concentrate on or complete others. I have an incredibly hyperactive mind and fidget constantly. I have issues with task initiation, organising myself, and my own thoughts. My working memory and sense of object permanence are practically non-existent. And yet, it took till the ripe age of thirty-one for me to be diagnosed. Why?

Why?

This is the question that has been echoing around my mind for the last few months since my diagnosis. Why if I was so textbook was I not diagnosed as a child? Or even a teen? Why was this such a surprise to myself and those around me? These nagging questions have been burning in the back of my brain and have sent me down dozens of research rabbit holes… and I have not liked a single one of the answers I have found.

NO GIRLS ALLOWED

One of the main reasons I went undiagnosed for so long is simply because we're told that ADHD doesn't *look* like me. When we think of ADHD we think of hyperactive and naughty little boys. Little boys who pull pigtails, swing on their chairs and disrupt classes. We're told it looks like unbridled hyperactivity, boundless energy and a cheeky dimpled smile.

While ADHD certainly *can* look like this it can also look remarkably different. It can look like the little girl who always has her head in the clouds. It can look like the girl who can't ever seem to get her head around spelling and basic maths. She's the one who's always putting her hand up before the teacher has finished their question because she just can't wait for her turn to speak. She may be hyperactive and impulsive but she's learned the hard way that showing her energy outwardly often leads to reprimands. What is often thought of as harmless boyish naughtiness, (after all *boys will be boys*), is seen as unacceptable behaviour in girls, and she is punished harshly for what her male peers get away with. ADHD in girls can look like the report card that says *she has so much potential but needs to apply herself more*. It can look like the girl who cries too easily at inconsequential things because she simply can't regulate her emotions.

I was that little girl, and I still am in many ways. Eventually, I learned to not make a fuss, to keep quiet and hide my fidgets. Where some, mainly male, children around me showed their neurodivergence without shame, I was taught that it was something to iron out. Soon, when my rejection sensitivity dysphoria would rear its head, I learned to swallow my feelings and if I was compelled to cry I learned to do so silently so as not to disturb the class. Instead of kicking my table legs or swinging on my chair, I began to switch my fidgeting to more invisible tactics. I would twirl my hair, rip at my nails, bite the inside of my cheeks and scratch my skin till red welts appeared. These things, though they caused physical harm to my body, seemed much more acceptable to my teachers and those around me. In fact, I was rewarded for it.

I vividly remember one primary school assembly, the type where small awards badges were given out to students for achievements such as neat handwriting, a high score in a test, or helping a teacher with some menial task. Names were being called, a shuffling line was formed and badges were being pressed into sticky little palms. My name was eventually called. Of course, it took a few attempts to grab my attention as I spent most of my time in assemblies completely zoned out in my own inner world - yet another symptom missed. As I lined up to collect my prize badge it was announced that the reason I was nominated was *For having a happy face all week and not crying once.*

A punch to the gut.

Until this moment I hadn't realised that I cried much more than others in my class. I hadn't realised that this was something that was considered not normal, a nuisance even. I was embarrassed and felt chastised when I was supposed to be celebrating. People liked me better when I hid my feelings. They liked me better when I pretended to be more like the other children in my class - normal.

I didn't realise it at the time, I was only 6 after all, but I think that's when I started to wear the *mask.*

WEARING THE MASK

Masking is an incredibly common trait in neurodivergent people. It's the face we wear day to day when we want to be accepted and get through life. Often we don't even know we're masking, as it's a coping mechanism that's become second nature to us. Instead of presenting ourselves how we truly are, we've unconsciously trained ourselves to mirror the actions and personalities of the neurotypicals that surround us. We rehearse conversations in our heads, we practice facial expressions and speech inflexions in the mirror when no one else is around. We use all our strength to make eye contact and restrain our urges to fidget during conversations. Often we misguidedly focus our attention and energy on *appearing* to be listening rather than *actually* listening to what is being said to us. We appear bubbly and effervescent because people seem to like us better when we act this way, even when it's false. We do all of this to the detriment of our own mental health and wellbeing. It's indescribably exhausting carrying out this unseen labour to pass as *normal* and many of us are unaware that we are even carrying this weight. I know I wasn't. All I knew was that something was wrong and I could never put my finger on what. Something just felt hollow and cold inside me.

I was 9 years old when I first started feeling depressed. I didn't have the vocabulary or the life experience to describe what I was feeling to myself, let alone put it into context for the adults in my life. Instead, I called it *feeling homesick*, even though I was safe at home. I was confused as to why I felt so numb and restless - now I know it was due to my brain lacking dopamine, the hallmark of ADHD, and the stress of relentless masking. Now don't go assuming that my childhood was all doom and gloom - far from it. I was loved and cared for and had plenty of joy in my life. But I did also have this dark cloud that phased in and out of view as my self-esteem and confidence faded thanks to living undiagnosed and masking.

The older I got, the more this dark cloud would obscure my world. My teen years, though filled with wonderful things, were steadily melancholy as I struggled greatly with everyday life. My self-esteem and confidence nosedived as the peers that surrounded me moved from strength to strength, milestone to milestone, while I internally struggled and began to burn out from all my interests, from school and from socialising. My bodily focused repetitive behaviours steadily turned to more severe self-harm and substance abuse. Obviously, I hid these things too. It wasn't even particularly hard to do so. I was just another *emo kid* who wore black, listened to angsty music and suspiciously wore long sleeves even in the height of summer. We were ten a penny in the early 2000s. Just a trend - a phase. I now know that self-harm and addiction are incredibly common in undiagnosed girls (and all genders) with ADHD, a toll taken from masking and not receiving the support you need to fulfil your potential. A blind attempt to self-regulate and self-medicate. It's the tragic intersection of ADHD's raw, unregulated emotions and unbridled impulsivity.

Living life while undiagnosed is painful. As you start to fall further and further behind your peers there's a certain ache that intensifies. You know that you are trying, in fact, you're trying harder than many of those around you, yet you can never seem to measure up. You're constantly chastised and punished for your lateness, your forgetfulness and your distracted mind. But it isn't down to *laziness* as you're so often told. You care too much to be lazy - you actively don't want to act this way. Yet still, the patterns repeat. The farther behind you fall, the lower your self-esteem becomes and the more you attempt to mask your symptoms. Further and further down the rabbit hole of depression and anxiety you tumble.

TREATING THE SYMPTOMS, NOT THE CAUSE

My mental health continued to decline throughout my teenage years, often hidden behind a bubbly facade or simply dismissed as typical teenage angst. It was during these years that I first learned that many care and support systems can fundamentally fail young women - especially neurodivergent young women.

When I first complained to doctors that I felt unhappy and discontent in myself, my hormones and puberty were blamed. Conversations around starting the contraceptive pill were had, the issue was swept under the rug. At fifteen I developed a debilitating chronic illness after a viral infection. I was nursed back to a baseline of health, yet left on my own to manage my newfound normal. No counselling was offered to help me transition from non-disabled to disabled, no treatment plan was formed as there was no cure. Instead, I was just told to set my sights lower and pace myself. I was ill, but not critical and so I had to navigate my way through the grey gully of chronic fatigue and pain alone. All the while I was spiralling further and further into depression.

I had my first panic attack at sixteen. I was convinced there was something dreadfully wrong with my heart as it fluttered like a terrified bird in the cage of my chest. My breathing was shallow, my head swam and I had a relentlessly foreboding sense of doom. I went straight to the local doctor's surgery and was seen straight away, disturbing the doctor on his lunch break - the Boots meal deal sat open and half-eaten on his desk while he examined me. After checking my heart rate, my blood pressure and serving me a steely gaze the doctor announced that there was nothing wrong with me. I was hyperventilating which was causing the *"symptoms to present"*. He delivered this news matter-of-factly and without any empathy. In fact, he seemed cross that he had seen me so urgently for such a non-event. Just a panic attack.

Just a panic attack...

I was told to breathe deeply, stop panicking and sent on my way. I was dumbfounded. I was embarrassed. I was angry. Something was wrong enough to trigger a panic attack, yet no moves were made to ask me what might have triggered the event. No questions were asked about how I was feeling or if I needed to talk to someone. No enquiries at all into the cause of my anxiety, let alone any solutions offered. No, I was sent away like an annoying child mewling for attention. I didn't seek help for a good few years after that. Instead, when I did see doctors, I reverted to masking my way through interactions while, underneath, things continued to fester.

Years later, after rather spectacularly crashing out of university, I had my first breakdown. I had finally lost the battle of trying to keep up with my peers. I was physically and mentally unable to do it any longer. I couldn't keep up with the reading, was forever getting my timetable mixed up and always seemed to be attending the wrong lecture halls on the wrong days. My coursework was non-existent and my tutors were tired of my excuses. My impulsivity was completely unchecked which led to some fantastically awful decisions. After several intense and ill-advised benders, recurring physical illness and some stays in hospital, I was done. My depression had hit a new depth. My self-worth completely evaporated. I was a failure who was unable to get myself out of bed. Even when I did manage to crawl out of my pit I started to have panic attacks when I left my tenement building. The sky felt too large, the faces all seemed unfriendly and the world was too loud. Slowly but surely my world shrank smaller and smaller as my breakdown reached its peak. Soon I could not leave the flat without the cold clutch of a panic attack wrapping its icy fingers around my heart. Not long after that, I could not even leave my rented room.

My partner eventually managed to coax me to a doctor's surgery, where I blurted out all the thoughts and feelings that I'd been struggling with. This time I felt listened to. This time I *was* offered help, but not in the way I needed.

I was diagnosed with Generalised Anxiety and prescribed beta-blockers.

Now there was no doubt that I *was* struggling with anxiety and depression, that much was painfully clear. However, I now see that these were just symptoms of living with undiagnosed ADHD. It was a surface manifestation of a much deeper problem. Something that tranquillisers could not fix. This pattern of burning out, breaking down and seeking help continued for years. The locations and the doctors changed, hell, so did the names of the diagnosis and the medicine prescribed, but the cycle steadily continued. One year it was labelled as *"anxiety"* and I was prescribed beta-blockers in doses as high as a severe angina patient would receive. The next year it was *"low mood"* and I was sent on mindfulness courses and prescribed Cognitive Behaviour Therapy. The most recent was "*clinical depression*" and I was prescribed a variety of different antidepressants until we settled on one which seemed to ease the pain enough with the least amount of side effects. Yet all of this was just treating the surface symptoms of my real underlying issue. The root cause remained painfully out of reach.

I now understand that my ADHD's cocktail of a lack of dopamine, rejection sensitivity dysphoria, low self-esteem and lack of emotional regulation create a perfect storm when untreated. A perfect storm that is almost guaranteed to cause severe anxiety and depression.

Sadly, my story is far from unique. In fact, it's almost laughable at how typical an experience it is for neurodivergent women. Many GP's are woefully underprepared for the realities of spotting both mental illnesses and neurodiversity in their allotted 10 minutes of patient contact time. Even worse is the fact that many of the diagnostic criteria for ADHD are based solely on the symptom presentation in young males. Young women like me are often doomed to remain undiagnosed or misdiagnosed and enter into this endlessly repeating loop of misunderstanding. Doctors not listening to and dismissing women is a problem as old as medicine itself. Yet the chronically underfunded and overstretched national health service is not solely to blame here.

Our western, patriarchal society is socialised to believe that young girls who are partaking in self-harm, risky behaviour and even suicide attempts are simply attention-seeking, making a fuss over nothing, being *hysterical*. This fact is particularly painful as those with undiagnosed and untreated ADHD are at a higher risk of death by suicide. Worse still is the fact that mental illness and the *quirkiness* of neurodivergent women is actually romanticized in our culture. We're seen as the charmingly broken, *"manic pixie dream girls"* who appear to spice up our partner's worlds and become an interesting footnote in the tapestry of their lives. We're assigned roles as the crazy ex-girlfriend, the offbeat muse who shakes up their stagnant imagination, the mentally ill girl he *"saved"* and who gave his Uni years meaning.

Then there is the ever-present stigma of poor mental health. Culturally we're constantly bombarded with messages to *"speak out"* when we're suffering, to reach out to those around us… but the reality is that most don't really want to hear about the ugly, gritty reality of mental illness. It's not the cinematic sadness of the movies, it's vile and upsetting. It's stale body odour, self-imposed isolation and permanently tear-rashed cheeks. It's admitting to loved ones that you don't want to continue on anymore and seeing them recoil in horror at a statement that is simply too upsetting to face. And so when we speak out we are collectively gaslit into thinking that things can't be as bad as we say, we are dragged into the role of consoling those who are supposed to support us, the feelings are pushed down for the sake of others' comfort, and the cycle begins anew.

FAKE IT TILL YOU MAKE IT

The cycle of pushing down my undiagnosed ADHD traits, hiding my mental illness and perpetually masking continued as my late twenties rolled around. Only now, as I pursued a career rather than *"just a job"* and became a *"real adult"*, I discovered a new cultural mantra that sanctioned and even encouraged my destructive behaviours.

"Fake it till you make it"

We've all heard this phrase before. We've had this gleefully repeated to us by friends, work colleagues and lifestyle gurus alike. It's a phrase with good intentions and innocence behind it. It's the type of phrase designed to comfort you and support you while you find your way in the world. It's also a phrase that can be dangerous for neurodivergent minds and disabled bodies.

At the heart of *"fake it till you make it"* is the sentiment that as long as you are seen to be trying, eventually you'll catch up with your outward presentation and things will all fall into place. For many that is exactly what happens, things do start to align, the pretence of knowing your stuff and having your life together does gradually manifest into reality. It can be an empowering message - for neurotypicals. For people like me, however, the phrase and practice can take on a far more toxic air.

For many neurodiverse and disabled people, the hustle and grind culture we find ourselves in can be toxically ableist. Not only are we expected to act and perform a certain way in the working world, but now, with the rise of *wellness culture*, we're expected to perform a false reality constantly. Wellness culture asks us to strive for unattainable constant happiness and implies that we have failed if we do not reach this state of nirvana.

For me *"faking it till I made it"* came in the form of doubling down on masking and hiding my physical and psychological symptoms. In my undiagnosed naivety, I had wrongly assumed that everyone felt like a hostage in their own brain and body. I thought it was normal to have one personality for one situation and a completely new one for the next. I thought it was normal to people please and smile over my pain and sensory overload - I genuinely thought that was how all adults did things. How wrong I was.

It may sound ridiculous to take such a throw away phrase so to heart, after all it's the type of saccharine, pro-hustle culture slogan you're likely to see printed on mugs and t-shirts. Harmless right? Yet these constantly repeated messages that are ingrained in the capitalist culture of the modern world were steadily telling me, and others like me, that we need to change in order to fit in, in order to be productive and therefore valuable.

And so we seek out the dopamine we lack through external approval, we smile and nod and agree to things that hurt us to feel included and accepted. We blindly search for answers in all the wrong places.

THE SELF HELP TRAP

I have a confession to make - I am a recovering self-help addict.

In my attempts to find the missing puzzle piece that would enable me to see things clearly and put my jumbled life in order, I desperately clung to any fad, book or lifestyle that floated through my vision. I tried everything. I tried fad diets, juice cleanses, and countless supplements that were marketed as anxiety busters and brain boosters. I tried mindfulness, minimalism, meditation, stoicism, aromatherapy, inner-child work, dream boards, manifestation and bullet journaling. I tried various different incarnations of daily routines, life organisation methods and I have an ever-growing pile of forgotten planners and Filofaxes. I read all the books, did the workshops, attended group meetings and all of it, though it successfully helped others, left me high and dry in the relentless flow of my boom and bust cycle.

With every new lifestyle change came the repetitive formula of learning, which turned to hyper fixation and reckless, impulsive spending. (After all, every self-help movement seems to involve some sort of financial cost like we can purchase our way out of depression.) This phase was always followed by eventual failure to keep up the routine and the pretence which led to even more despair. Yet I still soldiered on looking for that one method, that one item that I could hang all my hopes of stability and normality on.

Of course, this desperation is precisely what many in the wellness and self-help industry are actively preying on. There are entire business models based on capitalising off the discontent of others. Now I don't for one minute believe that every person working in this industry is a predator as these methods and regimes can provide comfort for some - but they are usually designed to work on neurotypical brains. They are designed to help brains and bodies that have correctly functioning reward systems and mine simply does not.

As I swung from movement to movement the traditional trappings of ableism and toxic positivity followed me.

"You need to want it more..."
"If you just tried a bit harder to stick to the routine..."
"Have you tried just not thinking so much about it?"
"Just think positively and good things will happen."

Harmless platitudes to some, but triggering and painful slights to me as I relentlessly fought an unseen battle in my own mind. Every newly failed attempt to gain the upper hand just dragged me closer to the edge and farther away from my own sense of self. The same negative questions constantly swam in my mind: Why wasn't anything working? What was I doing wrong? Why am I like this? As much as the bright and welcoming adverts splattered across my magazines and social media claimed to have the answers, I needed to turn away and forge my own path.

BREAKING FREE

I wish I could say that I came to an incredible epiphany, met a GP who truly understood and fought tirelessly for my diagnosis and treatment, which I triumphantly received in record time, but the truth is rather less satisfying - albeit more absurd.

What finally pushed me towards seeking an accurate diagnosis was the algorithm.

With the spread of Coronavirus in 2020 and sweeping government-imposed lockdowns, I began, like many others, to spend a lot more time alone and away from my usual routines. Without realising it my constant mask began to slip. I was furloughed and removed from my usual environment so there was no urgent need for these secretly practised coping mechanisms anymore. Subconsciously I started to phase them out. What this meant was my symptoms, for the first time since childhood, were allowed to surface openly. It was chaotic, confusing and I felt frighteningly out of control. Without the context of a diagnosis, I just assumed I was getting worse and becoming unhinged.

Like many others furloughed and faced with months inside, I turned to social media to pass the time. Some would say I spent an unhealthy amount of time scrolling various feeds but this is where things started to change for me. With each interaction and piece of engagement I fed the great machine, a clearer picture of my inner world was formed in code and the algorithm refined. Before long social media sites began to show me countless memes, videos and posts featuring the things I was feeling, the things I had lived. For the first time I saw myself, my true self, reflected back at me through the phone screen. The thing all these pieces of content had in common was the #ADHD.

The real research began in earnest. With each medical article, I saw myself appear clearer and clearer. I empathised with every statement, saw my outline sketched between each line of text. Every description felt like it had been pulled directly from a snapshot of my life, written precisely to describe me. And so, after some pestering, my GP referred me to a specialist. I eventually received my diagnosis and my treatment plans are being drawn up as we speak.

Of course, this isn't the end of my story, it's only the start of a new chapter. I have a diagnosis now, but I have years of disordered thinking and destructive behaviour to overcome and heal from. A diagnosis gives a tidy name to my issues but it does little to dull the pain of three decades of living undiagnosed. At the age of thirty-one I now have to relearn many of the life skills that most around me take for granted - it's terrifying. But it is also strangely liberating.

I can finally step away from the things that don't serve me and create coping mechanisms and support systems that *do* work for my neurodivergent brain. Gone are the endless planners and to-do lists in notebooks. I've now replaced them with highly visual whiteboards and coloured post-it notes. I've *"gamified"* care and hygiene tasks to increase the likelihood of me completing them and I'm upgrading my storage to ensure that everything is visible all at once. I'm setting up colourful displays to remind me to take my medication and I am learning how to navigate and regulate the stormy tides of my emotions. These tiny, seemingly insignificant changes are making huge differences in my life. I'm even beginning to learn how to unmask safely, by fidgeting and stimming in social situations, working on my communication methods and letting my true emotions surface. I am taking steps to no longer minimize myself in order to appease neurotypicals and I am also learning to ask for help when anxiety and depression rear their heads.

The biggest change in my life is how other people see me. The frustration and resentment are easing in most of my personal relationships, more space is being given and a new level of openness and authenticity is being reached. I feel like less of a burden now that I understand how my brain works and what its true strengths are. Nothing is a magical panacea and nothing drastically changed overnight following my diagnosis; it may not change for years, but I am beginning to feel like the cycle might be truly broken for the first time in my life.

The pain, anger and confusion of living undiagnosed for so long still remains of course. But I'm entering into a new period of radical honesty, learning and understanding.

I am mush, but I am newly diagnosed and empowered mush.

One Million Hearts Healed

Kathleen Brigidina

I grew up grounded, with my toes either buried in grass, water, or mud. Like my Irish parents, their parents, and their parents before them, my love for the Earth runs passionate and deep. Our Celtic lineage is one of intimate relations with trees, herbs, the elements, moon and sun. It is rich with Earth wisdom keepers who were threatened not to speak their truth, who were forced to stop their dancing, to abandon their culture of healing. Those nature language keepers crawled under the hedges; they silenced their songs and storytelling. They disappeared into the dark forests, like night owls, blue mushrooms, and rare moon flowers, rarely to be seen in the light of day. They muffled their voices and their instincts along with their beating drums until they all but forgot. They pretended they were not creative beings who conferred with birds, gave birth in the moonlight, or spoke the language of Trees. Covered in cloaks and veils, they concealed their truth, pretending to be the obedient followers of the ones who carried the bigger sticks and swords. Nestled beneath the hedges, the truth was alive, hidden but never fully uprooted. It was held in the substrata of their hearts, woven skilfully into the music, art, poetry and storytelling they passed down to us.

Generations later, my parents came to America in search of a better life. They set about turning a fertile parcel of land four blocks from the Des Plaines River into a miniature Ireland, complete with street signs and county markers. It was a haven for Nature that kept us safely hidden away. Barely anyone outside of our family was to be trusted; we weren't allowed to leave.

It was our own world, an oasis where fruit trees filled my mom's jams, grapes were squeezed from our vines, and garden potatoes filled our Sunday table. We learned of life from a menagerie of animals including my favorite baby ducklings. We played in water, in rivers, lakes, and anywhere we could splash around in it. We conserved water washing our hair in wheelbarrows full of rain after running free through it. Our well was dug deep.

Still, I longed to touch the land of the "Old Country". Saving my earnings from babysitting and small restaurant work until I had enough to go, I flew to Ireland when I was 18. My younger sister came with me and we stayed with our older sister who already lived there. One night soon after we arrived, I snuck over a fence into a farmer's field, to befriend a gorgeous white horse and ride her bareback in the moonlight. Holding my arms around her neck, I had never felt so wild and free. So me. We roamed Ireland for almost 4 years, traveling mostly on foot. Inhaling the earthy essence of that lush, green land. The magic of my ancestors took even deeper root in me and still guides me today.

Back in the U.S. I volunteered with a small, local environmental group in the late 90's. Most people were unaware of how our footprints leave an imprint on the Earth that will be felt far into future generations. Those who were aware were unsure of how to make changes that could make any real difference.

Our local group gave presentations on sustainability, sharing awareness and offering solutions. It was all small gatherings, here and there. The task seemed insurmountable. We were getting nowhere. We needed to do more, and do it faster.

One morning, as I put my foot on the floor beside my bed, I had a full-scale vision, complete with body length goose-bumps. Energy was moving up from the ground, tingling through my feet, through my whole body. It was like being on that wild white horse again. I was seeing through Earth's eyes, feeling my inter-beingness with all light, with all good Heavenly and Earthly spirits. It was like watching a movie about a large community event that would awaken the whole community. Everything, the place and every detail, was there.

In the vision, a building with two-story windows looked onto a beautiful pond of water that was surrounded by trees. The hallways were all rounded. Wherever you started, you would go in a full circle to experience it all. The place was packed with people. There were speakers, government representatives, all kinds of sustainable businesses teaching about alternative energy: solar, wind turbines, geo-thermal. In one area connected to the pond, there was a flurry of local organic gardeners sharing produce and farm fresh eggs, as well as conservationists and native plant specialists. State and local officials were planning carbon cutbacks and real solutions. Artists were creating unique sculptures from recycled materials. Some were reclaiming and giving new life to old furniture; others were crafting eco-dyed clothing. A twelve-foot tree made of recycled paper had leaves where people were writing their promises to the planet.

It took my breath away. With my heart pounding out of my chest, I was downstairs writing up a plan before

I realized what had happened. I had never felt such enthusiasm. Saving the planet felt truly possible. I couldn't wait to share all of it with my eco group.

My enthusiasm was swiftly dampened by the chorus of scorn that arose from the group. "Your ideas are too big…You do not *seriously* believe it was Earth speaking to you, do you?" "That's crazy and much too big for our little group! We do not have time." One very wealthy woman burdened with control issues resulting from an abusive childhood smirked at me, "You could never do it on your own."

I shrank with disbelief as we moved to the next agenda item. I retreated, utterly deflated. My heart had popped like a balloon. Dejected and unheard, I went stone quiet, praying for the meeting to end so I could leave and keep what felt like the last of my dignity.

At home, I crawled under the covers and cried, thinking they had broken me. People were not to be trusted. Later that day wearing a tired cloak of defeat, the tingling surge of Earth's creative energy came up through my feet again. I stopped instinctively to listen and heard Earth saying, "Are you going to hide again? Are you going to let them break you, stop you? Or are you going to trust that I have your back and follow my lead?" My body refilled with energy. Reconnected to all that is, my heart expanded. It was bigger than ever. I was back on the horse. My eyes filled with tears. I was seeing through Earth's eyes again. Earth was whispering to me, in me. I made a choice: to feel safe and be brave, to step into the unknown and trust what I was feeling. I would not let them stop me. I had no idea how it happened but I didn't need to know. My gratitude was too enormous to ignore. I took a deep breath and leapt.

Two days later, the local leadership academy called to inform me that a group of fourteen local leaders, business owners and influential people had chosen to volunteer and bring this event to life. To this day, no one recalls where they heard about it. In my heart, I knew it was Earth's plan and her miraculous guidance at work.

I went back to our eco group to announce I was going ahead and had a brilliant, powerful crew of volunteers for the event. Even if they did not want to help, the event could be named after the group. They tried to hide their shock and agreed. The Universe was obviously behind this!

One of the community leaders who had volunteered was the president of the local community college. He didn't have any spare time, but he could provide a school building. I was elated. The next day, as he showed me around the building, I recognized the two-story glass windows overlooking a pond, the curved hallways, the many auditoriums and rooms for presentations. I cried right there looking out of those windows. The doctor, a man from Jamaica, bowed his head and told me how grateful he was to be part of this beautiful mission for Earth. It all felt so surreal, but, again, too powerful to doubt.

Throughout the six months of non-stop, no-sleep work that followed coordinating details I had never handled before, self-doubt was a frequent visitor. I pressed on. I went to the woods or to the river and, like magic, I was re-inspired. I was growing. New awarenesses were flowering. Earth was teaching me, showing me how completely she supported me. I could feel her roots mothering me, guiding me, shaking each personal fear and self-doubt loose. She was calling me to my strengths and planting her seeds in me. After each breakdown, I just kept saying YES! I surrendered to the wild beauty, to the constant confirmation of goosebumps and synchronicities. Gratitude and trust were all I needed to continue. I was on a mission to reconnect people and the planet.

The volunteers' creativity was on fire. Their desire, inspiration and innovation were exploding, guided by love for Earth, and their own unique quality of inner knowing and connection. The eco group eventually got on board; no one was immune to its attraction.

Over 2,000 people attended. Over 100 vendors participated. We had 45 speakers and presentations on sustainability, including support of the mayor and the governor. When reporters arrived, the mayor offered to make it an annual town event on the spot. This would become a staple of revival and reconnection to the guardian hearts of the original peoples of this beautiful River Valley.

Afterward, the woman I referred to earlier from the eco group began driving for ownership of the event. In a concerted smear campaign for small town domination, she maligned me wherever possible, turning others against me. She was practiced and strategic. Gunning for woman of the year, she ended up getting it. It was heavy and ridiculously competitive.

Listening to my own spirit, I knew that I had accomplished what was needed. I did not need accolades. I brushed myself off in gratitude, grabbed my trust and moved on. I spearheaded Earth Day and green business events in Chicago and a few other towns; wrote the first Earth Day proclamation for the mayor of one town, and the Food Day proclamation for others. I brought people together every month to showcase speakers and panels about Sustainability. Coordinating a group of teachers, we designed a syllabus and Sustainability curriculum for five local community colleges, with course work ranging from organic farming to alternative power sources and everything in between. The differences these communities were making were real. I was more connected and hopeful than ever for Earth. Being pushed aside had been a blessing. It had given me a wider range, deeper work and other thresholds to cross.

Years later, out of nowhere, the woman who had wrested control of that original event came to a holistic healing center where I was offering reiki sessions. When she signed up to have a session with me, I was shocked. My first impulse was to sneak out of the back door. But I centered myself instead. I was there to be a channel for healing and she had come for that. I went into the treatment room, cleared my energy, filled my bra and pockets with every healing crystal I saw, and placed them underneath the bed. After taking twenty deep breaths, I greeted her in the waiting room. She looked unwell. She remarked that she was probably the last person I expected to see. I agreed and led her to my healing room, where I asked her to lay on the table. Realizing she was putting herself at my mercy, I relaxed. She was trusting me despite knowing I might want revenge. Before I placed the lavender eye mask over her eyes, I asked her if she wanted to share her intention for the day's session.

My body shook when she calmly told me she was dying and had been in intensive care. Before leaving the hospital, a little troll-like man had come down a magical staircase in the ceiling to tell her she had unfinished business and needed to apologize to me before she could go. She held her hands over her heart and said, "My intention is to heal my heart."

There was no need to respond in the intensity of that sacred moment. All I could do was what I was there to do. I covered her eyes, pulled a blanket over her feet, lit a candle, and held my hands out just above her heart. Once I felt the pulsing energy of her heart, I simply held space for her highest good to come through. Time stood still. I felt her heart opening. I saw beautiful, sparkling white light flowing through me into her. I felt surrounded and held by Mary and all her Angels. The essence of rose oil I had sprayed in the room was becoming stronger. I felt my feet barefoot in the grass, though I was standing on a wooden floor. Then I heard a voice clearly say, "One million hearts have just been healed across the planet."

After the session, she sat up to drink the water I brought to her. Her eyes were filling with tears when she quietly said, "I knew I was supposed to come to see you. Thank you."

She passed away six months later, from what the doctor called heart failure. But I knew it was only the organ that had failed, not the loving heart that was freed, the one that she had reclaimed for herself and many others around the world.

We can all wear solar panels on top of our heads. We can have a garden of organic vegetables infused into our body every morning. We can win woman of the year for what we do in our community. But as long as we are not connected heart to heart with each other, as long as we are not treating each moment and each living being as sacred, we will never be sustainable. Love is the sustainer.

I have found that heart-to-heart connection with the Earth. I have found it in the loving tapestry of all beings in Nature, as well as human beings. This Universe is shot through with being. Earth and all beings need our love, attention and care. We can and must reconnect to the sacred in everything. If we do, my experience confirms in ever-so-many magical ways that Earth, life, Trees and even wild moonlit rides will speak through us, guiding us home to our hearts and helping us heal our world.

Ruminations on a Body

Liz Clayton-Jones

When I was young
I could run
For what seemed like miles
Laughter and smiles
Through fields
Over styles
Climbed haystacks
Swam stream and sea
Fed my body
Stolen fruit
Penny sweets
Mum's treats
To rest was to read
Under the sheets
Straining to see
To learn
Just one more adventure
Body and Mind together
Instinctive
Free

Then a revelation.
Short. Myopic. Muscular.
Unattractive. Un-feminine. Ugly.
Striving for outer approval
A teenage rollercoaster ride
Of diet, exercise
Of eating, inertia
Body as traitor.
Safety was Study.
Brain not body.
Work became life.

Despite all
Gifts beyond measure
A child
Imperfectly perfect
Body as carrier
As gift giver
As life maker
Even as it resisted
Even as it was resisted
It gave.

And yet
Child is life
Work is life
Body not yet loved
Just a thing
To carry the load
Of stress
So tired
Too tired

Another rollercoaster
Of diet, exercise
Of eating, inertia

Must keep going
Must do all the things
Must be all the things
Pushing
Ignoring
Berating
This body

Now
A late love
Seeing my imperfect as perfect

Another change
A midlife kick
A revelation.
Body as life.

Acknowledgement
Appreciation
Gratitude
Knowledge
Brain *needs* body
Body as Study

Nurture
Nature
Nourish
Energise

Breathe

A journey back to freedom

***

The freeform poem above is a small miracle borne
out of the last line.

For five decades my body has been largely ignored.
And when I wasn't ignoring it, I was actively repelled
by it.
Sporadic bouts of fitness have been interspersed with
periods of deep personal dislike. During those years
my weight has varied by six stone (I'm now
somewhere in the middle) and ranged from peak
military fitness to couch-potato (I'm now also
somewhere in the middle).

I've had to sit with the guilt that my own relationship
with my body may have contributed to the one my

daughter has of hers, further complicated by her hEDS [1] And I've pondered on the western obsession with female appearance that leads us to loathe the very receptacle of our being.

But, in honesty, those wonderings were quickly pushed to the side in favour of doing all the things. From the age of eight I learned that an easy retreat was study and work. It was so easy to create busyness to occupy both mind and body. As an adult, following an abusive first marriage (a relationship I now recognise was inevitable considering how I felt about myself and my worth), I was a single mum for sixteen years; my beautiful daughter, her activities, her friends, her physical and mental health were the focus of life away from work. I was embedded in a high-performance corporate environment for over thirty years and was able to use the drive within the company as an excuse to hide within the busyness and blame the company culture for something that was largely of my own creation.

Being busy meant I didn't have to **be**.

Midlife has been a reckoning of sorts.

A wonderful man entered my life and adored both me and my daughter; he saw us as beautiful without and within. My toughest moments in this unexpectedly wonderful relationship have been centred around my ability to accept that he sees this beauty as real. Midlife hormones have run their own riot too, leading me to use my science wiring and my coaching and mentoring experience to support other women finding this sudden shift in body and mind unsettling and even traumatic. And yet turning those very gifts inward has eluded me.

As my corporate career neared its natural end and my daughter blossomed into an extraordinarily capable and independent woman, I realised I needed to shift. That sounds like it was immediate, which it was not. I ploughed on with the busyness, setting up a business, still doing all the things. The shift came about subtly, sneaking in past the armour of habits built up over years. New teachers came into my life, some deliberately sought, some incidental. Conversations about trauma, addiction (to work) and the science of our bodies sat alongside conversations about joy, playfulness, and creative expression. Conversations that brought vulnerability and pain sat alongside conversations that spoke of love; that started to fill my heart with something expansive, like filling a deflated balloon with air.

This is a journey just beginning.
The poem—the first outpouring from a heart and head unused to working together, a rumination on how my relationship with this body of mine has changed through the decades.

We are remarkable, us humans. We think all the thinks and we feel all the feels but we forget that the only reason we can do all of that is our bodies. We have 100 trillion cells all working together to create each one of us unique – that's 30 times more than the stars in the known galaxy! But where we might stare in wonder at a clear night sky, how often do we reflect that curiosity and wonder inwards and marvel that we even exist?

Whatever life stage you are at, no matter your different abilities, take some time to reflect on your own body now. It's the only relationship you cannot walk away from; you're married to it for life. It is incredible technology, but like any technology it needs care, maintenance and fuel. Come to love it now. Don't leave it as long as I did. Journey back to yourself.

[1] hEDS = Hypermobile Ehlers Danlos Syndrome; if interested, see https://www.nhs.uk/conditions/ehlers-danlos-syndromes/

Acceptance and Affirmation

Danu Sivapalan

For generations women have played pivotal roles in our lives, whether that be helping the poor, looking after their families, nursing wounded soldiers, peacemakers, influencers and activists fighting for female education, women's rights and climate change all with the aim of changing the world for the better.

For me, I play many roles; a Daughter, Wife, Mother, Sister, Daughter-In-law, all which come with certain expectations, responsibilities and a sense of 'duty' which has been ingrained in me from a young age and is part of who I am. This has its advantages, however at times I feel I am at war with myself not always knowing what is right and in turn this adds strain on myself and my relationships.

I am a first generation, British born, Sri-Lankan female telling a story about the influence of society's expectations and my life's journey of acceptance and self-belief in becoming the person I am today. I am speaking from my own experience and observations and I hope that other women will be able to relate to my story.

The beginning

My mother came to the UK as an immigrant in 1980.

I arrived into this world three years after my mother first stepped outside of her world, the country where she was born and grew up, leaving behind her home, friends, family and everything she had ever known.

England was alien to her. A place of unfamiliarity, difference in environment, culture, surroundings and way of life. She did not have a support network aside from her husband. The one thing she had going for her was her ability to understand and speak the English language.

My father was considered privileged, having had the opportunity to study Engineering at Stafford University. Once he completed his degree, he did what was expected of him and returned to Sri Lanka to get married and brought his wife back with him to the land of opportunity.

Sri Lanka is an island in South Asia with a population of 21.8 million. It was under British rule from 1815 to 1948 and was known as Ceylon, where the famous Ceylon Tea originated from. There has been political unrest since the country gained independence and it was the beginnings of the civil war which caused immigration and the arrival of refugees into Britain.

The eighties were a difficult time for immigrants and refugees. My father and many others had to work extremely hard to survive. My father worked two jobs to support his family. My mother tried to seek employment before I was born but was not able to cope with the racial abuse she received whilst working as a cashier at Woolworths in Brixton. She had returned to work soon after my 1st birthday when my parents discovered that I was being abused by my child minder. At this point my father thought it best that my mother become a full-time housewife. My brother was born 5 years after me.

Wife

Becoming a wife and mother made me reflect upon my upbringing and form a realisation as to why I am the way I am.

To my friends and family looking at my life from the outside, they see a woman following the path of a postcard Sri Lankan girl who listened to her parents and got married to a 'nice Sri Lankan boy' at the age of 26, who had a child at the age of 28, who conformed to society.

The reality is, I had a sheltered upbringing and lived at home with my parents up until I got married. I did live away whilst I was at university but would be back at home every chance I got, mostly during weekends and therefore did not experience the reality of living independently without the safety net of my parents.

I was raised mainly by my overprotective mother, whilst my father worked long hours to provide for the family. Growing up, I felt like an in-betweener who did not know where I truly belonged. I am one of many who were stuck in a limbo, being brought up with Sri Lankan traditions in a Western world.

My teenage years were a testing time for me. I was extremely naive, mainly due to my sheltered upbringing. I was a curious child with many questions, but anything my parents deemed as controversial would not be spoken about. They did not teach me how to deal with sadness or failure. I was even protected from death, not being allowed to attend any funerals as it was 'inappropriate for a child'. I went to my first funeral at the age of 24 and it was a traumatising experience.

My mother and I did not have an open relationship. This was mainly due to the fear I had towards her and her lack of emotion and affection. A daughter should be able to go to her mother to seek help or guidance but the very thought of speaking to her made me feel nervous and anxious. She never spoke to me about 'taboo topics' such as sex or puberty. I approached her when I needed my first bra and it was my friends who explained what periods and sex were before I had sex education at school. She always told me not to talk to boys but that made me want to talk to them even more. I was condemned for showing emotion and expressing myself.

A **young child** relies on **its mother** for **comfort**, affirmation, and **encouragement**. These were lacking in my relationship with my mother and this has haunted me throughout my life to the present day where I lack in self-belief and confidence and consequently suffer from anxiety and find myself seeking reassurance in things I do at home, at work and in general.

My mother wanted me to follow in her footsteps and had the idea of bringing me up the same way she was back in Sri Lanka. Her father died when she was young and her eldest brother forbade her from pursuing her education beyond the age of 18 as a woman's role was to get married, have children and look after them and the husband and generally 'run' the home.

My brother and I were brought up very differently due to our difference in gender. I was taught the basics of cooking, cleaning and general household duties whilst my brother was encouraged to pursue his education. He was given a lot more freedom and independence but for me it was quite the opposite.

My mother's expectation for me was to get married to a rich husband, have children and to look after them whilst being a housewife. She said that having a degree under my belt would make me marriage material! However, my father understood the importance of education regardless of gender.

Whilst I was studying for my degree at university, she started her search for a suitable partner as she thought the best thing for me was to marry someone whose stars aligned with mine as soon as I graduated. I think that she wanted to shed all responsibility of her only daughter as she saw me as a liability. Deep down, I knew this was not the life I wanted for myself. Yes, I wanted to get married and have children but before this I wanted a career, to travel the world and live independently. I felt so pressured not only by my parents but by my family and society.

Our culture is very much society driven and consequently all eyes are on you. You make one wrong move and you are the subject of unnecessary gossip. My parents were very conscious of what other people thought of our actions and behaviour, so even if they themselves were happy with the choices we made, society's opinion took precedence because if we did wrong it would reflect badly on them. This then resulted in secrecy, lack of openness and the inability to be yourself, hiding from society.

As long as I lived under their roof, they had complete control over me. I had no voice and merely did as I was told for the first 25 years of my life. Marriage for me was a 'get out card' escaping from the suffocating life I was leading under their roof.

I married my husband who was introduced by a friend of the family. We were engaged after six months of knowing each other and married a year later. I left my job, home, friends & family and moved 150 miles away to an unfamiliar place, but I did not find this daunting. It all happened so fast but I saw this as an opportunity to start a new life and lead it how I wanted to with the support of my husband. I suppose I was after a fairy tale where life would be rosy and I would be happy. However, it was far from it. I felt lost and alone.

Being the first out of my circle of friends to get married they had their concerns that it was moving too quickly and they were aware of the pressure I was under. They would tell me to stand up for myself, but I was scared. I felt like I didn't have a voice and whenever I had an opinion or did stand up for myself it was seen as being disrespectful. I was not one to shout, raise my voice or any form of confrontation. This resulted in me becoming an introvert within the four walls I was living in.

What made matters worse is marrying an only child and his family. At the beginning of our marriage my mother-in-law welcomed me into her home and told me that she would treat me like her daughter. However, over time, the more I got to know her, the more I felt I could not be myself around her. She made herself out to be a liberal Sri-Lankan woman, which she is somewhat in comparison to some others - but when it comes to her son and her family there were different rules and expectations.

She is a 'traditional' wife who does everything for her husband (like in the 1950's.) Her upbringing and values are obviously different to mine and although she integrated with society more than my mother had, the Sri-Lankan mindset remained. Her words and actions over the years did not make me feel like a daughter at all. She is a strong woman with extremely high expectations of people and, due to her values, she has distanced herself from family members and maintains relationships with very few people. There is nothing wrong with that. This is what she chooses to do, but I do not see the world in the same way she does and I simply cannot live up to her expectations. Our lives and experiences are incomparable. I imagine that my lack of maturity at the time may not have helped our relationship but at the same time I felt that there was very little 'margin for error'. The geographical distance between us certainly helped me manage this overbearing relationship.

Just before our 1st wedding anniversary I found out that I was pregnant. This was a surprise to my husband and me. I certainly was not mature enough to become a mother. Our families however were over the moon and suddenly I felt overwhelmed thinking about the journey ahead of me.

Motherhood

This has been a time of growth, reflection and acceptance. I have been a mother for over ten years now and it has taken me to this point to accept the journey I have been on to get to where I am today.

Solely using gas and air, 17 hours and a 2nd degree tear later my first child was born. A healthy baby boy weighing seven pounds and two ounces. This was specific information that I could share with our friends and family, leaving aside the gory details of labour - beyond this I had to learn as I went along. For the first week following the birth, I struggled to physically stand and walk. I spent the first night alone in the hospital and I did not sleep a wink. I trust this is common for new mums but at the time I did not know any different and I was so frightened.

I had NCT (anti-natal) sessions prior to giving birth which was the closest insight I got into motherhood, from how to change nappies, hold and bath babies and breastfeeding, to the consistency and colour of their poo. These were the most eye opening and informational sessions I had from anyone which goes to show how much I knew about having a baby! This was the time I would have benefited from the support of my mother.

I make my mother out to be some kind of monster. She was not at all. The only way she knew how to show her support was by being there. I would only have to ask her once and she always turned up when I needed her. This has its disadvantages.

Generally, in our culture everyone turns up. When there is a birth, death or in time of need people will be there. My concern when my son was born was this. I was so overwhelmed, had no clue what I was doing and to add to this the pressure of people wanting to come visit me and my baby.

When I arrived home with my husband and son for the first time as a family, we were greeted by my mother, mother-in-law and father-in-law. With my husband being an only child there was sheer excitement shown by the in-laws towards their first grandchild, so much so that they had no awareness of my feelings when they took my baby as soon as we entered our home. In their eyes, was this a way of being of help? Or were their actions complete selfishness out of love for their grandson?

Only a day old, he was passed on from one grandmother to the other whilst being filmed by his grandfather. I was in shot of the camera too, grinning nervously and hating every second of it. He let out a squeal and this soon turned into a full-throated wail. All he wanted was to be comforted by his mother but I did not have the confidence to speak up. I felt like screaming inside. Anyone observing this would ask me "why didn't you say anything?" This relates back to my upbringing. I was playing the role of an obedient daughter-in-law who does not voice her opinions. I thought I would hurt their feelings by taking *their* grandson from *their* arms. It took some time to process but I soon realised that he is *my* son before he is their grandson and he is my number one priority.

Something my mother-in-law said to me recently made me think about this very occasion. She thought that she developed a bond with her grandson because she held him at birth whereas she did not get the same opportunity to do so with her granddaughter and therefore does not have that same connection. My mother-in-law spent a significant amount of time away from her son during his early years due to personal circumstances. This was her choice, but I feel that because she missed out on her son's childhood she is making up for it by overcompensating with her grandchildren.

Since having my boy I had to grow up very quickly. I was the first one out of my friends and family to have a child. Living miles away from family meant I did not have the support network to help so I was very much on my own. My priorities changed and as a result I grew apart from my friends.

When my daughter was born three years later, I believe that I went through a period of post-natal depression but as a Sri Lankan woman you are taught to get on with things. You are not meant to think or reflect. You simply just do. There is a stigma associated with mental health and depression and seeking help is a sign of weakness.

I found a diary entry I had written at the age of 17, being thankful for a roof over my head and food at the table and how grateful and fortunate I was for being alive and surrounded by luxury in comparison to those who were less fortunate. However, I also wrote of my feelings of sadness due to the lack of affection at home. My mother did not hug me or kiss me that often. The only time I remember her kissing me was on my birthdays. I did not feel loved. I was disappointed in myself for not achieving the grades I wanted for my GCSEs and felt that I let my parents down. I knew that I could have done better but for whatever reason I did not have the motivation to study and lacked focus.

I understand my mother's position having been brought up in Sri Lanka with different values to those born into the western culture. I was born in England, as were my children and unfortunately the Sri Lankan culture is slowly fading as new generations are born. There are certain values I hold close to my heart which I can only hope my children value too. The difference is I will not dictate what they can or cannot do but will guide them to the right path. They will make mistakes and make their own choices and I will always be there to support them in whatever they decide to do.

I want my children to know that I am not perfect and that not being perfect is okay. I will apologise for my mistakes and learn from them. I will guide them so that they have the confidence to grab opportunities that come their way. I will listen to them and support them. I will bring them up with warmth, affection and comfort whilst encouraging them to believe in themselves and teach them real life-skills that they will take with them into their adulthood. I will hug them, kiss them and tell them that I love them at every opportunity. I will be the best mother that I can to my children, the mother I felt I did not have.

Me

People often ask, "who inspires you and has helped to shape you into the person you are today?" This person would be someone who has had a positive influence on you or someone who motivates you mentally and emotionally.

I cannot pinpoint just one person who has been on this evolving journey with me. There are many people even to this day that have an impact on me. My mindset through most of it was to do all the things that my mother didn't and to be someone who I want to be rather than someone who others want me to be. I'm not quite there yet but I take each day as it comes.

For a long time, I was a person who puts others' needs before my own. Growing up I wanted to please others but most of all my parents. After all, they did bring me into the world and cared for me in a way that they thought was right. As a parent you want the best for your child and you want them to be happy. The truth is, I don't believe that my mother was ever happy in her life and this reflected in my upbringing. I could sense her frustration in her behaviour and through her interaction with me.

I wanted more from my life than being a good mother, wife and daughter. Motherhood is a wonderful thing and is the hardest job I've ever had to do. It has taught me a lot but it was not enough. I want to play a part in helping others and make a difference to the world. I want to be a role model to other women who've had a similar experience to mine and young women who aspire to be a mother and have a career. My parents made sacrifices in their lives so that I could have a better one. They did not invest time for themselves or their relationship like we do today. The concept of 'well-being' and 'date-nights' is alien to them. My mother's form of exercise was cleaning the house and my dad was always working and he did not have time for anything else. Seeing my parents struggle made me want a different life for myself. I needed to prove to myself that I was capable of more.

I was not established in my career before starting a family which was extremely frustrating for me. I would have liked to have been financially stable and self-sufficient before having children but things do not always go to plan. I felt that it was important for me to spend quality time with my children during their early years and decided to put my career on hold until they were of school age. Whilst working part-time I thought about what I wanted to do and when it was time, I started climbing the career ladder. It has been quite a journey with many hurdles and success but with hard work, determination and most of all self-belief, I have progressed in my career and intend to continue until I achieve my goals.

Since getting married and escaping from my parents' reins I was exposed to a whole new world. A combination of real-world experience and my husband's influence has made me change both as a person and in my outlook of life. I decided to take full control of my life and as a result am overly independent. I don't rely on anyone and do not open up or get too close to people as I have lost trust and have felt let down many times.

We all make choices in life and we have to hold ourselves responsible for the choices we make. I held resentment towards my parents for a very long time as I felt that my fate was in their hands and they took away my future, the opportunity to live my life independently and the choice of whom I would spend the rest of my life with. My judgment was clouded and I rushed into making a choice that I was pressured into making. The bottom line here is that they simply held me back.

Turning 30 was a significant milestone for me. It was a time of reflection looking back at my past, the choices I made, the people who were no longer in my life and what I had achieved up until that point. At that time, I felt deflated and dissatisfied by what I had not achieved and I was comparing myself to others around me of a similar age. I know now that was not the right thing to do. There has always been fire within me, but it took a while to find that spark.

"You can be anything you want to be and do anything you set out to do. Just believe in yourself and be the best version of you."

For a long time I relied on others to make me happy and realised that no one or thing can make you happy. This happiness is short-lived. I have learnt to let go and learn from the past to help guide my future but most of all learn to love myself and find happiness and peace within.

It is time to close this chapter and enter a new one that is waiting for me, to move forward stronger and sure-footed in what I want and who I am. I have grown courage and resilience and with each day I am growing and ever-changing.

It is only now that I accept who I am and the circumstances that brought me to this point

Leave Room for Magic

Sheena Hales

At the start of this year I framed the words of Meghan Markle "My New Year's resolution is to leave room for magic"; I even put the word Magic into a snow globe to help create it in every moment.

As I lie in the dark in my hospital bed on a cancer ward some ten months later, recording these words, I feel magic all around. I choose to believe the magic isn't just external, that it has been within me all this time, energetically flowing and gathering power. Looking after me. I feel so tingly that I could burst with joy. Like this moment was always meant to be experienced. I feel safe, at home, connected, loved and no longer a victim. I feel alive in every sense. I acknowledge in these moments that it is peculiar that it took this extreme moment to slow me down and awaken me.

Over the past year I have been awarded a British Empire Medal from the Queen for my service to the finance industry, turned 50, got divorced from the father of my son and a man I love(d) and discovered I had breast cancer *and yet still* it has been my best year ever.

I am honoured. I believe the universe opened up this masterclass to allow me to become present and to feel love and communicate in a way I have never experienced before. Who knew that when I went looking for love and adventure for the second part of life, that cancer would provide the master key.

Being awarded a British Empire Medal

I work for a major bank and was nominated and awarded a British Empire Medal from the Queen for my service to the Financial Services industry. This was really for my services to my community. I pioneered an idea and led a team to repurpose part of our Head Office as an emergency distribution centre. The intention was that it would take mass donations in support of the charities on the ground helping the most vulnerable during the height of the Covid19 pandemic.

My reflection at the time was that it is odd to be recognised for doing something that felt natural – my zone of genius even. I approached the logistics problem with a single thought – what if this was easy? So, I penned a compelling request and sent it directly to one of our executive team. I asked three short questions. It took ten minutes to compose using simple words and with no fancy justifications. I knew I had to put impact over the voice in my head saying, "this won't work, will I embarrass myself, what if they say no, or worse, don't even acknowledge it". To my joy and fear, within 20 minutes it had been tabled at an executive board discussion. The Board replied to say the conference centre would be open tomorrow adhering to the covid measures, would be staffed and managed by our security team and our marketing team would help me promote it.

The work I led went on to help deliver over two million meals to those impacted by food poverty and to distribute for example 240,000 garments of essential clothing for refugees and the homeless, over 200,000 kettle meals for those isolated in hotel rooms without access to cooking facilities and 200,000 new children's books and education packs to children without technology in their homes. It also galvanised support from our colleagues and customers, such as a farmer in Aberdeen who sent truckloads of fresh potatoes and carrots. Each time I asked he said yes, and our catering partner turned these and other donations into thousands of simple healthy meals for those in need.

The work incidentally delivered over 25 million pounds worth of free positive or neutral advertising as people spread the story about our kindness and how as a bank we had changed to be purpose led. The work our volunteers did has changed their lives, they have spent two years helping others in a way they have never done before and provided our colleagues with tangible examples of our purpose in action. It created sustainable change in ways we had never imagined; our in-house cafe chains are now run by a social enterprise whose profit supports the homeless. That still blows my mind.

But the euphoria of getting the medal soon turned to stress; I did not feel worthy; it was too easy; I felt an imposter and embarrassed that those who helped didn't get a medal too. Instead of feeling in awe of myself, I felt depressed; I realised that even getting a medal from the queen wasn't enough to make me feel happy. Bonkers but true. Was this it? Was this my full purpose in life? Was it over?

Later in the year I would learn from a coach who reads the lines on your face like a palmistry expert that I had all the hallmarks of a person who was highly successful but that did not *feel* success. She left me with advice, unless I understood what success was to me I would never feel at peace. Boom. There it was. My peace button. Except, I didn't know how to activate it. This was too frightening a prospect to ignore. The quest was on. So, I began looking for what success should feel like for me. I didn't realise my biggest masterclasses were yet to come and as I lie here tonight I am starting to understand.

My 50th year

This was also the year I turned 50, a year when we couldn't gather and celebrate together and I spent the weeks before my birthday cancelling everything I'd put in place. I would not be kissed or hugged and I would only see everyone virtually. It began an internal dialogue and intense curiosity about what love and being loved means, especially as I was single and didn't want to be.

A few days before my birthday my coach sent me a love letter. It was beautifully written, loving and very inspiring. Then I recognised the words; they were my words that I had spoken in a voice message to a friendship group. She encouraged me to let my heart listen to my wisdom. I realised how nourishing, loving and wise the words were; I allowed myself permission to let them settle and fill my heart; it made me feel deeply loved. She encouraged me: "now imagine how you'd feel if you choose to say those words more often to yourself".

This began a love affair with myself. Despite how I sometimes feel, I began to love who I am. Some days I took myself on a date: I booked a floatation, I went on a retreat, I read in a hammock or curled up with a blanket. I went to the supermarket and wiggled in tune pushing my trolley to my favourite songs with headphones on and realised how many people didn't laugh but engaged and smiled with me. I paused more when asked "how are you" and learnt to connect in a whole new way. On other days I cried for hours and simply allowed myself to welcome in my feelings and then let them come and go.

Over the course of this year, I had the joy of attending a workshop called "Love what is" and I learnt to fully let go and embrace the universe as it unfolds for me, experiencing the joy of the unknown without fear. To make plans and be ok if they break, to let go of something which isn't serving me, to set goals but be open to change and to play in the moment.

What this all made me realise is that success to me is not just about doing remarkable things, it can also be about having a life full of connection with people that you help, inspire, learn from and listen to. Together you can create magic by motivating and enabling each other to grow. I have never achieved anything on my own despite sometimes feeling alone. I've sparked an idea and people have followed, challenged, charged ahead, walked with me or picked up the pieces after me. My limiting belief that I was alone and not loved was a story and it was time to shed it. I needed to stop dragging it with me through life, hurting myself and all around me.

So, to my marvel, on my birthday I cooked my son and I the most beautiful breakfast, lit essential oil candles during the day and I began to experience love. A friend arrived and read a billboard 'Love Actually' style on my doorstep. Flower bouquets filled my house with colour. A high tea was delivered with balloons and sparkly lights, a gift from my sister arranged amazingly by my son and my neighbour. A friend made me the most amazing birthday cake; a work colleague sent me a playlist on Spotify of songs that reminded her of me. I was given an exquisite dressing gown to ensure I lounged like a queen, a beautiful print by Charlie Mackesy and an engraved bracelet. Most of all I no longer had any evidence that I was alone or that I was not loved. That's magic.

The Divorce

So, after all that love came the hurt. I was going to go into a dark cave by choice. I needed to get divorced to create space in my life for my future love. It needed to be this year. No one gets married to get divorced, do they? But I think in retrospect it took going through the process of getting divorced for me to really understand and feel what love actually is.

I had not been a perfect wife but whatever way I look at it, I never deserved to be put in a position that I would feel the need to put my fist in my mouth to scream silently in the shower to hide the noise from our 6 year old due to the adultery shock, or to react to another lie by curling up on the cold floor of a public toilet wearing an expensive suit after vomiting in the interval of presenting a bank-wide strategy. To experience the humiliation of finding the Victoria Secret (they couldn't be H&M could they!!!) knickers under the bed.

As I allowed time for self-discovery this year, I realised that I had in fact betrayed myself many years before my husband had. I had set no boundaries for him to follow. I didn't value or respect myself and I definitely did not teach my partner how I wanted to be treated. I had stopped being the entrepreneur, that independent, confident woman he met and I had lost my sparkle and infectious smile. I stopped being a friend and a lover when I became a mum. I diverted all my attention to our son, but I was exhausted working full time and taking full responsibility for running the house and our social life. I was a martyr and an angry one. I had no time left for me and I indulged only in food and alcohol for comfort and spent many years doing things alone. My energy was negative and edgy.

The divorce was substantially delayed due to courts not meeting during Covid19 and this allowed the healing to continue. Our divorce decree finally came through on 27th July, my now ex-husbands birthday.

For some the paperwork would feel like closure. For me, I knew I had unspoken words I needed to share with him. It was time to say goodbye and let him go. There was an urgency in my feelings. I was no longer a Mrs, which was an ego loss for me, and I could not continue to own him. I know that sounds very controlling. It's true. I'm not proud.

I asked for a face-to-face meeting and he agreed. He didn't ask why, he was brave and vulnerable, or maybe scared. I started by reassuring him I didn't want more money, I wasn't changing our childcare arrangements and I wasn't ill. He laughed nervously. I told him I wanted a lifetime moving forward of being able to look into his eyes and hold his gaze and at the moment I couldn't. I shared with him that I had thought it was because I was hurt or angry. Now I realised it was because I felt guilty, Guilty for making him the one to shoulder all the blame for our marriage breakdown. I apologised. I was wrong. We both messed up. I may not have had the affair but I had a choice how to react and I chose to not love him as much as I could, to be angry, resentful, annoyed with him and to get frustrated. By making him wrong, I realised I made myself the victim and that was not right. I wanted that to change for us both. Allowing him to walk with more pride.

This conversation took courage from both of us. I knew I could not say sorry if I expected him to apologise in return. He didn't. Which made me silently laugh a little. He listened fully and admitted he couldn't look back and that it is what it is. Sharing that with me was his way of being vulnerable and a degree of acknowledgement. I understood. He asked me not to be so hard on myself and I had an OMG moment thinking "he thinks I am taking all the blame back". But so be it. I needed closure. But what he did say made me cry. He said "Sheena you are the mother of my son and I will always look after you because of that, so if you are ill or get made redundant, I don't want you to worry. I will not see you on the streets, we will work something out".

I cried and I realised in that moment how fragile love is. I do have regrets and I will always love him. I had treated love as if it was transactional, and I withdrew it when I didn't get what I wanted. It was a tough lesson. Now I choose to care for him as the father of my son and that will always be true, unconditionally.

Three days later I called him, "Richie, I have just discovered I have cancer" and he said, "I'm here for you, what can I do?".

Embracing cancer was to be my greatest masterclass

Breast cancer to me looked like I was radiant, bursting with vitality and ready to go on adventures. I was newly divorced, had just bought a campervan and was ready to spice up my life with fun trips and dreams of a new hot man in my life.

Once I recovered from the shock, I was amazed and blown away by the magic that happened. An early mammogram identified something I couldn't see and couldn't feel and had no symptoms. Why did I do the test? Eventually, I had created space in my life to think about, value and prioritise myself.

When I got the call with the results at 8.10am, I was pouring coco pops for my son. The voice said, "are you sitting down somewhere we can talk easily". She had my attention, It was a life changing moment. I asked her to call back after the school run. In that wait I continue robot-like, as we all do. Smiling. Armour on, "have a lovely day, I love you".

I listened. Lots of words. Swarming. Only one landing, cancer. Then three "I have cancer" and then "I cannot die". She goes and I have a list of actions: to call my medical insurance, to book more tests. Who the f@ck are my medical insurers, where is the paperwork? I am alone. Of course, I googled horrible stuff. Breathe.

Thanks to my wonderful coach I realised that cancer was not going to be a fight or a battle. It was not going to be me against my cancer. My outcome would not depend on being a "winner" or a "fighter" or a "brave warrior". Those who die from cancer do not "lose a battle" because of their own inability to summon fortitude or strength. I realised I could choose the high-dream or the low-dream but the low dream would hurt myself, my son and everyone who loved me. Instead, with her guidance, I chose the high dream, in that I chose to take the positive outlook each step of the journey and when I couldn't and the dark moments came, she would shine the light. She kept shining the light and I began to learn to let it flow in.

I allowed myself to open up to being fiercely vulnerable. I embraced it. The closest I have felt in my body to this sensation before was when I learned to snowboard and for the very first time allowed myself to lean out away from the safety of the slope, heart open, arms out. This feels intrinsically wrong but totally exhilarating and frightening in the same breath. I was to face this part of my life, head on, each step of the journey, only seeing the next few hundred yards at a time. Taking shelter and being held by those I choose to walk with me.

I began to put down my armour and love and care for my body as much as I could. And that meant honouring how I felt at any given time. I allowed my body to express emotions, rest and relax, and tell me what it needed. I made the most of the good days and did what I could to hold onto a positive mental mindset. I remember my brother said "Sheena, remember I am one of your people, I am here for the light, the dark and the messy bits in between, please always show up and I will hold your hand". My sister said, "I invite you to open the book I gave you and read it out loud enough and with gusto for me to feel the vibrations in the air 400 miles away, the butterfly effect, and I will call you."

I was given wisdom by a neighbour that managing cancer takes a team, not an army, a loving, supportive compassionate team. Gentle kind love. I was given help to pick five of my people to take me through my cancer journey, with me at the centre of that team. Each knew and agreed on their role, so no one felt overwhelmed or burdened, allowing me to ask and receive help and love in the most profound way.

I began to notice that cancer was changing the quality of every connection. Everyone had become more honest, intimate and thoughtful. It has proven to enrich every conversation and deepen the relationships in my life. Other people stepped up without being asked in the most extraordinary ways. For example, I have a weekly 30-minute coaching call with a wonderful friend to help me explore how I keep asking for the help I need. How amazing is that?

The day of surgery - today

As I lie now in the hospital bed, I reflect on how funny and beautiful in many ways this day of my surgery has been.

In the morning my coach sent me a funny YouTube video about meditation and I sat in a hot tub I'd hired for the weekend to make isolation more enjoyable. I laughed as I looked across my garden and felt so grateful for the lovely safe home I'd created. That day my son cycled off, as planned, to school, with an army of people who would support him in my absence.

I was able to observe that I am often controlling, rushed and impatient. I'd asked my lovely friend, who was self-isolating with me, if she would mind changing my bed linen into white crisp sheets for when I get back. I could see disappointment in her face when she said, "Oh Sheena, I was going to surprise you by making it all beautiful when you get home". I realised people want to make magic if you let them; I want to be the person that leaves that space.

I made time to lean into a prearranged cuddle with a neighbour in the street and exchanged a caring gift for her as she was off to her mum's funeral that day. My other neighbour stepped in to cuddle us both and then she was my chauffeur to the hospital. En route she handed me this really valuable and sentimental rosary beads from the pope to keep me safe and left me with a beautiful message to encourage me to see that even though I'd not told my mum, as I did not want to worry her, my mum was still present, that her love was still here and she was still holding my hand and next to me during my treatment. I felt my body fall into her virtual embrace and I bathed in her love.

At the hospital, I check in. The staff are wonderful. As I go through the admission steps with the nurse my phone rings, stops, rings again and again. I realise I can't concentrate so I interrupt the nurse and ask if I can answer my phone to my ex-husband. My son has fallen at school and needs to go to A&E. My ex was in Leeds and too far away to help. So, with one call, my friend, staying to look after my son, is rocketed into rapid parenting skills and forced to speak to my ex who she has not spoken to since our separation. They find room in their hearts to be kind and welcoming to each other. It all goes like clockwork and even my son's bike is returned home by a classmate. Everyone played their part, helped and held me in my moments of need and took away the worry - like silent superheroes in waiting. This incident took the focus off me and reminded me that I was not central to the world even during my surgery and that everything else was still spinning.

The love I received was unmeasurable. I feel I have gone to heaven skipping death en route. My heart overflowed with love. I have received so many unexpected messages, rays of pink light, songs of strength, words of wisdom, reminders of how to care for myself, beautifully wrapped gifts, carefully selected to allow me to laugh, to nourish my body and to feel that I am deeply loved. I would not swap places with anyone, it has allowed me to see who really is special in my life and that feels awesome.

And boy I did laugh through my hospital stay. I was asked to take a pregnancy test - I imagined how funny it would be if I went in with cancer at 50 and came out with a baby.

Then just before I went in for my operation, there I was with my boob all marked up with a titanium clip (which I see as a mark of strength) and a wire marker inside leading to my cancer and a big arrow in marker pen identifying the "right tit". I looked at it and photographed it, for evidence and memories. I chatted to my life coach and shared that not only was my surgeon incredibly talented and had already saved people I knew with breast cancer, he was also very charismatic and hot. We laughed that I should write my mobile number across my good boob. Knowing he was happily married, and that I wasn't exactly looking my best, I settled for a biro-written message on my left boob to say, "Thank you", enveloped in a heart. Later the surgeon told me that when they discovered it, it made them laugh, it had never been done before and if it hadn't been unethical he would have taken a selfie. It was an important lesson I have been taught, you can always have a positive impact even when you think you have no control and your chips are down. You can smile even in the dark moments, and try to show up the best you can.

So here I am now, out of the operation, all bandaged up and told it is a complete success. I am cancer free unless proven differently by the biopsy and we will know that for sure in seven days. I feel immense relief, if you are going to have breast cancer, then a small, early and treatable version is a gift. Thank you universe.

As the quietness and dark of the ward at night surrounds me I feel that pink light coming from so many people that make my life remarkable and isn't that wonderful. Isn't that what life should be like? The magic I had planned to leave room for at the start of the year was glistening and filling my heart and the room to an intoxicating electric level. It demanded my attention. I knew I had to breathe it into every pore to replenish and energise my body. It was magical, overwhelming and real.

In the midst of this life changing event, I feel I am home. It is the best place I have ever been. I know the next chapter of my life is just beginning, so much has changed, and yet I am still to discover who I am becoming. I feel overwhelmed with joy that I get to roll again. I don't know what my next bold move will be but I am so excited and scared. I realise that life is like a game of snakes and ladders, sometimes you get to move forward and other times quite unexpectedly you get to step back. It is adventurous. It is my life and I have grown to love it. My mess has become my message and become my way of living and I realise in this moment, that I love what is.

Creating Community

Sara Steffey McQueen

I don't think my story is one of crazy wild talent or skill. But it is a story of Light within that needed to radiate and be seen. It began in my early 20's, but it wasn't necessarily youth that called it to me. I believe the Light is a growing thing that can be watered to sprout and shine within us at any age when the need and time are right.

When I graduated college in 1972, I had a sense of potential and joy that from then on, I could study whatever I chose. I recognized myself as a lifelong learner, gatherer, and sharer. Books have always been a special gift to me. They were and are my best teachers. I didn't have a grandma to share a family heritage or teach me the "old ways." It was books that kindled the ideas of the inner life of Spirit: the one that is free and that holds us. As an extrovert full of hope and living in the 1970's in the U.S.A, I'd been introduced to the writings of Aldous Huxley, Herman Hesse, Viktor Frankel, and the art of Georgia O'Keefe. I discovered Indian Philosophy in school, including the idea of a Unity of Self from the Upanishads. I felt I had come home and was intellectually ready to create a life of my own.

I craved the freedom to unfold, to explore, to live a creative life, not knowing what that would be. One thing was clear: I wanted to live in nature and with others of like mind. After graduation my friend introduced me to a man. She thought Mike had goals compatible with mine. She said she thought we might even want to collaborate. Mike and I both wanted to open a storefront: He wanted to refinish antique furniture, and I wanted to open an art gallery and store. We had a soul recognition. I sensed and believed I had met a person who would be able to accommodate my needs and was interested in living in a rural setting, as I was. I felt his openness and flexible strength and I appreciated his gentle ways. We both shared a deep happiness and joy in being together. Our relationship has endured and deepened with each passing year.

What I most want to share is that we didn't make a big plan for how we'd live our life, we just **did** it. We had a vision with no details. It was just a passion and a magnetism toward an idea. We didn't study how, or research living in group situations. Books about the lifestyle we began to live hadn't been written yet. We just told a few friends, rented a big house with a few bedrooms, and began what is now my life.

Idealism has taken me a long way. TRUST was integral and necessary. Not that I thought about these qualities. They were natural, with perhaps some naiveite added into the mix. I like to share my experience because over the years I've heard and met so many people who say they want community or to buy land with others. They place stipulations and expectations and details such as looking for the "right" people or the "perfect" location. Often, they don't have the money to follow their dream. I believe that our success was based on a simple faith or trust in human goodness and a shared commitment to live softly on the land as best we knew.

Our group began remodelling an old rental house to serve as a studio/gallery and refinished furniture business we called "Country Comforts." Even my dog was named Country. I was doing everything to "get to the country." After 9 months of working on the house, in the last room on the last window, while stripping and removing old paint, I sparked a piece of steel wool as I brushed across an uncovered electrical outlet. A fire broke out and within a short time, all our effort and intention were reduced to ashes.

It was too much to imagine restarting our project in a burned-out house. Instead, the six of us decided to move a couple of hundred miles south to the town where I had attended college. We found a large house to rent on the edge of town, and phase two "The Big Pink House" was created. We had a large backyard where I learned to compost. I learned to make soup stock too, and my Earth Mother self was awakened and happy.

I began reading Euell Gibbons' Stalking the Wild Asparagus [1] and that initiated a 50-year study of plant medicine. Our group lived together in a sweet harmony. On Saturdays we would turn the music up loud and clean the place. We just flowed in reciprocity. If I cooked, then others cleaned up afterwards. Simple common sense and courtesy prevailed and became habits. We fasted together once a week, scavenged grocery dumpsters for good fresh discards, and lived a happy "hippy" life, a simple good life.

I do believe when we're in an authentic place and somehow connected to our purpose, there arises a magic. Some call it synchronicity. I don't expect it. I don't think I make it happen. It's a grace of sorts. Perhaps faith. Not that we don't experience hardship or even tragedy and suffering. But in my life, I've noticed this response and feel much gratitude and appreciation when it arises. We have these moments in life when we're in a flow, where opportunities seem to arise, and things fall into place.

On a sweet warm spring day, I was downtown, perusing shops, and I walked up stairs to discover a little gem of a place called Threads. It was run by a beautiful woman named Yarrow. I immediately recognized a special connection, and within weeks she offered to GIVE me the shop! She had decided to move to Colorado and attend a new school called Naropa Institute. Yarrow said I could take over Threads and since most of the wares were used, I just needed to start paying the rent. This opportunity led to more synchronicity.

As my story of community and country living unfolded, Threads became another place of gathering and creativity. Rent was cheap, allowing my friends and me to not only sell the inventory Yarrow left, but to make blue jean embroidered skirts and create one-of-a-kind jewelry, using recycled African bead necklaces. We traded goods with our customers and enjoyed meeting travellers as they passed through town.

Our group still had no money or resources to buy land. We lived on very little but kept a clear vision of a place in the country. The next spring when the weather warmed, our town held a flea market weekend at People's Park, a corner lot close to the University. I decided to take advantage of the fresh air and take some wares to the park instead of opening Threads that day. Sitting on a blanket next to me was a couple selling a large antique trunk. We began chatting. They lived in the country and wanted to try living in a community. I was living in a community and wanted to move to the country. It wasn't long before we decided to try gardening together on their land.

They were renting an old, run-down hunting cabin in a different county on land farmed for generations. The cabin was small and in a rugged condition, but it was beside a creek with a small spring right outside. The garden was a hike up an old tractor path through a meadow past a dilapidated barn. They'd planted the garden at the top of a hill where the view encompassed both sunrise and sunset, giving a 360-degree view of woodland and meadow hills. There was even an old graveyard nearby. By Fall, our group had moved to this beautiful hilltop vista, sleeping in 3 or 4 pup tents. In a few months we added new friends to the group and used the cabin for cooking and storing our belongings. I think of this period as our commune days. And also, my honeymoon time with Mike.

We called our commune Blue Spring Farm. We'd done it. We'd created a community. We were learning skills together and deepening our love of Nature. We shared all our resources, which weren't much. We shared a sock drawer, cooked on an old wood cookstove, washed in the cold clean spring, and swam in the curve of Raccoon Creek. We had little money and spent a lot of time fixing an old car and hitching rides to town with the neighbors. But we were happy. "Sweet Owen" as the locals call this land. It had a unique beauty with ridges and valleys of goldenseal and acorns and walnut trees. It felt like this was a timeless life we were living together. Actually, it was only for a few months of my young life. Winter was approaching and living with no running water, heat, or electricity, not to mention an uncomfortable encounter with hunters one night, emphasized our need to change our situation. Some people left, to travel on, some moved into town. Four of us wanted to stay.

One morning as I stood on the beautiful rocks at this magical spring that I adored, I thought about how much I loved this area and wanted to stay. I wondered who owned the beautiful pristine woods across the Creek. I researched the local plat maps at our Courthouse and wrote a letter to the owners. Mike worked for the State Forest at the time, and I proposed we rent the land. We would put up tipis on the land and protect it from poachers or trespassers. I had never even seen a tipi. I hadn't camped as a child. I knew tipis are a southwestern shelter of the First Nations, but it was something I thought we could build. The Indian Tipi by Reginald & Gladys Laubin [2] became our resource. The book was our guide, and we found a local farmer with a small stand of pines he wanted thinned. Following the book closely, we thinned the pines, took the poles, and used draw knives to take off the bark. We ordered yards and yards of canvas which we sewed into long strips of fabric in the hallway at Threads. Soon we had created two tipis.

There was a zeitgeist going on in our town during those days; opening of whole foods restaurants, ashrams popping up; a food co-op formed, and alternative newspapers flourished. I met a go-getter who was the editor of one of these papers and we started talking about our shared vision of buying land we could live on and protect. We started holding discussions and gathering like-minded folks who were seriously interested in buying land together. We began looking at land parcels for sale. Months later, a 300-acre piece of land showed up on the southwestern edge of our county. It was mostly woods and had been logged recently so there was a logging road throughout. A beautiful stand of cedar trees lined the road down to a creek where a small waterfall bubbled. The top of the land was a high point in the county, and a meadow of 25 or so acres. It was beautiful. We knew the time had come to get serious. We agreed to purchase May Creek Farm for $10,000 down. About 48 people signed an agreement to put in $300 each to make the down payment, and we agreed to pay for 20 years. Some of the group knew no one, but we shared a common desire to be caregivers for the land. In our hearts, we all pledged to go forward into this mystery of building community.

That was 45 years ago. We had no idea what we were doing but we've grown and thrived organically over the decades. We had no infrastructure. As time went on, we saw the need to form a corporation and wrote rules and regulations, by-laws and so forth. But in the beginning, we started out living in tipis and before our first winter built a small shack as a shared community kitchen and meeting space. We built composting toilets, hand dug a cistern before we had resources to dig wells, lived without electricity and enjoyed learning about this magical place. Of the original May Creek Farm members, there are six founding members still present. We're raising our third generation and have become a family of friends. My greatest joy is sharing my ways of ceremony and magic in rituals in Nature with my granddaughter. I've now lived in this family/community longer than my blood family.

Our community is not perfect. We have challenges. For me, my original vision has not fully unfolded, but I'm seeing the possibilities still alive in our adult children. I have deep roots on this land, and I am still learning to listen and hear from Nature. My life is full of peace and gratitude.

I've shared my story to encourage others to follow a dream and pursue it with trust. It's taken tremendous faith in one another and the Benevolent Universe to stay the course. And, yes, times have changed for the younger ones. Land prices are exorbitant, and there are so many new challenges. Other times also had major roadblocks. May you nurture the sparks of your own inspiration. Blessings.

***"Our mission is to create and nurture community based on respect for each other and responsible stewardship of the land"* –**

[1] Gibbons, E. (2020). *Stalking the Wild Asparagus*

[2] Laubin, R., Laubin, G., & Vestal, S. (1989). *The Indian Tipi: Its History, Construction, and Use*

Empowered by Limitless Possibilities

Christy Caudill

Journal entry, June, 2017

It's felt like an uphill battle, but reading back from journal entries over a month ago, I have healed a lot and come a long way. Then, I had crippling pain from walking. Then, every step was delicately and slowly managed. I was so careful not to bump anything with my feet or place my steps on surfaces that might be uneven. It felt like every fiber of my being was dedicated to protecting my feet from the pain that would stop me, force me to close my eyes, breathe deeply through it, and focus on allowing the pain and the moments to pass. I did not want to give up on being able to walk again. I did not give up on it.

The main thing I am struggling with now is the numbness in my left hand and wrist. The numbness keeps me awake. I am getting 3—4 hours a night, and the night before last was the worst: I got a few hours of sleep but woke several times with numbness and SO much pain. When I finally just got up, I did everything I could to try and get the painful tingling to stop, for the feeling to come back. I did some kind of desperate exercise, jumping around the apartment in the middle of the night, the best I could to get blood flowing.

It's difficult to let yourself fall asleep when you know that's what you'll wake up to.

Last night though, I slept better than I have in weeks. I was motivated to journal about what I ate and did so

299

that I could recreate it. Let's start with what I did the day before yesterday, where I woke through the night with the worst yet numbness and massive associated pain…

More than 15 years on, I find this journey of healing from the autoimmune illness Rheumatoid Arthritis a miraculous one. When I was 17, just off to college on a cross-country running scholarship, I was abruptly stuck with an illness that would define my twenties...and I thought it would define the rest of my life. I was bedridden for months at a time, my knees locked in place; the swelling in my fingers prevented me from using zippers or buttons, opening bottles, or grasping a toothbrush. I sat in Rheumatologists' offices surrounded by the elderly who shared my suffering. As a young person who did not yet even know myself, the disconnection from the active, physical person I had always been was deeply emotionally painful. I was told that in a best-case scenario, I wouldn't become wheelchair-bound until I reached the ripe old age of 40.

Yet, something transformational found its way into my life: desperation. It broke me open. At 26, I decided I would not choose a life of suffering through constant *medication cycling*, with their every-present companion, sickness. The looming threat of medication-induced lymphoma was ever-present with the multiplying and growing nodules under my skin. The medications didn't really allow me to even function that well. I still felt like some version of the Elephant Man, joints bulging at grotesque proportions. For better or worse, I made a decision that I didn't want to live that way, even if it meant not living.

For a year, I put my ardent western scientist mind—thinking dictated purely by the rational—on the shelf, and became truly open-minded for the first time in my life. A search for any way of healing that others had found before me–anything other than the singular and insufficient avenue I had been given–became my motivating force. I acquired a small library of books on a topic I had never before given any credit at all: alternative medicine.

I tried some of the healing methods described in the books, but did not see any successes. I was really flying blind, but I was trying. I was ready. I was open. One day, a work friend of mine mentioned to me, in passing, that she was seeing a Traditional Chinese Medicine practitioner that changed her health completely with a simple dietary change. To this day, I still don't know why I went to see this healer; I was still unaware that my own worldview had kept me an artificially small self, narrowly confined to a limited reality that dictated my version of "possible". I am not proud that I held subconscious bias about the superiority of western ways of thinking and being. I now feel as though it was all, simply, exactly as it needed to be.

I worked with the practitioner to develop a method of self-healing through self-discovery, which started with keeping a detailed food (and everything else) diary for 3 years. It was a diet and symptom tracker, a long method of food elimination and reintroduction, a decade before I had ever heard these terms. (The internet resources and its embeddedness in our lives were not quite what they are today.) After only 3 months of this process, I made the decision to come off my medications—all of them: the infusions, the multiple injections, the pills. I have never taken them again.

The decision came to me one day when I was at the gym. I had finished a light cardio session on an elliptical machine and went to sit on the floor to stretch. Without thinking, forgetting about the guards I normally used to carefully protect my body, I pulled my legs up, bringing my knees up to my chest.

Wait, wait. My knees don't bend. They don't bend that way. They don't bend in this normal, natural, easy, pain-free, comfort.

The feeling of gratitude that arose was powerful. It was bursting out of me in tears, in heavy breathing with eyes closed, rocking back and forth as I held myself at my knees. I held myself so tightly. There, on the floor of a gym full of people, I was fully in it. I was completely lost to this world and consumed with *being gratitude*.

Once I began to recognize that my diet was healing my body, I lived with this sense of *being gratitude* at an intensity that was completely foreign to me before. And so, something bigger was happening that I could not intellectualize. It was the first time I had ever trusted anything outside of my intellect. I did not enter these states early on in my healing with the intention of self-love and gratitude. I never sat down and decided that I was going to focus on gratitude. Perhaps focusing on gratitude has a way of making it ever-more elusive, as though the trying (largely performative and disconnected from the source of gratitude) subverts the being. The self-love and gratitude seeped in slowly, over time. The more I kept my focus on trusting and working through the process, giving everything and working with a singular focus on it, the more I became enlightened to guiding feelings like gratitude and love, because they simply arose. I say *enlightened* because I had never before been able to access those emotions at that depth, and it seems as though, after these experiences, I never truly had felt them at all. I had never really understood them.

Perhaps this is what is referred to as *post-illness growth* or *post-trauma growth*. Many who have lived through an intense and life-altering circumstance hold that it was the best thing that ever happened to them. For me, it allowed me access to emotions that were not possible before, simply because they were buried under too many other things that simply did not matter. It opened me to actually feel the blessing of life.

When I say that this life experience broke me open, it seemed to reset my orientation to life and my expectations about what is possible in this lived experience. I now feel it as a knowing: when living in reality, it is reasonable to expect miracles. When living in false realities—the limited confines of mind-stories—it is perfectly reasonable to accept limitations.

I have experienced a handful of flare-ups over the years: a recurrence of pain, inflammation, and debilitation with varying degrees of severity. But this reorientation to life and its possibilities gifted me that there is a cyclical nature to all things. At 39 years old, I now live the overwhelming majority of my life without a trace of the illness, and it has become so distant that it feels like these experiences were another life, that they are the stories of another person. I am a weight lifter and avid rock climber. I hang off of those fingers which could not before hold a toothbrush. *Every single day* I revel in the joy it is to be in my body, to physically express without pain and limitation–that deep joy and gratitude has never left, and it has never wavered. (My sister said to me once, "You're not even physically capable of frowning, are you?") Like my journal entry from 2017, when I experience a sense of regression in my life, I take stock of myself and my actions. I have learned to be empowered by limitless possibilities, and refuse to be resigned even when things feel the most dark, the most immovable. When I am in a flare-up, I become focused, steely-eyed; I stare it down; I do not fear it, *it fears me.*

Sometimes Hope

Y. Yi Pang

Stretch

Sometimes our love must
stretch so far as to continue to
encompass the beloved who
is walking away from us…

And we must hold them in our
hearts while letting them go
and the pain will sear through
us while we try to hold our
heads up and carry on
without the ground upon which
we had been standing
And though our wings are
battered and broken,
our feathers stripped of
all flight, our hearts so very
broken…
They beat, they leak
—fighting to stay open
pretending to be a stone

Sometimes Hope…

Sometimes hope is a thing with
Ridiculously huge wings that lift me
So high above my troubles and cares
Proffering the infinity of possibility

Other times holding on to hope
Is grasping an anvil with one finger tip
While hanging by an absurdly thin thread an inch
From the event horizon of a black hole

Yet still, I hold…

Let it Go…

Let it go
Accept the pain
Embrace the darkness
Hold the heartbreak

Let it break
B r e a k
S..h…a…t.t…e….r
M
…e
……l
………t

Cherish that little
Vulnerable heart
Falling, falling apart
Feel it explode…implode
Both at once

And when you think you've no heart left
Look inside and see…

.

.

.

.

.

.

More

The Abyss of Truth

Holding my gaze in the abyss of truth
I see the wrinkled, decrepit thing that is me
Without a shred of courage to hold my hand,
Shaking in utter fear and aching for denial
Can I love this me deeply enough?
To reach a tender hand down to her
To touch her with such compassion that
This cowering me might willingly shed her grotesque
armour?

A few years ago, my father passed away suddenly and unexpectedly, and my world was shattered. Meeting that grief, traveling through it (which I am, of course, still doing), wasn't something I could easily write about while it was fresh and raw, and then rarely ever directly. But it taught me so much, and I thought I had reached a rather mature perspective on grief and its meaning for me.

A couple of years after that, my husband suddenly and unexpectedly (not quite in the same way as with my father's death) announced that he didn't love me anymore and wanted to live his life unencumbered by our partnership. It was a loss that would rock my world in ways I could not have imagined. Thus I began another grieving journey that would teach me I have so much more to learn about love, loss, pain, acceptance, and letting go.

These poems are my attempts to describe some of the more poignant lessons that imprinted themselves on me during these two grieving journeys. I want to note that some of these insights I had already embraced intellectually, but experiencing these two losses deepened my understanding in ways that maybe nothing else could. I hope some of that comes across in the poems.

STRETCH describes a perspective I only reached after a rather gruelling journey. I knew I wanted to go there but my subconscious had all kinds of objections that came to me in wild dreams my conscious mind found quite incredulous. I believe those dreams were a necessary part of the journey to accomplish the 'stretch'; I had to fully embrace the pain (the sadness, anger, sense of betrayal, etc.), to feel the full range of emotions without judgement. I didn't get beyond those feelings so much as I came to have a different relationship with them. No longer wanting to escape them, I learned to integrate them into a new ecosystem of emotional being.

In every challenging journey, hope has a central role to play and I have written about it a number of times already. This one came in visuals after some wild ups and downs in my journey and I realised that no matter how desperately bleak my situation might feel, there was always a tiny thread of hope that I never abandoned and that never abandoned me. With a nod to Emily Dickinson, whose poem must have somehow been playing in my subconscious—though I oddly didn't recognise it until much later—SOMETIMES HOPE… recognises the shapeshifting superpower that is our hope.

Letting go is something we all struggle with, I think, and not just when it comes to the kind of grief I was navigating. Surely there is always some grief in letting go of things we hold dear. The poem, LET IT GO…, was written as a kind of pep talk to myself, an acknowledgement of how difficult it is to let things go and an acceptance, even an appreciation, of the pain involved. When I stopped fighting the pain, I realised that it was exactly right that I should be heartbroken and that the pain of grief was but an expression of my love. And the end of the poem points to a deeper lesson yet, that it seems our hearts were made to break.

THE ABYSS OF TRUTH came as a reflection of some visualisation exercises from the second Courage to Shine course offered by TreeSisters. We were asked to visualise and engage with parts of ourselves that were rejected. This poem came in visuals many months after the course and I didn't realise it was a mirroring of that exercise until just now as I ask myself what exactly sparked this poem. It helps me every so often to gaze into this abyss of truth and see what is there to greet me. The challenge is to meet whatever I see with all the compassion I can muster.

The Monk and The Traveller

Kelly Herrick

A monk once said to me,

"You wear your need to belong like a smell".

She was right and I had become noseblind. We've all been in a house with an unpleasant fragrance, wet dog, kitty litter, cigarettes, and we politely pretend not to notice. The owner has become so used to the smell they don't notice it either. We don't tell, they don't smell. The monk had done me a huge favour at the right time. I needed to notice and crucially *I was ready*.

I was ready to hold up this feeling and look at it, to sit with the discomfort of looking at it and then look some more. I was at a point where the nastiness of the smell was outweighing the benefit of wrapping myself in it to hide. That was the key thing, I wanted to spring clean this bad smell out of my life.

If it hadn't been the right time I would have probably thought the monk was being rude, or didn't know the importance of the smell, or didn't get the point of it. I would have found dozens, if not hundreds, of ways to convince myself that hanging onto the fug was way more important than having fresh emotional air to breathe. We are so good at sitting in our own unpleasantness because it's what we know, and what we know feels comforting and safe even if it isn't so good for us.

Belonging has always been wrapped up in worthiness for me. Am I good enough to be in this group or that one? Will they like me enough to let me in? Will I be good enough for them to want to stay? I realise now that trying to belong has been a lifelong quest I didn't know I was on.

I've proudly called myself a 'rebel', a 'free spirit' and an 'independent woman' for years. Sometimes that's been true, other times it's been a total fantasy. These labels were armour against the need to belong. On one hand my inner self has been trying to belong my whole life, whilst my outer self has been saying 'belonging is for sissies, you don't need to belong - be strong!'.

I had created a tiring and endless irritation and tension; a desire to belong and a desire to stop *wanting* to belong. It's hard to live in opposition with yourself.

Here are the roots of my belonging story, the challenges believing I didn't fit in put me through, and how I have found a way to finally belong.

Let's go back to the beginning.

We tell ourselves stories every day and mine has been 'you don't belong' since I can remember. It's important to know where these stories crop up, where they are anchored, because then we can set them adrift and sail away. Recognising that we even carry stories is the first step to freeing ourselves from them.

My story starts on the British travelling fair. It's how generations of my family lived and how I was raised, living in a huge caravan, travelling from place to place every week or two. It's a tribal kind of life, outside the typical cultural norms. It's fiercely loyal and tight knit, so belonging was almost a birthright. I was (and am) a Traveller. That name defined us, bonded us and separated us from everyone else.

Thinking back to those early childhood years I often feel a sense of unease. A slight jarring or misalignment. I recall that I didn't like doing what the other kids did. There was a wild rough and tumble to a childhood on the fair, some of my strongest memories were fights. I was upset about the fighting, I certainly wasn't a natural, and it wasn't the physicality of it, or the name calling; for me it was always a haze of confusion, I didn't know why we were fighting. I knew there was a purpose to it but I couldn't quite work it out, I didn't understand the rules. I didn't belong in this social group.

I didn't realise how shy I was back then. When the other kids would play boisterously together I'd often be on my bike, or building dens for bugs or ceremoniously burying dead hedgehogs. I'd talk to the colours on my bedspread, pretend elderberries had magical powers and imagine my Chicaboo coming to life. I was definitely one of the quieter ones.

My family was just as noisy and overwhelming. They were loving and close, but it was a busy life for my parents, who always seemed elsewhere; and my sisters, who were older than me, would often be working or socialising above my age group.

I felt like an intruder in my own life, like someone was going to discover I was play-acting any moment. I'm not sure where that feeling came from, but it always seemed to be there. The lack of structure and freedom seems like every kid's dream, but I remember chasing the adults around, trying to work out what next, never feeling settled and always slightly anxious. This is where my desire to belong came from because it *felt safe*. I knew that if I was useful, if I fitted in, then I would be looked after and loved. I would be safe. That was my story trigger.

For as much as I felt out of step on the fairground, nothing would prepare me for what came next. When I was 8, and for all the right reasons, I was sent to boarding school.

It was the first time I'd ever lived in a house. I lost my family, my home, my culture, my friends, my dog, everything that was familiar to me overnight. I hadn't been going to school much before, I had been mostly free to roam and play, and all of a sudden I was confined to a uniform, to sit still, to live by a bell. To this day I don't think I've fully absorbed what a trauma that was to me, or how much it has shaped me since.

Immediately I knew I didn't belong here either. I didn't talk the same, I didn't know what the other kids knew, the adults were different, I didn't feel how everyone else felt. When the other girls were homesick it was for their parents, their house, their toys; for me I was homesick for my entire lifestyle, from the food we ate, to the words we used, the sounds at night, to the place I slept.

What confused me was that in order to belong here, I felt I had to *not* belong to my fairground life. It felt like I had a choice to make, one that would stay with me forever, and at the age of eight I was in no way prepared to make such a huge decision. And so the tension began.

I would go from reading *Mallory Towers*, horse riding and hockey, to making candy floss, sleeping in a caravan and roaming fairs at night. I was living in directly opposed cultures who both disliked the other. I was betwixt and between, a creature of the margins. I would hear derogatory things about travellers at school, then go home to hear derogatory comments about non-travellers. I owned all of that negativity, when the kids at school would sneer 'Gyppo' that was me. When the kids on the fair would shout 'Flatey' that was me too. I took the insults from both worlds, and they hurt because they highlighted that I didn't truly belong to either of them.

Over my ten years of boarding school I became happy there, I think I became institutionalised in many ways. The tensions of two worlds and two lives would bubble up, but I'd try to suppress it and be soothed by the rhythm and repetition of life at school. I felt a strong attachment to my school, even if it wasn't belonging. Then it ended.

My friends all moved forward in a straight line, along a lifeline that was the same before they came to school, a life of houses and jobs and university. I was standing at a split in the path. I had been balancing two lives until that point but now I had to travel in just one direction. Which would I choose to try and fit into?

Cue the drama. How my story dictated my life.

From here on in my not belonging story started to turn into a full blown, subconscious drama. I didn't always realise it but it drove me to make dubious decisions, it over-sensitised me, it made me reckless.

I did carry 'I don't belong' like a smell back then. I can see now that trying to fit in and being fearful of not fitting in, triggered me to do some things that altered the course of my life and took me years to disentangle myself from.

I left my university drama course. At the time I put too much attention on creating my 'safe' relationship to replace my displaced family...which didn't last. I put myself out in the margins on purpose then was surprised when it didn't work out.

I played around with a few drugs. It was the 90s dance culture. I wanted to fit in. It was risky but it was a short cut to belonging and happiness, so I took it.

I married my first husband way too young and we weren't a good match. I was trying to recreate a tribe where I felt I belonged. I ended up in heart ache after it finished.

I didn't take the opportunity for a second interview with a big London ad agency. I predicted I wouldn't fit in before I even got there, so I safely minimised my own dreams and opportunities.

I lost touch with some of my best friends. Because obviously they were all in a wonderful group together that I wasn't good enough to be in. I flitted in and out, playing the rebel. I felt too vulnerable to commit, so I missed out on friendship and love.

I married my second husband and let myself completely disappear in order to fit into my own marriage. It grated on him and me. Instead of enabling us to belong as a couple, this efforting was one of the reasons that we eventually drifted apart. I was left heart-broken with two small children, lots of debt and deep emotional trauma.

I climbed the corporate ladder, bigger, better, faster, more. I turned the volume down on my soul so I couldn't hear my heart's desire to be elsewhere. I believed I could fit in, do well, be safe, have everything I needed. I was wrong.

I created a lot of theatrics I could have avoided because I was making decisions from a belief that I didn't belong. Where I wanted life to be simple my story actually made it deeply complex; where I longed to be safe, I put myself in some of the most vulnerable and risky positions I had ever been in. Making decisions based on a falsehood led me into dark days.

Over time my story of not belonging had come to own me. My story had become a script for how I behaved, what I felt and what I believed.

How I started to edit my own story.

Speaking to the monk was a gateway for me. It was the link between what was and what could be. I was in a place where I felt able to stop and scrutinise.

The first thing I had to do was recognise the truth of what she'd said.

Then I had to watch my story on replay, pausing it, rewinding it and really being curious, not judgemental, just ever so curious about what it all meant. I used a lot of helpful stuff to delve deep, writing my childhood as a fairy tale, journaling, talking about it, mind mapping, drawing, listening to my younger self...

Once I had navigated the waters of my old story I could see the course I wanted to plot to travel away from it.

I wanted to own my heritage and my experience. I wanted to care less about what other people thought. I wanted to enjoy myself. I wanted freedom *and* security. I wanted to trust my intuition more. I wanted to define my belonging based on how I felt in myself, not how others made me feel.

I wanted to create and not react. I wanted to forge my own sense of belonging and I knew it was within my power to do it.

It was then I had my epiphany - fitting in and belonging are two entirely different things. And who else do I want to belong to but myself? Fitting in is an external desire motivated by others, belonging is an internal desire coming only from our true selves.

Over the last few years I've done a lot of 'the work'. I've created a life I am really happy with. There have been a lot of people to help me along the way but none so much as myself. I feel that now I am living the true version of myself and not the version I thought I had to be.

It's taken time and in places it's been hard, but I've navigated my way based on where my home is, inside of me. I belong in *that* place, I like it, it is cosy, sometimes chaotic, creative, fun, natural. It's a million miles away from the stifling and boring home I tried to create for myself populated by everyone else's expectations. I even have a detailed vision of it that I visit in my mind when I need to, it's beautiful. This then is where I belong.

Belonging is a blank page not a finished story.

"I've worked it out," I said to the monk, "I know how to belong."

And I went on to explain how my tribe was me and that I could choose how to move around this world belonging to myself, extending that outward to the world when I chose to.

"I see people forming villages of their tribes all around me. Villages of this type, towns of that. But I like to be the Traveller in the wagon travelling between. I connect deeply but freely, choosing when to be linked, when to explore elsewhere, and when to return. I get to be in lots of tribes, connected but not bound.

I thought for a long time I needed a tribe but instead I am connected to many. I believe this is my natural way. I believe accepting this and all the joy it brings, and stopping worrying about finding a tribe, will unlock a huge sense of peace. To quote Fleetwood Mac: "back to the gypsy that I was."

If belonging to myself is my destination then being the Traveller in the wagon is my method of transport.

It's no surprise to me that I am happiest in a free-spirited, travelling, exploratory life. I only left the fairground in one reality, not all of them. When you are travelling through this world it really is just yourself you need for company, everyone else is a beautiful gift bestowed on us by space, time and magic.

There's no need to find a tribe – it's just a bunch of people afraid of their own wilderness, trying to fit in. What if you chose to belong to yourself? To enjoy who *you* are? To play in your own wild heart? I bet you'd have room to be you wherever you went.

I think the monk would agree with me on that too.

References and Support Links

British Red Cross mobile apps: First aid skills and techniques. (n.d.). British Red Cross. https://www.redcross.org.uk/first-aid/first-aid-apps

Davidson, E. D. (2019). *Wild Path to the Sacred Heart.* Star Tree Press.

Ectopic pregnancy information and support. (n.d.). Tommy's. https://www.tommys.org/baby-loss-support/ectopic-pregnancy-information-support

Encounters on Belonging, with Toko-pa. (2022, January 28). Toko-Pa's Official Website. https://toko-pa.com/encounters-intimate-conversations-on-belonging-with-toko-pa/

Gagliano, M., & Simard, S. (2018). *Thus Spoke the Plant: A Remarkable Journey of Groundbreaking Scientific Discoveries and Personal Encounters with Plants.* North Atlantic Books.

Get support | Endometriosis UK. (n.d.). Endometriosis UK. https://www.endometriosis-uk.org/get-support

Gibbons, E. (2020). *Stalking the Wild Asparagus* (Illustrated ed.). Stackpole Books.

Gilbert, E. (2022). *Eat, Pray, Love: One Woman's Search for Everything Across Italy, India and Indonesia by Gilbert, Elizabeth (2007) Paperback* (Twenty-fifth Printing ed.). Penguin (Non-Classics).

Interplay. (n.d.). Interplay. www.interplay.org

Laubin, R., Laubin, G., & Vestal, S. (1989). *The Indian Tipi: Its History, Construction, and Use, 2nd Edition* (2nd ed.). University of Oklahoma Press.

NHS website. (2021, November 18). *Ehlers-Danlos syndromes*. Nhs.Uk. https://www.nhs.uk/conditions/ehlers-danlos-syndromes/

Niestadt, L. (2019, May 11). *Podcast #46 An Easy Rider's RoadMap to Manifesting, navigated by Kathrin Zenkina.* Lou Niestadt. https://louniestadt.com/episode-46-easy-rider-roadmap-to-manifesting/

Ph.D., C. A. (2021). *Woman Between the Worlds: A Call to Your Ancestral and Indigenous Wisdom*. Hay House UK.

Sams, J. (1994a). *Earth Medicine: Ancestor's Ways of Harmony for Many Moons* (1st ed.). HarperOne.

Sams, J. (1994b). *The Thirteen Original Clan Mothers: Your Sacred Path to Discovering the Gifts, Talents, and Abilities of the Feminine Through the Ancient Teachings of the Sisterhood* (1st ed.). HarperCollins.

Sudden Cardiac Arrest UK. (2021, December 4). *Bereavement*. https://www.suddencardiacarrestuk.org/get-support/bereavement/

Sudden Cardiac Arrest UK Facebook Support Group. (n.d.). Sudden Cardiac Arrest UK Facebook Group. https://www.facebook.com/groups/SuddenCardiacArrestUK/

Webster, B. (2022, January 6). *What Is Sovereignty? 13 Elements*. Bethany Webster. https://www.bethanywebster.com/blog/what-is-sovereignty-13-elements/

Authors

Amaya Lupe

Amaya Lupe is Founder of Casa Boas, lives by the principles of the Sacred Feminine in honor of Mother Earth and loves her shamanic work as a women's Circle Keeper/Ceremonial Leader, Ritualist and Native Art-Artist.

Barbara Brown

Artist/author/forest-walker, Barbara Brown shares the beauty and the wonder of the forest, inspiring people to fall back in love with Nature.

Bethany Carder

Bethany Carder is a singer, dancer, musician, ecologist, writer, and humble student of the Earth and the Cosmos.

Christy Caudill

Edge walker, tree talker, writer and Earth and space scientist; kin and interbeing in a mad love affair with the Earth.

Claire Frame

Claire is a well-travelled, energetic, resourceful graphic designer and artist; consistently finding new and creative ways to share her passion for the planet through precision, vibrant colour and the simple joyful celebration of life.

Clare Dubois

Clare Dubois, founder of TreeSisters, is a poet, a writer, public speaker, edge walker, planetary dreamer for what's possible when we remember who we are as elements of nature, and stands for the ultimate embrace that is love.

Danu Sivapalan	A mother, cyber professional and an advocate for gender diversity in the workplace, instilling positivity in others and inspiring future generations to believe in themselves and their ability to achieve whatever they set out to do.
Daphne Helvensteijn	As a tea-lover, contrarian thinker and blogger, Daphne lives her life in a thoughtful, but at times theatrical and eccentric way, learning from nature, sensing energies, knowing that all is inclusive.
Dawn Foote	Mum, wife, vizsla-owner and collaborative co-founder of Katapult, creators of themed attractions & experiences, Dawn also uses her creative skills to indulge her passions for travel, exploration, nature and photography.
Donna Hicklin	Helping women to heal and expand to their true potential, Donna is an intuitive holistic therapist, healing landscape artist, meditation creator and workshop facilitator.
Dr Jacqui Leaman-Grey	Jacqui is a wife, mother to 5 sons, grandmother to 9 and now lives along with 2 golden retrievers in Somerset(!), having been a 'successful corporate suit', a global presenter, author and secret hippy.
Ellen Dee Davidson	Wild path, nature worshipping, sitting with redwoods, mother, grandmother, author sometimes speaker for trees.

Heather Pearson

Heather is a writer, musician, artist, and entrepreneur in service of the Voice of Mother Earth.

Isabelle Blum

Isabelle Blum has a background in environmental sciences, marketing, and Taoist Arts, and is offering possibilities to transform oneself and the world through nature connection.

Jane Toy

Living the New Zealand country life, co-creating and rewilding with Mother Earth, Jane Toy is a proponent of permaculture, regenerative agriculture and land-based art.

Jean Ferguson

Jean Ferguson is a hands-on adoring granny and helps non-profit organisations in Scotland deliver more value to the people they support.

Jennifer Comeau

Poet, singer-songwriter, Earth Ally, and founder of Sunrise Hill Sanctuary, Jennifer Comeau inspires humans to remember and restore our sacred partnership with the more-than-human world.

Kathleen Brigidina

TreeSisters Community Engagement Coordinator and Artist Liaison, mother of two incredible daughters, believes we are all one with Earth and all beings; conscious, creative, and healed by Love.

Kelly Herrick

Kelly Herrick is an artist, writer and creative strategist who shifts people into a more inspired and optimistic state about themselves and the world.

Lale Wilson   Lale Wilson is a proud mama, devoted wife, grieving daughter and corporate leader who has entered her transformational journey into deep self-exploration, and is returning home to her core.

Liz Clayton-Jones   A recent corporate escapee and post-menopausal woman, Liz uses her lived experience, love of science and passion for Strengths coaching to guide women in work through a transformational menopause experience.

Martina Naversnik   A recovering workaholic, Martina now spends her time finding more sustainable models of income generation that enable and support wellbeing.

Maya Spector   Maya Spector is a poet, ritualist, SoulCollage® facilitator, and retired children's librarian who has authored a book of poetry, The Persephone Cycle, and has a second book in the works.

Naomi Puri   A mother and once a daughter, Naomi helps young people to build skills and confidence through the employability programme she leads and her voluntary role for a youth mental health charity in Edinburgh.

Nüv   Nüv is an authentic soul who strives to learn and evolve; her loving disposition leads her to lighten and nurture all who surround her.

Rachel Herzig
Rachel Herzig engages ecological embodiment, entangled spirituality, and socially engaged art and performance in service to a more just and joyous world for all beings.

Rhianna McGonigal
Brand new mum not content with sitting still, normally scheming up a new project or planning a trip away, at her happiest when spending time with friends and family.

Sara Lesley Warber
Holistic family physician, researcher of nature's effects on health, and sometime creatrix, Sara Lesley Warber is the founder of Mutual Reawakening where dreams of nature, health, and a balanced life are nudged into daily lived reality.

Sara Steffey McQueen
Artist, Intuitive Astrologer, Ritual Circle Gatherer, Creativity Coach, Tree Sister, grandmother, and co-founder of May Creek Farm an intentional community in Indiana, U.S.A.

Sarah Pepper
Wife, mother, carer, IT professional, Sarah's positivity, drive and mental resilience are her core; she is extremely active in her local community and a keen advocate for women in Tech.

Sarah-Anne Forteith
A Scottish girl living in England, an avid bookworm, lover of fairy tales and wearer of bright colours who takes too many pictures of her dog.

Sheena Hales	Sheena Hales is an inspirational speaker whose passion for encouraging purpose and contribution led to a British Empire Medal for Service to the Community.
Y. Yi Pang	TreeSister and deeply entangled Earthling, on a journey of open-hearted listening.